BUILDING CULTURES AND CLIMATES FOR EFFECTIVE HUMAN SERVICES

EVIDENCE-BASED PRACTICES

SERIES EDITORS:

David E. Biegel, PhD
Elizabeth M. Tracy, PhD
Jack, Joseph and Morton Mandel
School of Applied Social Sciences,
Case Western Reserve University

Family Psychoeducation for Serious Mental Illness
Harriet P. Lefley

School Social Work
An Evidence-Informed Framework for Practice
Michael S. Kelly, James C. Raines, Susan Stone, and Andy Frey

Mental Health Treatment for Children and Adolescents
Jacqueline Corcoran

Individual Placement and Support
An Evidence-Based Approach to Supported Employment
Robert E. Drake, Gary R. Bond, and Deborah R. Becker

Preventing Child and Adolescent Problem Behavior
Evidence-Based Strategies in Schools, Families, and Communities
Jeffrey M. Jenson and Kimberly A. Bender

Supporting Families of Children With Developmental Disabilities
Evidence-based and Emerging Practices
Mian Wang and George H. S. Singer

Evidence Based Treatment with Older Adults:
Theory, Practice & Research
Nancy P. Kropf and Sherry M. Cummings

Screening, assessment and treatment of substance use disorders:
Evidence-based practices, community and organizational setting in the era of
integrated care.
Lena Lundgren and Ivy Krull

Building Cultures and Climates for Effective Human Services:
Understanding and Improving Organizational Social Contexts with the ARC model
Anthony L. Hemmelgarn and Charles Glisson

The Evidence-Based Practices Series is published in collaboration with the Jack,
Joseph and Morton Mandel School of Applied Social Sciences
at Case Western Reserve University.

BUILDING CULTURES AND CLIMATES FOR EFFECTIVE HUMAN SERVICES

UNDERSTANDING AND IMPROVING ORGANIZATIONAL SOCIAL CONTEXTS WITH THE ARC MODEL

Anthony L. Hemmelgarn and Charles Glisson

OXFORD
UNIVERSITY PRESS

OXFORD
UNIVERSITY PRESS

Oxford University Press is a department of the University of Oxford. It furthers
the University's objective of excellence in research, scholarship, and education
by publishing worldwide. Oxford is a registered trade mark of Oxford University
Press in the UK and certain other countries.

Published in the United States of America by Oxford University Press
198 Madison Avenue, New York, NY 10016, United States of America.

© Oxford University Press 2018

Library of Congress Cataloging-in-Publication Data
Names: Hemmelgarn, Anthony L., author. | Glisson, Charles, author.
Title: Building cultures and climates for effective human services :
understanding and improving organizational social contexts with the arc
model / Anthony L. Hemmelgarn and Charles Glisson.
Description: New York, NY : Oxford University Press, [2018] |
Series: Evidence-based practices | Includes bibliographical references and index.
Identifiers: LCCN 2018003372 (print) | LCCN 2018005292 (ebook) |
ISBN 9780190455293 (updf) | ISBN 9780190455309 (epub) |
ISBN 9780190455316 (Online Component) | ISBN 9780190455286 (pbk.)
Subjects: LCSH: Human services—Management. | Social service—Administration. |
Corporate culture. | Organizational change.
Classification: LCC HV41 (ebook) | LCC HV41 .H438 2018 (print) |
DDC 361.0068—dc23
LC record available at https://lccn.loc.gov/2018003372

1 3 5 7 9 8 6 4 2

Printed by WebCom, Inc., Canada

CONTENTS

PREFACE

WHY WAS THIS BOOK WRITTEN?

The work in this book responds to decades of ongoing failures that have often accompanied efforts to improve services within human service organizations. Failed efforts to create sustainable improvements in human services can be found across a variety of service areas, including behavioral health, social services, and other providers such as education and health care. We share over 40 years of our research and implementation efforts working within human services organizations to address these failures. Based on empirical data we have published and our experiences in improving organizations, we believe a core determinant of these failures is the inability of improvement efforts to address Organizational Social Contexts (OSCs), including organizational cultures and climates. Social contexts play a powerful role in the success of human service organizations, efforts to alter or improve organizations, and the adoption and implementation of new technologies, such as evidence-based practices.

In this book we share our research and experience in human service organizations to help readers understand how OSC affects their services. Our ultimate goal, however, is to improve human services and the client outcomes that follow. To do so, we describe three core organizational strategies applied in our empirically tested organizational intervention that is designed to improve OSCs and services. Referred to as ARC, the acronym represents the key characteristics of effective service relationships: Availability, Responsiveness, and Continuity. Three key strategies of ARC are described throughout the book to explain how organizational effectiveness can be improved by altering the social contexts of human service organizations. The reader is provided with information on how we assess OSC and how ARC structures, processes, and mechanisms are employed to improve these social contexts. The presentation of research findings, the mechanisms that underscore change, and the strategies and tools of ARC are provided to assist the reader in understanding how we have helped organizations improve their social contexts and the services they provide. In short, we hope to support researchers, administrators, funders, organizational leaders, and other stakeholders in their efforts to build more effective human services organizations—ones that positively affect the lives of the clients they serve.

HOW TO USE THIS BOOK AND ITS CONTENTS

This book is designed for both researchers and practitioners. Based on "gold standard" research evidence and decades of practical experience in human service organizations, the content blends technical research and practical applications. This allows readers to choose their focus as they read, whether attending to research findings, practical case examples, or details of our intervention. The case examples provided throughout the book are designed to aid both researchers and practitioners in experiencing firsthand the impact of social contexts within human service organizations. These examples include experiences collected by the authors during the implementation of our ARC organizational strategies within organizations nationwide. The examples provide a visceral experience of the effects of social contexts within human services organizations as well as a vicarious look at real changes that have occurred when employing ARC's core strategies. Case examples highlight the mechanisms through which change and improvement occur, and they are integrated with research and empirical evidence throughout our book. Our empirical and case examples connect data and theory to the practical mechanisms for change that are illustrated in real-world examples. For example, influencing the deeply held beliefs, mindsets, and reasoning of organizational leaders in ways that enhance their ability to lead others in achieving effective services is supported by a discussion of research in social learning and cognition. Our work on mental models highlighted in this book demonstrates the impact of cognitive frameworks and underlying beliefs and assumptions shared among organizational leaders. More specifically, these frameworks and beliefs influence the interpretations, reasoning, and decision making of organizational leaders and members, leading to behaviors that influence client outcomes.

To assist the reader, we provide a brief overview of the book chapters. Chapter 1 introduces readers to the concept of organizational social contexts and provides an overview of our more than 40 years of research on social contexts within human service organizations. This introductory chapter summarizes the ARC organizational change strategies that are designed to improve OSC, including improvements in the key elements of organizational culture and climate. This introductory chapter also explains how social contexts influence human service effectiveness and efforts to improve services. Chapter 2 examines the impact of OSC with two actual case examples. These case examples illustrate the variability across organizations in OSC and the differential effect, both negative and positive, of social contexts on staff, client, and organizational outcomes, including the ability to promote innovation and change. These case examples are integrated with supporting research findings, and these case examples are used to further highlight our ARC strategies for improvement. The mechanisms of influence of organizational social contexts on services and organizational effectiveness are reviewed. Chapter 3 summarizes our OSC measurement system to provide an understanding of how social contexts can be assessed within human service organizations. This chapter documents the research support for our OSC measure and its relationship to staff, client, and organizational outcomes. It details key areas of assessment, including culture, climate, and work attitudes. It also describes the use of empirically derived personality profiles for organizations, profiles that provide a powerful tool to initiate and drive organizational change. Chapter 4 introduces the three core strategies of ARC that improve social contexts within human service organizations. These three strategies include: (1) embedding five ARC principles, (2) installing ARC's organizational component tools, and (3) introducing and altering mental models. A heuristic model of ARC's key strategies illustrate how the three strategies are integrated to provide the tools, processes, and thinking that ensure effective OSCs, improved services, and successful client outcomes. Key ARC processes are explained, including the importance of aligning the priorities enacted by organizations with ARC principles, developing relationships characterized by availability, responsiveness, and continuity; and developing innovation capacity.

Chapter 5 reviews the empirical evidence that supports the ARC strategies and process. This chapter describes the randomized controlled trials that support ARC's effectiveness in improving staff and client outcomes, as well as ARC's success in supporting the use of evidence-based practices. The empirical findings presented in this chapter and throughout the book are reinforced with actual case examples. Chapter 6 describes the infrastructure, initial preparation, and key strategies that are employed to begin ARC. This infrastructure includes the individuals and teams required to implement ARC and their accompanying roles and responsibilities. Preliminary training is described and additional features of ARC are highlighted to prepare the reader for the more detailed description of ARC strategies that follows.

Chapters 7 through 13 describe ARC's three core strategies. First, Chapter 7 details ARC's 12 organizational component tools to improve organizational effectiveness. Chapter 8 reviews ARC's use of mental models to alter beliefs, assumptions, and reasoning. Chapters 9 through 13 describe each of ARC's five key principles, respectively, that guide the application of component tools and mental models. The three ARC strategies of principles, component tools, and mental models are integrated closely to establish work norms, perceptions, and attitudes that are associated with successful innovation and service improvement efforts. These three strategies provide the tools and the thinking that guide behaviors and processes to assure that human service organizational leaders and members select and enact priorities that align with effective social contexts and services for clients. Similarly, these three strategies help foster shared beliefs, assumptions, and mental representations among organizational members that ensure consistency in decisions, processes, and practices that contribute to improved service quality and outcomes.

Chapters 7 and 8 include research that supports these strategies, the practical tools and activities deployed to enact these strategies, and case examples that bring to life both the importance of organizational tools and mental models. Case examples of the authors' work in organizations to successfully deploy these strategies are reviewed to illustrate improvement in staff, client, and organizational outcomes. ARC's five principles are designed to guide their deployment. At the same time, deploying the two strategies of ARC components tools and mental modes further embeds the ARC principles within the practices, actions, behaviors, beliefs, and reasoning shared among organizational members. Each principle is highlighted in its own chapter (see Chapters 9–13) and includes its influence on the use of component tools, mental models that impact beliefs and reasoning, and the accompanying expectations, perceptions, and attitudes that make up OSC. Each chapter provides research support for the principle and an integrated description of how principles, tools, and supporting beliefs are integrated to build social contexts. This description includes in each chapter a real case example of ARC embedding these principles in a way that improves staff and client lives. The order in which the chapters are read can vary depending on the interests of the reader. For example, those who desire a practice-based introduction to improving OSC may choose to read Chapters 1, 2, and 4 followed by the ARC principle in Chapters 9 through 13, before delving into the details of OSC measurement, the ARC process, and its empirical support, that are included in Chapter 3 and Chapters 5–8.

The final chapter of this book suggests future research and development efforts focused on four areas to refine organizational strategies for providing the most effective services. The four areas are interrelated and together describe how more specific information about these organizational strategies can increase their capacity for improving human services. The chapter explains that the future challenge for both practitioners and researchers is to determine which tools, principles, and mental models are most effective for various organizational profiles and characteristics, the mechanisms that link each organizational strategy to each desired outcome, and the combined sequence of strategies that is most effective. This information is needed to direct the most efficient combination and sequence of strategies that are likely to meet an organization's needs. The authors welcome comments and questions at ahemmelg@gmail.com and cglisson@utk.edu.

ACKNOWLEDGMENTS

First, we want to thank the human service providers and leaders we have worked with across the nation: They work tirelessly to improve the lives of our fellow human beings, often with little recognition or reward. Their persistence and dedication to the complex and challenging work within human services inspires all who work with them and serves as an impetus for our own efforts to improve those services.

We have enjoyed a long and productive collaboration, but the research and practice summarized in this book involved many colleagues. We extend our gratitude to all of our colleagues who have supported our work in so many ways, from providing insightful ideas and perspectives to practical assistance in finalizing professional publications and preparing ARC intervention and OSC materials. Of special note are Denzel Dukes, Joanna Cheatham, Philip Green, and Nate Williams, all of whom collaborated in our research center's work with service organizations and the production of research proposals and publications that directly contributed to this book.

Last, but most importantly, we would like to thank our families for their help in our efforts to balance family and work. ALH thanks his wife, Kimberly, and children, Isabel and Oliver, for enduring many hours of negligence during the completion of this book. CG thanks his wife, Joyce, and children, Matthew and Erin, for their support and understanding over his many years of weekends and holidays spent writing research proposals and publications.

BUILDING CULTURES AND CLIMATES
FOR EFFECTIVE HUMAN SERVICES

1

IMPROVING ORGANIZATIONAL SOCIAL CONTEXTS FOR EFFECTIVE HUMAN SERVICES

Our lives are immersed within organizations as employees, customers, clients, volunteers, or members that affect how we feel, think, and behave. When we join an organization as an employee, we enter a complex social setting with shared norms, expectations, and attitudes that influence our priorities, guide our work values, and impact our psychological functioning and well-being. Organizations can motivate and inspire us, or they can demoralize and disappoint us. In the same way, organizations that provide human services affect the behavior, functioning, and being of those who are served. For the past few decades, we have worked with hundreds of organizations that provide human services such as health care, education, behavioral health, and social services to understand why some are more effective than others. This book explains what we have learned about how these human service organizations affect the individuals who work in them, the quality of the services they provide, and the outcomes for those who receive the services. It also introduces strategies for changing human service organizations. These strategies influence service providers' behavior, perceptions, and attitudes in ways that improve the quality and outcomes of their services.

The following chapters are the product of four decades of research in human service organizations. Much of this work has focused on understanding and addressing key elements of organizational social context (OSC). OSC is reflected in organizational culture, climate, and work attitudes. These elements include the social norms guiding behavior within a work setting (i.e., culture), the perceptions organizational members hold about their work settings (i.e., climate), and their attitudes toward these work settings. Supported by the National Institutes of Health, the W.T. Grant Foundation, the John D. and Catherine T. MacArthur Foundation, and other public and private funders, we have studied organizations in all regions of the United States and reported our findings in scores of peer-reviewed publications. Our research includes nationwide studies, large multicounty tests of organizational improvement efforts, and randomized controlled trials of organizational strategies to improve the services provided by both public and private organizations. Our primary goal throughout our decades of work has been to develop, test, and refine methods for assessing and changing organizations' cultures and climates that support improved service outcomes. We have written this book to describe what we have learned in a way that benefits executives, clinicians, and researchers who share our goal of improving human service organizations. We believe our book is unique, providing a marriage between gold standard empirical methods and practical experience gained during our extensive organizational research and development efforts. This integration of science and practice provides insight to both researchers and practitioners into how organizational culture and climate affect human services and how organizational strategies can be used to improve services. It also offers case studies that illustrate the connection between OSC and human service effectiveness.

The following chapters describe the complex challenge of improving human services and the roles that organizational culture and climate play in those efforts. This book also introduces organizational strategies that compose the availability, responsiveness, and continuity (ARC) model for changing OSCs, along with the practical and research experiences that have informed those strategies. This chapter begins with a summary of what we have learned in the development of our evidence-based organizational strategies with five basic points.

First, we know that human service organizations vary greatly in their social contexts and that those differences have consequences for the way services are provided. Our studies of nationwide samples confirm that organizations providing the same types of services (e.g., behavioral health) can vary substantially in the cultures, climates, and work attitudes that characterize their social contexts (Glisson, Green, & Williams, 2012; Glisson, Landsverk, et al., 2008). Our studies also provide evidence that the variation in social context is linked to differences in service quality and outcomes, even when the organizations serve similar populations with similarly trained service providers (Glisson, 2010; Glisson & Green, 2006, 2011; Glisson & Hemmelgarn, 1998; Glisson, Schoenwald, et al., 2008; Glisson, Hemmelgarn, Green, & Williams (2013); Glisson, Williams, Hemmelgarn, Proctor, & Green, 2016a, 2016b; Glisson & Williams, 2015; Olin et al., 2014; Williams & Glisson, 2013, 2014b; Williams et al., 2016). Moreover, our work is part of a larger body of work showing that OSCs are linked to differences in a range of human service provider behaviors and client outcomes in a variety of service settings (e.g., Aarons et al., 2012; Aarons & Sawitzky, 2006; Aarons, Sommerfeld, & Walrath-Greene, 2009; Greener, Joe, Simpson, Rowan-Szal, & Lehman, 2007; Morris, Bloom, & Kang, 2007; Olin et al., 2014; Schoenwald, Carter, Chapman, & Sheidow, 2008; Schoenwald, Chapman, Sheidow, & Carter, 2009).

Second, our studies show that the social contexts of human services can be changed with carefully implemented organizational strategies and that those changes can improve the quality and outcomes of the services that are provided (Glisson, Dukes, & Green, 2006; Glisson, Hemmelgarn et al., 2012, 2013, Glisson, Williams et al 2016a, 2016b; Williams & Glisson, 2014b; Williams et al., 2016). We know from our research and experience that an organization's capacity for innovation explains the effects of social context on service improvement efforts. That is, the capacity of organizations to innovate (i.e., identify service deficits and make changes in practices and policies to address those deficits) is either enhanced or constrained by its social context. Some deficits can be addressed by the adoption of best practices at the service level. Others require altering organizational policies and processes that impact services. The success of either of these approaches requires the capacity for innovation, which depends on social context (i.e., culture and climate). We know from research on the diffusion of innovations that social context is instrumental in facilitating or inhibiting the adoption and implementation of new practices in all social systems (Rogers, 2003). In a similar way, OSC explains the readiness of an organization to engage in change and predicts which organizations will be innovative (Glisson et al., 2016b; Klein & Sorra, 1996; Hemmelgarn et al., 2006; Williams et al., 2016). OSC is critical to successful innovation across an array of human services from medical teams implementing surgical procedures (Edmonson et al., 2001) to the adoption of evidence-based treatments in mental health services (Glisson et al., 2016b; Williams et al., 2016).

Third, organizational social contexts are essential to innovation because they reflect the power of social systems to resist or promote changes in individual behavior. Social contexts are composed of interrelated networks of individuals who interact and share norms, expectations, and perceptions that influence their behavior and the characteristics of their networks. These context-based characteristics and behaviors are acquired through group learning, mimicry, sanctions, schema formation, and meaning construction, all of which explain the similarity of behaviors observed within specific social contexts as well as the variation of behavior observed between different social contexts (Bandura, 1986; DiMaggio, 1997; Fiske & Taylor, 2013; Scott, 2008; Strang & Soule, 1998). OSCs affect individual behavior in a variety of areas related to successful innovation, including the adoption of new practices, tenacity in solving complex problems, collaboration, commitment to change, and task engagement (Hartnell, Ou, & Kinicki, 2011). These same social phenomena explain why organizations vary in their capacity to improve and why some are more likely to adopt and implement innovations successfully (Greenhalgh, Robert, MacFarlane, Bate, & Kyriakidou, 2004; Katz, 1961; Robert, Greenhalgh, MacFarlane, & Peacock, 2009).

Fourth, organizational research in a variety of sectors, including medicine, customer services such as banking, and various professional fields such as information technology illustrates that OSCs affect the implementation of best practices introduced within organizations to improve effectiveness (Carr, Schmidt, Ford, & DeShon, 2003; Hartnell,

Ou, & Kinicki, 2011; Parker et al., 2003; Patterson et al., 2005; Sackmann, 2011). This occurs at each of three phases, namely, adoption, implementation, and sustainability of new best practices in human service organizations (Aarons, Hurlburt, & Horwitz, 2011; Damschroder et al., 2009; Greenhalgh et al., 2004; Harvey et al., 2002). Nonetheless, few actual service improvement efforts in community-based human service organizations address OSC in their efforts. Instead, most service improvement efforts focus exclusively on technical training in best practices at the individual service provider levels. Neither assessing nor altering the contextual characteristics that affect the success of the training is typically addressed. (Beidas & Kendall, 2010; McHugh & Barlow, 2010).

Fifth, it is important to note that the authors' efforts at creating strategies for improving an organization's capacity for innovation and performance build upon over a century of work on improving organizational effectiveness that has direct implications for human services. The history of organizational improvement strategies to improve effectiveness traces a dramatic transition from early mechanistic assumptions about individual work behavior in organizations to more complex views that include the roles of social context, cognition, and perception (Burns & Stalker, 1961; March & Simon, 1958; Van de Ven & Poole, 1995). Early organizational improvement strategies, such as Frederick Taylor's (1911) well-known model of scientific management, assumed a centralized, top-down approach that specified work behavior in a detailed way, linked work activities in an assembly-line fashion, and tightly controlled work behavior to improve productivity and efficiency. Early mental models or mindsets associated with these strategies framed organizations as machines with humans forming the cogs and gears. Subsequent empirical studies and increasingly complex views of work settings and performance challenged these early mechanistic assumptions. Nevertheless, as Lisbeth Schorr (1997) noted almost a century later, the underlying philosophy of the early mechanistic models remains evident in the managerial approaches taken in human service organizations in the 21st century. Schorr argued that this mechanistic management philosophy is so focused on eliminating the possibility that human service providers will do anything wrong that it makes it virtually impossible for them to do anything right. We argue in the following chapters that many human service organizations remain steeped in mechanistic models and engender norms, beliefs, and mindsets that fail to support effective human services. Given the complexity, unpredictability, and uncertainty of human service provision, this failure continues to plague many human service organizations nationwide.

THREE STRATEGIES FOR CREATING OSCS THAT SUPPORT INNOVATION AND IMPROVE SERVICE OUTCOMES

The association we describe in the following chapters between OSC, innovation, and service quality show that three complementary organizational strategies for changing social contexts can improve service outcomes. This introductory chapter provides a brief description of the three strategies that comprise a planned, team-based, participatory, and phased process (ARC) that increases an organization's capacity to identify and address service barriers through innovation. The first ARC strategy embeds *five principles* of service system effectiveness within the organization to align organizational priorities with effective organizational processes and decision making. The second ARC strategy trains teams of line-level service providers and leaders in the use of *twelve organizational component tools.* These tools are necessary to build an organization's capacity for innovation and its ability to identify and remove service barriers. The third ARC strategy promotes *shared mental models* such as openness to change and psychological safety among clinicians and administrators to support service innovation and improvement efforts. This strategy seeks to introduce new assumptions, framing, and reasoning shared by organizational members that support innovation and the key principles of ARC.

All three strategies are adapted from the work of many previous investigators but the ARC intervention is the first to combine the three strategies into a single model. Also, the strategies have been redesigned within the ARC model to complement each other while improving human services. Although many organizational improvement models have been proposed for improving OSCs, few have been tested in randomized controlled studies in actual work settings (Parmelli et al., 2011). The randomized controlled trials of the ARC model show that services can be improved with the three strategies by creating an OSC that engenders capacity for innovation (Glisson, Dukes & Green, 2006; Glisson, Hemmelgarn et al., 2012, 2013; Glisson et al., 2010; Glisson, Williams et al, 2016a; 2016b; Williams et al., 2016). We summarize the three strategies in the sections that follow.

Strategy one: Five principles of effective human service organizations. A variety of strategic goals and operational demands compete for emphasis in organizations as they attempt to survive and succeed (Quinn & Rohrbaugh, 1983; Schneider & Bowen, 1995). Organizations that do similar work differ in the priorities they place on the competing goals and demands they face and in the extent to which they align organizational priorities in a way that complements their efforts to be effective. When aligned with key organizational principles, these priorities help forge decisions, actions, mindsets, and processes that lead to human service effectiveness. For example, within health-care organizations the priority of high-quality patient care may be balanced with building new service lines to increase revenues. In hospitals that are guided by an unwavering principle of delivering high-quality care, planning and action taken at all levels ensure that quality of care is not lost. In those that have displaced this principle with a sole priority on increasing revenue, quality care is often espoused but not practiced sufficiently.

An organization's priorities reflect what is most important to the organization, but an organization's espoused and enacted priorities can be different—that is, organizations can say one thing and do another (Argyris & Schon, 1996; Pate-Cornell, 1990; Simons, 2002). Moreover, an organization can enact inconsistent and even conflicting priorities (Weick, 1979). Similar to other types of organizations, human services face *competing demands* (e.g., the demand for service quality versus the demand for service quantity—or the demand for resources to develop a highly trained staff versus the demand for fiscal restraint). Organizations also face the *difficulty of enacting espoused priorities* (e.g., ensuring that a priority on improving client well-being is reflected in organizational practices or ensuring that the needs of the identified target population are actually being addressed). Moreover, organizations face *conflicts created by inconsistent priorities* (e.g., enacting rules to control clinician behavior that are inconsistent with specified treatments requiring clinician discretion, or assessing program performance based on client outcomes while placing limits on the use of treatment options that individualize care). The priorities that take precedence specify what is most valuable to the organization and help define the driving principles of that organization. Alignment of enacted and espoused priorities helps ensure that the organization's actions reflect what it says is most important. Furthermore, the consistencies in enacted priorities reflect the extent to which the organization's priorities complement rather than conflict with each other (Zohar & Hoffman, 2012). ARC uses five guiding principles as described in Chapters 9 through 13 to enact consistent, espoused priorities focused on improving the well-being of those who are served (Glisson et al., 2016a; Hemmelgarn, Glisson, & James, 2006).

ARC uses written manuals and an ARC specialist to explain the principles and help organizational members align organizational priorities consistent with the principles via the use of organizational tools summarized below. The principles are based on the idea that common barriers can emerge in any organization that misdirect the attention and efforts of individual-level providers who serve clients. The five ARC principles guide an organization's efforts to identify and address those barriers by maintaining a focus on improving the well-being of the clients. This focus is critical to improvement efforts because a clear focus on client well-being and principle-based, contextual support for individuals to achieve client success is important to providers who feel they have made a prosocial difference through their work (Grant, 2007).

Each of the five ARC principles are described in a separate chapter: Chapter 9 describes being mission driven versus rule driven so that all actions and decisions contribute to the well-being of clients; Chapter 10 describes being results oriented versus process oriented to measure success by how much client well-being improves; Chapter 11 describes being improvement directed versus status quo directed to continually work to be more effective in improving the well-being of clients; Chapter 12 describes being participation based versus authority based so that policy and practice decisions that affect client well-being involve everyone with a stake in the decision; Chapter 13 describes being relationship centered versus individual centered to focus on the network of relationships that affect the organization's performance and the well-being of clients.

Strategy two: Twelve organizational component tools applied in three stages. As described in Chapter 7, the ARC intervention includes 12 organizational component tools that are introduced within the planned process and structure of ARC. Aligned with and designed to embed the ARC principles, these organizational components are introduced to develop OSCs (cultures, climates, and worker attitudes) that place an explicit priority on fostering innovation in pursuit of high-quality services that enhance client well-being. Selected from several decades of organizational research (e.g., Neuman, Edwards, & Raju, 1989; Robertson, Roberts, & Porras, 1993), the 12 components are adapted for human service organizations and are introduced in ARC materials, including the ARC Training Manual and ARC Facilitator's Guide. As described in Chapters 4 through 6, the ARC manual and guide support the creation of a structure and process within each organization for using the 12 tools. This structure includes an ARC specialist (external consultant), ARC liaison (internal champion selected by the organization's leaders), executive leadership team, Organizational Action Team (OAT), and ARC line-level teams of service providers.

The structure of ARC develops as the 12 organizational components are introduced in three stages within ARC. First, in the *collaboration* stage, the ARC specialist helps organizational leaders explain the ARC change process and goals to organizational members. Central to ARC's component of *leadership development*, this work clarifies the organizational structures and processes necessary to support service improvement efforts while engaging leaders in their active role of supporting ARC and embedding ARC's components in their organization's everyday practices, processes, and procedures. The assessment of the organization's culture and climate profiles (see Chapters 3 and 4) and of existing processes, systems, and priorities that influence both the profiles and the enactment of ARC's five principles begins in this stage. These initial efforts focus on communicating the commitment to the ARC process, the five ARC principles of service system effectiveness outlined above, and practical information about the ARC organizational structure and process to all organizational members. These efforts are reinforced with the components of *network development* and *relationship development*. An ARC liaison is identified in this first stage as someone who champions the ARC effort within the organization, and the OAT is created from representatives at each level: leadership, middle management, supervisors, and front-line staff. These entities engender *network development* as the ARC specialist and liaison foster the necessary interpersonal connections to support change. Similarly, the OAT team structure requires networking among members across organizational levels to enact adaptations, improvements, and alterations that improve organizational functioning and service quality.

The ARC specialist (an external consultant) and liaison cultivate *personal relationships* with members of the organization (e.g., OAT team), external stakeholders (e.g., consumer advocates), and supervisory and front-line staff to facilitate ARC efforts. These relationships are integral to framing the rationale and work of the OAT and ARC teams that follow and are carefully developed with explicit expectations of engagement characterized by availability, responsiveness, and continuity (ARC).

Second, in the *participation* stage, the external ARC specialist supports OAT team members and front-line teams in the use of five ARC component tools, including *team building, information and training, feedback, participatory decision making,* and *conflict management*. These components build decision-making and problem-solving capacity within ARC teams to address service barriers that are identified and addressed within the ARC process. The ARC facilitator's guide helps supervisors conduct team meetings that identify service barriers, develop proposals for addressing those barriers, and submit the proposals to the OAT for implementation. The OAT and ARC teams are trained in the use of criteria for assessing the relative advantage of a proposed innovation, applying the ARC principles in decision making, and supporting efforts to identify and address service barriers.

Finally, in the *innovation* stage, the ARC specialist trains team supervisors in four ARC component tools for changing policies, procedures, and protocols to improve service quality and outcomes. An organization's ARC teams are taught to use the component tools of *continuous quality improvement* and *goal setting* to identify and assess performance criteria, as well as establish challenging but feasible goals. Job characteristics are redesigned (i.e., *job redesign*) in this stage to address service and innovation barriers. Improvement plans within ARC include transforming job tasks, changing program practices, and training front-line staff to support the change. The development of plans to ensure the *stabilization* of innovation adoption and implementation processes is the last step.

The ARC structures and processes support a variety of innovations as a function of the unique interests and service barriers identified by the line workers composing the ARC teams. Examples of innovations proposed by the ARC teams of direct service providers can range across streamlining client referral processes, identifying and eliminating unnecessary paperwork, adopting and implementing new practice models, establishing new records systems, modifying decision-making processes, establishing linkages with other institutions (e.g., behavioral health clinics, schools, juvenile courts), or redesigning job characteristics and roles to improve efficiency.

Strategy three: Shared mental models to support innovation and service improvement. A third ARC strategy develops shared mental models among agency administrators, mid-level management, and front-line service providers to support innovation and service improvement efforts. That is, ARC introduces mindsets, assumptions, and frameworks to organizational members that influence reasoning and decision making consistent with innovation, ARC principles, and the use of ARC components to improve services. As explained in Chapter 8, mental models (such as openness to change and psychological safety) are heuristic-based cognitive representations that form the basis of reasoning and interpretation of organizational events that influence behavior (Hysong, Best, Pugh, & Moore, 2005; Mohammed, Ferzandi, & Hamilton, 2010). Service improvement efforts depend on shared mental models among organizational members that support adoption and implementation success. These models are associated with organizational culture and climate; they are also malleable and, in turn, can be developed to support improvements in culture and climate (Hysong et al., 2005; Mathieu, Heffner, Goodwin, Salas, & Cannon-Bowers, 2000). The model of psychological safety, for example, promotes the participation and commitment of line-level workers in critically examining service barriers and proposing improvements in job-related tasks without fear of reprisal from peers or supervisors. There is evidence that health-care and other human service teams that share assumptions and beliefs supporting psychological safety are more effective in implementing best practices that positively affect client outcomes (Edmondson, Bohmer, & Pisano, 2001). Similarly, studies in a variety of settings show that learning and performance are enhanced with the shared belief of work team members that it is psychologically safe to take interpersonal risks in improvement efforts and problem solving such as constructively critiquing existing practices or openly accepting suggestions for improvements from colleagues.

This third strategy is based on the idea that to be successful in improving services, the beliefs, reasoning, and mindsets that compose shared mental models among an organization's members must reinforce the use of organizational components (Chapter 7) in identifying and addressing service barriers. They should align with organizational priorities and be consistent with the ARC principles (Chapters 9–13). In this way, the thinking and behavior of organizational members complement the priorities specified in ARC's five principles of effective human service organizations while reinforcing the practical tools that support these principles.

THE EVIDENCE FOR USING ORGANIZATIONAL STRATEGIES TO CHANGE INDIVIDUAL BEHAVIOR

Using the strategies outlined in this book, we take a systems approach to understanding and improving the effectiveness of human service organizations. That is, the focus remains on the whole organization. Multiple levers often need to be pulled to create change behavior within an organization, including the need to address multiple processes and systems as well as the reasoning and assumptions of organizational members that influence their decision making and actions. At the same time, we understand that success requires practical changes in individual service provider behavior—and that behavior that is intimately tied to the organizational social context in which it occurs. For this reason, we argue in the following chapters that social context plays a central role as a change mechanism that links ARC strategies to the individual-level behaviors required to improve services (Schneider, Brief, & Guzzo, 1996).

The term, change mechanism, is widely used to describe the intermediate changes that are triggered by intervention strategies and serve as the basis of the intervention's effect on individual behavior. The three ARC strategies of embedding guiding principles, enacting organizational component tools, and altering mental models are change processes that affect both organizational-and individual-level change mechanisms. At the organizational level, the ARC strategies improve OSCs and remove service barriers (Glisson, Dukes & Green, 2006; Glisson, Hemmelgarn et al, 2012; Glisson, et al., 2016a). At the individual level, the ARC strategies affect practitioners' intentions to act in a way that leads to improved service outcomes (Glisson et al., 2016b; Williams et al., 2016). In other words change occurs in social contexts, such as the norms and expected behaviors, and at the individual level where intentions for behavior that support service quality and client outcomes are affected. Therefore, improved services are a function of

ARC change processes (principles, mental models, and organizational tools) that affect organizational-level and individual-level change mechanisms to change service provider behavior.

Mechanisms that link ARC strategies to changes in individual-level behavior are important because they teach us how to be more effective in our service improvement efforts (e.g., Grol, Bosch, Hulscher, Eccles, & Wensing, 2007). Understanding how strategies influence the shared organizational cultures, climates, and priorities that alter individual behavior of organizational members is essential. Our development of the ARC model therefore relies on research methods to identify the change mechanisms in planned behavioral change efforts in human systems (Doss, 2006; Kazdin, 2007, 2009). We conducted randomized trials to study the effects of ARC strategies on targeted outcome criteria, to identify change mechanisms, and to describe the links between the two. Our view is that the improvement of OSCs is the most effective and sustainable change mechanism to link organizational development strategies to effective services to individual clients; one that generalizes beyond any single treatment model, group of employees, leader, or organization. This underscores the value of a model such as ARC that provides guiding principles, organizational tools, and mental models that contribute to an organization's capacity for building social contexts that can identify and address unique service barriers that influence services effectiveness.

To support our work, we integrate organizational culture and climate theory with well-established social cognitive theories of individual behavior change to achieve the goal of improving human service systems (Ajzen, 1991; Ajzen & Fishbein, 1980; Bandura, 1986; Fishbein et al., 2001). A wide range of human service related behaviors, including the behavior of providers in health care, behavioral health, and other human services are explained by social cognitive theories (Armitage & Conner, 2001; Perkins et al., 2007). For example, these theories explain how team norms and behavioral patterns support the strategies that are developed or how teams can help maintain a sense of efficacy among coworkers who face complex client issues. In another example, environmental barriers that facilitate or constrain the enactment of behavioral intentions are addressed in social cognitive theory and in culture and climate theory (Fishbein et al., 2001).

Our point is that a great deal of behavioral and cognitive research supports the idea that organizational social context contributes to individuals' intentions to act in a way that improves service quality and to the presence or absence of organizational barriers to enactment (Ajzen, 1991; Godin et al, 2008). Our own research has shown how improvements in social context and organizational capacity for change affect clinicians' behaviors such as seeking out and adopting evidence-based treatments (Glisson et al., 2016b; Williams et al., 2016). The dual effect of organizational social context on the intentions of individual providers to act in certain ways and on the organizational barriers to those intentions parallels research on innovation in general. It also helps to explain the influence of social context on the implementation of best practices (Aarons et al., 2009, 2012; Baer et al., 2009; Carlfjord et al., 2010; Cummings et al., 2007; Doran et al.,

2012; Friedmann, Taxman, & Henderson, 2007; Glisson, Schoenwald et al., 2008; Glisson et al., 2016b; Henderson et al., 2007; Henggeler et al., 2008; Jones, Jimmieson, & Griffiths, 2005; Lundgren et al., 2012; Williams et al., 2016). Ebp implementation, in other words, further complements the evidence that organizational social context affects employee behaviors related to service quality and support the central role of social context in our ARC model of service effectiveness (Aarons & Sawitzky, 2006; Glisson & Green, 2006, 2011; Glisson & Hemmelgarn, 1998; Glisson & James, 2002; Glisson et al., 2016a; Hartnell et al., 2011; Hemmelgarn et al., 2001; Olin et al., 2014).

CONCLUSION TO INTRODUCTION

Our understanding of improving human services has evolved over several decades of consulting and research with a large variety of public and private organizations. During that time, we moved from describing differences in social context among human service organizations to linking those differences with service quality and client outcomes. We then began our efforts to test strategies for changing organizational social contexts in a way that improves service quality and outcomes. As illustrated in the case studies in Chapter 2 and throughout the following chapters, our practical experience in working with organizations to improve services confirms what we have found in our research: that is, organizational social context is a complex construct that is central to innovation and effectiveness in human services. The dimensions of culture and climate that help characterize an organization's social context affect service provider's attitudes and behavior in working with clients and in their efforts to improve services. For this reason, we are convinced that an organization's social context must be addressed in any successful effort to improve services, including those focused on issues such as the adoption, implementation, and sustainment of evidence-based practices.

The practice and research efforts we describe in the following chapters rely on assessing an organization's social context, comparing the results to similar organizations to determine the culture and climate profiles of the organization and reassessing to monitor changes in social context over time. For these reasons, as explained in Chapters 3 and 4, we describe the OSC measure we developed to assess the organizational culture and climate profiles of behavioral health and social service agencies for both practice and research. We have linked OSC profiles to clinician behavior, service quality, and client outcomes in numerous studies. From a practice perspective, these profiles are indispensable during change efforts as ARC specialists provide feedback to organizational members who want to improve their social contexts and subsequent service quality and outcomes. The profiles are essential to providing leaders with an accurate view of the work environments as experienced by their service providers and to document changes in that environment as the result of their service improvement efforts.

There is much more to be learned about how to improve human services. However, we know that the social contexts of organizations that provide services affect service quality and outcomes by influencing the behaviors of individual service providers. Successful change efforts must address social context whether the improvement effort is focused at the policy, program, or practice levels. Although improvement efforts limited to the individual service provider—such as training in new practice models or implementing new employee selection criteria—constitute the most common attempts to improve services. Our experience suggests that the social context within which services are provided determines whether an improvement effort is successful.

2

CASE EXAMPLES ILLUSTRATING THE IMPORTANCE OF SOCIAL CONTEXTS IN HUMAN SERVICE ORGANIZATIONS

We include something new in this book that we have never published previously. Our research and consulting over the last several decades have provided us with the opportunity to work closely—sometimes for several years—with staff and leaders in many organizations, ranging from the top CEOs to middle managers to those who provide direct services. Our personal experiences from working with members of these organizations have been as important to our learning about organizations as the findings of our large national surveys and our randomized controlled trials. This book explains what we have learned from these experiences and illustrates the theoretical and conceptual models we developed from our research with real-world examples. We believe the combination of theory, empirical data, and personal experience included in the following chapters provides a comprehensive and compelling method of understanding and describing the strategies we have designed and tested for improving human service organizations.

To begin, we present two case examples from distinctly different organizations, each illustrating contextual characteristics that affect how services are provided. In each of the two cases, unique organizational characteristics that create barriers to effectiveness are highlighted. These two cases illustrate a single contextual continuum (i.e., rigidity) along which the organizations with which we have worked can be placed. This is one of many continuums that characterize OSCs and affect service quality and outcomes. Our focus on a single continuum is to illustrate the complex challenge of understanding and improving organizational effectiveness, and most importantly, the mistakes in improvement efforts that can result from associating effectiveness with a single organizational characteristic such as rigidity.

The two case examples also illustrate that the indeterminate and uncertain nature of providing services to human beings distinguishes human service organizations from other types of organizations such as manufacturing. The distinction of providing human services is a function of multiple factors, including the diverse practices and technologies used in serving human beings; the variation in abilities, motivation, needs, and responses of those being served; and the extent to which the outcomes of the myriad service approaches and practices being applied are unpredictable. For this reason, we argue in the following chapters that successful human service organizations are especially dependent on a combination of shared principles, behaviors, and reasoning among its members to manage effective services without relying simply on bureaucratic structures and routinization. But as the following case examples illustrate, a lack of rigidity can have a negative effect by creating disorder and confusion that is as deleterious to human service outcomes as that imposed by a rigid bureaucracy. Our point is that social contexts are multidimensional and that efforts to improve service quality and outcomes require an array of organizational strategies to improve social contexts along multiple dimensions, depending on the unique profile and capacity of each organization. Our intention is to illustrate these strategies and to explain with this book that the effectiveness of the services provided by a human service organization is, in part, a function of a complex, multidimensional, social context.

TWO VERY DIFFERENT ORGANIZATIONS THAT STRUGGLED TO IMPROVE SERVICES

The following case examples represent two very different organizations. We worked with both organizations for several years. Although their names are omitted, they represent actual, real-world examples of the challenges faced by organizations that attempt to improve the services they provide.

Agency A. Agency A is a large, community-based mental health services organization in the Northeast. Our description of the agency begins with Jessica, who had served as a clinician for seven years in this organization. Jessica was praised by colleagues and leaders for her skill, expertise, and strong work ethic. She received excellent performance evaluations and two promotions, but was immediately fired following the suicide of a teenager under her care: a case that gained considerable attention from the media. Jessica was told in a formal letter of dismissal that she had not paid attention to information that indicated the teenager's risk of suicide. Jessica responded that she had not received the information indicating the risk of suicide before the death occurred.

Jessica filed a subsequent lawsuit, and it became clear that the information she was blamed for ignoring had indeed not reached her. It also became evident that similar errors in information sharing had occurred many times previously in the organization due to recurrent, persistent organizational barriers to communication. However, front-line staff and supervisors had given up mentioning the problem of poor information sharing to middle management because their expressions of concern generated negative responses from management. That is, staff within Agency A were often told they should take responsibility for problems and fix them, but in fact they lacked the means and authority to make the necessary changes. Front-line staff believed they were blamed for problems they could not control, a belief that was substantially reinforced by Jessica's dismissal. No one in the organizational hierarchy above Jessica discussed the barrier regarding information sharing with top leadership prior to or following Jessica's dismissal. We also discovered that the barriers had never been disclosed to executive leaders in the past despite the fact it was well known to line workers and middle managers. As described by a mid-level manager after Jessica's dismissal: "Everyone was worried that they might lose their job if they spoke up about the problem."

To illustrate and underscore the complexity of organizations' social contexts, it is important to note that leaders in this organization held high standards for staff and took pride in what they believed were clearly defined systems, processes, and training for providing quality care. The organization allocated more resources than many of their competitors to data management, staff development, and technical resources such as information systems, computers, and training in best practices. The organization's leaders worked hard to document procedures, rules, and regulations for staff to follow and provided clear job descriptions for new staff. Staff admitted that expectations for their work were clear, as were the divisions of labor and lines of authority. Most importantly, leaders had disseminated and engrained a clear priority that all organizational members maintain strong personal responsibility for their work, task completion, and errors. Executive leaders and most managers believed, and their organization's economic health confirmed, that they were dedicated to making their agency one of the best in their community.

At the same time, organizational leaders expressed frustration during our initial meetings. They believed staff members were not fully benefiting from training opportunities, improvement strategies, or data sources that leaders had worked hard to make available. Further, leaders shared a belief that staff members were not as committed to doing a good job as they had been during their own early years in the organization. When leaders talked about solutions for poorly performing programs, they chose strategies for closely monitoring the activities of staff that relied on work checklists, procedural guidelines, and rules to guide staff. When faced with a crisis due to an error or performance issue in a program, the inclination was to move or replace staff to reestablish in their words, "a more effective program culture."

During staff meetings, there was an acknowledged hierarchy of authority. Subordinates were cautious in speaking or offering ideas in front of superiors, particularly if the information suggested that a potential error, negative perception, or organizational barrier needed to be addressed. In fact, the organizational consultant from our group was cautioned about this issue before entering a meeting that the CEO arranged with the consultant and top leaders. The CEO wanted to discuss potential problems and areas for improvement that had been identified, but one executive pulled the consultant aside prior to the meeting and warned, "Nothing too negative about the organization should be shared. We want to stay positive." Throughout our work with the agency and at multiple levels the phrase "be careful or you'll get thrown under the bus," was repeatedly used to caution colleagues about speaking too freely. It was clear that the organization placed a priority on managing impressions, leaving the consultant constantly deciphering truth from what was said. Front-line staff perceptions of organizational protocols, such as discipline and feedback, were mixed in their assessments. Staff acknowledged many protocols were clear and more detailed than in other places they had worked, but they expressed caution, anxiety, and a feeling of risk that the discipline and feedback systems would be used to point out their own failures.

The front-line staff perceptions of these organizational characteristics were reflected in their responses to our organizational climate and culture assessments. Organizational profiles included moderately high scores in some areas such as staff reporting clarity about work roles and how things should be done. Staff responses in other areas, however, indicated a negative climate, such as the staff members' descriptions of high levels of stress and poor engagement with clients. The organization's culture profile showed that front-line staff reported having little discretion or flexibility in their work, indicating a particularly rigid culture: and they believed that change would be difficult and unlikely to occur, indicating a resistant culture.

Jessica's lawsuit was settled out of court, but the organization continued to be affected by the experience. We worked for two years with the agency's leaders and staff from Jessica's previous program before the limited access to information that led to her dismissal began to be addressed.

Agency B. Agency B is a community-based mental health services organization in the Northeast that is similar in its scope of work to Agency A, but it has a very different work environment. The staff members have little anxiety or fear of being at risk and interactions among leaders, managers, and front-line service providers are consistently positive. In our work with Agency B, the staff members were open, cordial, and genuinely interested in working collaboratively. Everyone was quick to participate and openly discussed organizational problems. Both leaders and staff focused on how well their clients were doing and welcomed suggestions from our group's consultant. Overall, the leaders and managers of Agency B contributed to an open and psychologically safe work environment for their clinicians where suggestions and input, even about problems with leadership, were invited and welcomed.

During meetings, staff members listened carefully to each other's ideas and built constructively upon each other's views. At the same time, however, there was almost no note taking or recording of the ideas and suggestions offered during the meetings. The focus of each meeting tended to change during the discussion and the purpose of each meeting was not always clear. When a purpose or goal for a discussion was initially stated, the original purpose was often lost as the meeting progressed. Most importantly, the meetings usually ended without final decisions, action plans, or the delineation of next steps. Based on these experiences, the consultant from our group worked with the organization's service teams to establish protocols for running meetings, taking notes, creating action plans, and in establishing expectations and actions for following through with decisions. Repeatedly, staff and leaders would apologize for not having completed their allocated tasks, often pointing to a client crisis or other event that arose since the previous meeting. These explanations for not completing tasks were cheerfully accepted by colleagues within the agency. Everyone was satisfied that improvements could be made at some point in the future if work continued.

Our work with Agency B subsequently identified poorly functioning organizational systems in several areas including feedback, training, and discipline. For example, feedback information to front-line supervisors and staff was virtually nonexistent. Data were used internally in a haphazard fashion and gathered primarily to meet minimum funder requirements. As another example, Agency B's training system provided limited orientation to new staff and no structure or process for ongoing training. Nonetheless, members were consistently willing to share advice and ideas with others experiencing a difficult client problem. But processes for establishing training needs, acquiring training, or ensuring that training was implemented simply did not exist. As a third example, although a discipline system had been established, managers reported that it was not used consistently and was not clearly understood by most managers. Managers were not sure what to do if a staff member was behaving inappropriately but suggested that problems were infrequent.

It was clear to our group that the agency struggled with planning and follow-through despite their commitment to improving client well-being. As one program supervisor stated, "We generate a lot of good ideas here, but nothing much comes of them." When asked about note taking, another supervisor said, "I sometimes write down notes for myself, but as a whole, we don't take a lot of notes." A third staff member indicated that their CEO was well liked and well intentioned but that she lost track of projects that were initiated by her and other members of the organization: "She turns a lot of important things over to others and doesn't follow-up to ensure that new things stick." In conversations with the consultant, the CEO indicated that she struggled with follow-through on long-term projects because critical problems or incidents with clients always came up along the way. The CEO stated, "I don't want staff to think client problems are secondary, so I get involved when clients' crises occur. That distracts me from other plans."

We worked with the leaders and managers to prioritize planning and follow-through and to establish structures, processes, and mechanisms within the organization to ensure participation at all levels. Building on their important, shared belief that staying focused on client well-being was critical to success, we focused on linking planning processes and norms for follow-through with client success. Our initial baseline profiles of culture and climate for the organization revealed shared expectations among service providers that change was unlikely to occur and that roles were frequently unclear. The staff in Agency B reported much less rigidity and lower stress in their work environment than described in Agency A. But, the staff in Agency B also described a less functional climate than described by staff in Agency A, and Agency B was resistant to change for a very different reason than Agency A.

Given the baseline social context of the organization, trust developed quickly between the consultant and leaders in Agency B who readily acknowledged concerns about the economic viability of several programs. The leaders' inability to help the programs reach productivity goals necessary to sustain the program was identified as a critical issue. The leaders also remained open and receptive to recommendations and support throughout their participation in the ARC process. However, leaders and staff required considerable support in developing and following through with plans at all levels. The consultant devoted a great deal of time in building the team's skills in planning activities, note taking, and monitoring progress as plans were implemented.

ORGANIZATIONAL SOCIAL CONTEXT (OSC)

The two case examples of Agency A and Agency B illustrate the complexities and challenges of improving the effectiveness of human service organizations, complexities and challenges we will revisit in this chapter and throughout this book. They also highlight the multifaceted role that OSC plays in generating problems and creating barriers and solutions to addressing those problems. That is, these case examples introduce the unique nature of individual organizations and the influence their shared norms, priorities, attitudes, and beliefs have on member behavior and organizational success. These examples help the reader understand what we have concluded from our four decades of research and consulting work within human service organizations. Organization social contexts are central to understanding the success or failure of human service organizations and to building and then sustaining highly successful ones. As you will learn from the following chapters, there are multiple dimensions to social context that can be measured and changed to improve services. Organizational culture and climate are primary factors composing social context, as are the work attitudes (e.g., job satisfaction, commitment) that are shared within a work setting. These elements are common to all organizations and as described below, are particularly important to the effectiveness of human service technologies.

OSC's influence on service quality and outcomes. Organizational climate is associated with individual job performance, job satisfaction, psychological well-being, withdrawal from work, organizational commitment, motivation, and turnover, as well as organizational-level outcomes such as innovation, performance, and productivity (Carr,

Schmidt, Ford & Deshon, 2003; Patterson, West, et al., 2005). Meta-analyses across 84 different studies link organizational culture to product and service quality, innovation, employee work attitudes, organizational growth, and performance (Hartnell, Ou, & Kinicki, 2011; Ogbonna & Harris, 2000; Sackmann, 2011).

Within settings providing behavioral health, social services, medical, and other human services, organizational climate and culture are associated with service quality, service decisions, adoption of empirically supported treatments, sustainability of new programs, access to services, staff turnover, service outcomes, and the practices of those providing the services (Arons & Sawitzky, 2006; Aarons, Sommerfield, & Walrath-Green, 2009; Glisson & Green, 2006, 2011; Glisson & Hemmelgarn, 1998; Glisson & James, 2002; Glisson, Hemmelgarn, Green, & Williams, 2013; Greener, Joe, Simpson, Rowan-Szal, & Lehman, 2007; Hemmelgarn, Glisson, & Dukes, 2001; Morris, Bloom, & Kang, 2007; Schoenwald, Chapman, Sheidow, & Carter, 2009).

It is important to note that the effects of culture and climate are found across a variety of types of organizations, including those in hard technology industries where the materials and processes are well defined and linked closely to product quality. The reliability of Toyota cars, for example, is dependent on the quality of materials, engineering skill and knowledge, and explicit manufacturing practices and processes. Yet Toyota's success in building high-quality vehicles depends as much on their organizational culture as their technology (Liker & Morgan, 2006). This includes the norms and expectations associated with innovation and change at Toyota, such as promoting staff input and participation in improvement efforts. As another well-known example outside of human services, early research recognized the significance of social context in the coal mining industry, where disruptions of established social norms from the introduction of new technologies for coal extraction negatively influenced organizational performance, innovation, and effectiveness (Trist, Higgin, Murray, & Pollock, 1963). And, there are many other contemporary examples in hard technology areas unrelated to human services, such as the Space Shuttle Challenger disaster where established norms of NASA's social context prevented adequate responses to the concerns of engineers who had identified design problems that led to the shuttle's disintegration.

We argue that the outcomes of soft technologies used in behavioral health, social service, and other human service agencies are even more vulnerable to OSCs than are hard technologies. Human service technologies, such as varying treatments for depression, address complex and evolving client problems with multiple approaches. These approaches often differ between and within organizations and individual providers with varying degrees of success. Outcomes associated with these soft technologies are often unpredictable, and success is not always guaranteed—even when highly skilled and knowledgeable providers implement them. These characteristics of soft human service technologies are, in part, a function of the unique characteristics of those receiving services as well the knowledge of how to best serve the unique needs of individuals. What we do know is that human services depend on the quality of relationships and interactions service providers establish and maintain with clients, their families, and other service providers. Service providers depend on these relationships to assess, monitor, and intervene in client problems. Strong relationships ensure that clients, families, and others view the services as available, responsive, and having continuity (the origins of the acronym ARC) and ensure that providers are engaged and clients are more likely to comply.

The indeterminate and unpredictable nature of human services and its dependence on social interaction present both a challenge and opportunity for influencing socially constructed interpretations of organizational events, behavioral expectations, work perceptions, and attitudes that are shared among organizational members. It is these shared expectations, perceptions, and attitudes that create an organization's social context. In uncertain and unpredictable human service work, staff rely on social interactions and social learning to maintain a sense of control and direction in their work. Staff monitor others and interact to understand and establish consensus on acceptable problem-solving approaches and behaviors. Beliefs and assumptions about clients and effective approaches form through communication and social learning as staff process experiences with clients, stakeholders, and their organization's leaders. Shared perceptions of their workplace and their attitudes regarding work develop as members observe and discuss work experiences. In turn, the judgment, decision making, and reasoning of staff and leaders are interpreted through their shared social context. That context defines work norms, patterns of behaviors and expectations that guide organizational members in understanding what is important, what work priorities should be emphasized, what is rewarded, and how to react and behave in the face of uncertain outcomes.

The power of social context to affect individual behavior, perceptions, and attitudes explains the effect of social context on effectiveness. For example, when organizational norms communicate priorities that emphasize and value completing paperwork, rule adherence, and hierarchical decision making, organizational members focus their efforts on completing paperwork and following specified hierarchies and procedures—regardless of whether those activities contribute to improving the well-being of their clients. In these settings, completing the paper correctly and promptly is doing the job well. When organizational norms emphasize the importance of improving the well-being of clients and allow service providers the discretion and flexibility to address unanticipated client problems, the unique needs of each client are more likely to be the focus of their efforts. In these settings, the job is improving the functioning or status of the client.

Mindsets, reasoning, and OSC. The effect of OSC is supported by socially constructed beliefs, assumptions, and inferences that are shared among members. Because human service organizations use soft technologies that vary in their application from organization to organization, staff members within each organization depend on shared beliefs and assumptions to explain success, to understand failures, and to plan on how failures can be avoided in the future. In other words, reasoning about cause and effect and differentiating between appropriate and inappropriate action depend on the beliefs, assumptions, and attributions that are shared within the members' social context. The beliefs, assumptions, and reasoning shared by staff guide their reactions and behavior both implicitly and explicitly, whether explaining positive or negative outcomes. For example, if staff members believe improving client well-being is not a top priority for their leaders—such as what occurs when client headcounts or billing is emphasized over client outcomes—staff interpretations and reactions to organizational events reflect their shared beliefs and lead to interpretations of events that reinforce their beliefs about leadership and their organization. Given their shared beliefs and inferences, staff members in these work environments react to improvement efforts focused on clinical skill development with minimal engagement and effort. They assume that the development effort will have no effect given the true emphasis on headcounts and billing. In another example, an organization that has a shared leadership belief that staff members are unmotivated might adopt more rigid approaches to control staff behavior. From their shared framework of beliefs, leaders would not consider a strategic approach that allows increased discretion for staff for making decisions as rational or effective.

The irony is that organizations that need the most change are often the most resistant as the result of shared beliefs, assumptions, and reasoning that present barriers to change. In overly rigid and resistant cultures, improvement efforts such as continuous improvement processes are implemented as top-down efforts, reflecting the leaders' distrust of their staff's ability or motivation to address difficult barriers, as well as stifling the staff's involvement in the process. It is important to emphasize that these underlying beliefs and assumptions can be implicit, guiding behaviors and approaches with minimal conscious thought (see Chapter 8). Even conscious and thoughtful decision making are subject to selective attention and inferences that drive attributions, influence reasoning, and transform conscious thought and subsequent action. Extending our previous example, when supervisors believe that staff are unmotivated, they attend unconsciously to examples of work not being completed and implicitly attribute failures to this negative trait. Thus, OSCs guide our behaviors and thinking in particularly powerful ways; they drive our reasoning and reactions quickly and often without our conscious awareness. As described in Chapter 8, addressing mental models (loosely termed "mindsets") are a critical part of altering and improving OSCs within human service organizations.

Attitudes, perceptions, and OSC. The psychological impact of work environments on organizational members, or organizational climate described in Chapter 3, is influenced through social learning and affects work attitudes and motivation within a work setting. Perceived stress and emotional exhaustion, for example, alter service providers' motivation, energy, and tenacity for addressing complex client problems (Glisson & Hemmelgarn, 1998). Similarly, these perceptions are closely linked to attitudes toward one's organization, including measures such as organizational commitment and job satisfaction (Glisson & Durick, 1988). Not unexpectedly, these work perceptions and attitudes are associated with work behavior, including the quality of interactions with clients and colleagues. (Broome, Flynne, Knight, & Simpson, 2007; Greener et al., 2007; Schneider, White, & Paul, 1998). This is important because the success of human services relies on relationships with clients and on the interactions among colleagues that support group problem solving, information sharing, and collaborative assistance in addressing complex and difficult cases. Supportive relationships among service providers assure continuity of care as they share common goals, strategies, and approaches for their clients and when assisting each other in a client's care.

When work environments are perceived as unsupportive and stressful, service providers are less engaged in their work and invest less effort in addressing clients' needs and concerns. With less provider engagement and investment, clients experience less service availability, responsiveness, and continuity in their care. That is, the providers support and services may not be accessible or available, adequate, or truly responsive to the client's needs, nor consistent with others to assure continuity. Staff in these types of work environments focus on meeting minimum work requirements with little commitment to addressing clients' unique needs. Less time is spent collaborating with colleagues to develop solutions to difficult client problems. Motivation for tenaciously tackling client problems is diminished, and focus shifts from improving client well-being to rationalizing client failure.

Revisiting Agency A. We know from numerous studies that an organization's social context influences its members' beliefs, reasoning, perceptions, and attitudes, as well as their expectations and behavior. In Agency A, as we described previously, front-line colleagues were frustrated and angry with organizational leaders over Jessica's dismissal. At the same time, they were afraid to express their opinion that Jessica had been treated unfairly. They believed she was another example of staff being blamed for problems that they had no control over. They indicated that the agency worried more about appearances and impression management than addressing clients' needs. Their perceptions were reinforced when an additional manager was disciplined after the legal settlement for not sharing information about the error with upper leadership. As a result, staff morale decreased further and turnover increased in the program following these events.

The leaders in Agency A attempted to understand their agency's problems and believed that the organization's problems were evidence of low commitment among staff. The leaders concluded that they should monitor staff and program performance even more closely and establish additional procedures and guidelines to increase their control of work behavior, representing an escalating commitment to a flawed leadership plan focused on rigidity and control. In this organization (and in others we have been employed in), leaders blamed staff, and staff blamed leaders for many problems, creating a cycle of frustration, distrust, and mutually ineffective behavior.

Our view is that both staff and leaders in Agency A were working hard, performing many hours of unpaid overtime; they wanted their organization to be more successful in serving clients. Despite these positive intentions, the leadership team's authoritarian, rule-driven, controlling, and punitive approaches assured that their efforts would be frustrated. For example, written feedback in the initial stage of the organization's performance evaluations were uniformly perceived by staff members and many leaders as the first step in documentation for dismissal. As another example, feedback to staff regarding problems identified by leaders was accompanied by messages such as, "I don't care how it happened . . . get it fixed," without discussions of what barriers or resources might need to be addressed.

While leaders perceived problems mentioned by staff as excuses for not trying new and promising practices, staff avoided anything that deviated from well-worn paths within the organization for fear they would be blamed for a failed effort. Staff reported decreasing levels of motivation in their work, indicating their certainty that the leaders did not welcome their input or appreciate how hard they were trying. New training initiatives such as the use of EBPs or improving teamwork were therefore perceived by staff as merely additional demands being made without any input from those doing the work. At the same time, leaders were baffled that staff did not appreciate the training they were offered and had such a low level of commitment to improvement. For example, when leaders asked staff what data feedback they would like to receive, staff responded minimally because they expected leaders to use the data to further monitor and control staff behavior.

Staff responses to our own confidential assessment of OSC confirmed high levels of stress, poor engagement with clients, and a dysfunctional work environment. Turnover was increasing and accompanied by expectations of negative repercussions for openly discussing organizational barriers to service. There was little staff motivation for improvement. Negative attributions by staff focused on leaders not taking responsibility for solving problems that were then blamed on lower-level staff members. Negative attributions by leaders, in turn, focused on staff members' lack of commitment to improvement. Discipline, training, and performance evaluations continued to emphasize control and punishment rather than support and development. Staff described an OSC characterized by ineffective yet deeply held beliefs and increasingly engrained behavioral norms that ensured long-term failure.

OSC, innovation, and evidence-based practices. We found in our research and consulting work with organizations that poor social contexts have two effects: They hamper organizational effectiveness and at the same time prevent efforts to improve effectiveness. That is, contextual factors that harm performance prevent innovations and improvements from being successful at improving performance. In Agency A, for example, leaders failed in their improvement efforts to provide easily accessible client feedback data to service providers after installing a new data information system because of a poor social context. The data system provided easily accessed results, but staff subverted access to the data because they feared how the data would be used.

Agency B, on the other hand, had a much different problem. The history of failures in implementing new technologies and processes established expectations among staff that new approaches or innovations would fail. Previous failures occurred because behavioral norms of the organization did not include expectations for planning, monitoring, and follow-through. As a result, Agency B's past failures were repeated. In our work, we found that the lack of follow-through in an organization takes different forms but always with similar results: an acceptance of the status quo with little expectation of change. In another organization, for example, we asked a focus group of child welfare supervisors and leaders to list barriers that hampered their ability to succeed with clients. They spent two hours listing a variety of service barriers they encountered but were unable to respond when asked what specific ideas or action steps they had for eliminating any of the barriers. The cultural norm in that organization was focusing on problems, not solutions. The associated belief that it would be unreasonable to hold caseworkers responsible for improving clients' well-being, given the complexity of the problems, was so strongly embedded that being asked for solutions was perceived as inappropriate.

The association of OSC with problem solving, innovation, and the implementation of best practices has been recognized by organizational researchers with direct implications for improving human services (Aarons & Sawitzky, 2006; Aarons et al., 2012; Glisson, Williams, Hemmelgarn, Proctor, & Green, 2016b; Williams & Glisson, 2014a; Williams et al., 2016). Recognizing the impact of context on treatment outcomes, the National Institute of Health (1997) report, *Bridging Science and Service,* concluded decades ago that the clinical utility and effectiveness of new treatments in community-based practice settings are quite distinct from their efficacy in controlled clinical trials. For this reason, models to guide clinicians and researchers in assessing effectiveness beyond efficacy trials (Onken, Blain, & Battjes, 1997) and the development of practice research networks where new treatments and technologies can be tested within applied settings have been emphasized for some time (Borkovec, Echemendia, Ragusea, & Rusiz, 2001; Norquist, 2001). These efforts continue to be driven by the mixed success of disseminating and implementing efficacious clinical practices in community settings (Kazdin, 2015; NIMH, 2015; Weisz & Jensen, 1999; Weisz et al., 2015; Weisz, Ugueto, Cheron, & Herren, 2013). We conclude from our research and consulting experience that the influence of OSC on the adoption and implementation of new practices explain why EBP's are not consistently effective in community settings (Glisson et al., 2016b; Hemmelgarn, Glisson, & James, 2006; Williams et al., 2016).

Social context affects innovation from the initial stage of exploration to the last stage of sustaining implemented innovations. For example, we know that improving OSCs increases exploratory and preparatory behavior for adopting EBP's (Glisson et al., 2016b). Exploration and preparatory behaviors occur when staff members are embedded in cultures that expect staff to be up to date and proficient in their knowledge, skills, and practices. As a result, the success of EBPs can be improved using organizational strategies that target the social contexts in which the practices are introduced (Glisson et al., 2010).

Our experience in introducing a new child assessment tool in a state child welfare system provides an illustration. We designed a child assessment and monitoring measure to improve placement and service decisions for children in the care of child welfare and tested its reliability and validity in several studies (Glisson, Hemmelgarn, & Post, 2002; Hemmelgarn, Glisson, & Sharp, 2003; Tyson & Glisson, 2005). The leaders of a state child welfare system were enthusiastic about implementing the assessment and monitoring tool. We discovered in the implementation process, however, that their enthusiasm was associated with the expectation of controlling staff behavior rather than individualizing care. The goal of providing staff with a tool that could inform service and placement decisions was less important to the leaders than standardizing decisions in a way that could be monitored to reduce staff decisions. That is, leaders believed the assessment could be used as a cookie-cutter decision tool that minimized discretion and associated errors of their front-line staff. The agency's emphasis on control, centralized decisions, and organizational norms that placed a priority on paperwork allowed the assessment tool to be distributed, completed, and filed by front-line staff statewide within a short time. Following existing norms, the results of the assessment measure were quickly added to the paperwork packets completed on each child at intake.

The organization's culture ensured the assessment tool was completed and filed for each child. But the culture also ensured that the assessment did not improve services. The tool's intended purpose of providing information to improve client service and placement decisions was not realized. It was simply additional documentation to be completed and placed in each child's file. The norms for paperwork were so strong that caseworkers gathered the assessment information from anyone they could find who knew the child to complete the report, including reports from a parent who had not seen their child in 5 years. Sustainability, in one sense, was assured without improving services. The measure continued to be completed for many years, but our later work in the system revealed the assessments were never used for the intended purpose. The cultural norms that contributed to it being added to the intake paperwork also prevented the information generated by the assessment from being used to improve services. We learned from this and other experiences that new practices can be sustained by OSCs independently of effectiveness defined as improvements in service outcomes (Glisson, 2008).

THE CHALLENGE OF CREATING EFFECTIVE OSCS

Leaders and other members of service organizations do not purposefully create social contexts that impede their effectiveness. Nevertheless, data from two nationwide studies, as well as multiple regional studies, show poor OSCs are created as often as outstanding ones (Glisson, Landsverk, et al., 2008; Glisson, Green, & Williams, 2012; Olin et al., 2014). We have shown that organizational culture and climate profiles vary enormously across nationwide samples of social service and mental health organizations and that the profiles are associated with criteria such as staff burnout and turnover, as well as service quality and outcomes (Glisson, 2010; Glisson & Green, 2006, 2011; Glisson & Hemmelgarn, 1998;

Glisson & James, 2002; Glisson, Schoenwald, et al., 2008; Olin et al., 2014; Williams & Glisson, 2014b; Glisson et al., 2016; Williams et al., 2016).

There is significant variation in social contexts even when organizations with similar resources serving similar clients in similar communities are compared. In other words, leaders and staff as well as the nature of the processes and systems they support play a significant role in creating OSCs. This does not discount, however, the myriad practical constraints facing leaders and staff of mental health, social service, and other human service organizations, constraints that present complex challenges for efforts to improve social contexts. These organizations are fraught with internal and external challenges that create competing priorities, demands, and pressures that undermine and detract from positive social contexts. The following chapters describe these challenges and the strategies we have developed to address them. We explain how social contexts can be improved with these strategies and how service quality and outcomes benefit from the improvements.

Our efforts to improve services are based on the understanding that those served are individuals who vary in strengths and needs and are embedded in multiple social networks and community settings that present service barriers. As a result, human service providers address highly complex problems that require careful monitoring, adaptation, and individualized attention to the demands of each client, knowing that success varies and is only partially affected by their efforts. Moreover, external forces created by federal and state government rules and regulations, media coverage of exceptional cases, class action lawsuits, and associated consent decrees are a part of many service environments that place additional demands on social services, mental health, and other human services. The environment for service organizations is also shaped by financial, political, and community factors. Each of these influence what the organizations can and cannot do in the face of uncertainty associated with economic and political changes at state and federal levels. For example, the ebb and flow of economic and political support created by policies such as the Affordable Care Act and No Child Left Behind are associated with a multitude of technical, procedural, and resource-related challenges.

Although the list of external factors goes well beyond these examples, they illustrate that creating and maintaining effective human service organizations are most difficult for systems that resist innovation and change. Ironically, external funders, regulators, legislators, and others often create additional uncertainty and challenge for human service systems even with well-intended efforts to improve services. For example, human service organizations often depend on multiple funding streams, each of which requires additional documentation and, in many cases, unique measures of service quality and outcomes. This unwittingly results in overwhelmed and frustrated staff that must gather and record an ever-increasing amount of information to satisfy the need for accountability. Within this turbulent environment, improvement efforts can be perceived by staff as a burden rather than part of a solution. Leaders and managers respond by spending much of their time addressing the logistical demands of change, developing new training protocols for staff, and integrating new policy requirements within existing systems—all while attempting to continue the core work of the organization.

As suggested by Lundberg (1990), organizational culture provides "the reservoir of solutions to the organization's ongoing and recurring issues and fundamental tasks—from survival in the external environment to managing internal affairs, from handling crises to inculcating new members, from dealing with growth or decline to maintaining morale, from measuring performance to renewing product-service offerings." We discuss in the following chapters our strategies for creating organizational cultures that can provide the reservoir of solutions for improving human services faced with high levels of uncertainty and change.

3

UNDERSTANDING AND ASSESSING ORGANIZATIONAL SOCIAL CONTEXT (OSC)

Experience and research convince us that efforts to improve human services, whether through innovation, the implementation of best practices, or a reduction in bureaucratic red tape, require improvements in OSCs. Our conclusion rests on the fact that organizations are social systems defined by shared behavioral norms, perceptions, and attitudes that guide how its members act, what they believe is important, and how they view their responsibilities and contributions to their organizations' goals. These systems' characteristics include the mindsets and the priorities shared by organizational members as they provide service to clients, make daily decisions that influence care, and interact with colleagues to achieve the objectives established by the organization.

Both our research and consulting work with organizations have depended on our ability to assess their social contexts. We developed our measure of OSC to profile organizations' social contexts and to link those profiles to a variety of service outcomes. We use the OSC measure during our organizational improvement strategies to compare individual human service organizations with national norms and to monitor changes in social context over time. Nationally normed profiles for individual organizations are useful for creating the need for change, educating organizational members on the impact of OSC on critical outcomes and helping organizational members understand the shared behavior, perceptions, and reasoning that characterize their organization.

The complex social systems that define organizations are reflected in our measure of OSC, including their multifaceted nature. We begin this chapter by reviewing our approach to assessing OSCs and providing information about the use of OSC profiles for improving human services.

THE MEANING AND MEASUREMENT OF OSC

Our understanding of OSC identifies an organization's culture and climate as its central and most important elements (Glisson & Williams, 2015). We define culture as the expectations and norms that guide behavior in the organization such as resistance to change. It is the way things are done in an organization, what is expected, and what is rewarded and reinforced. Climate is defined as the psychological impact of the work environment on the members—such as the impact of stress on workers. Although the terms, culture, and climate are sometimes used interchangeably by researchers and practitioners, we define them as distinct constructs and have confirmed their distinct nature in two nationwide studies (Glisson, Green, & Williams, 2012; Glisson, Landsverk, et al., 2008). These two studies and many regional studies confirm that child welfare and mental health service organizations, respectively, each exhibit a variety of distinct organizational culture and climate profiles (Glisson, Green, & Williams, 2012; Glisson, Landsverk, et al., 2008). As reviewed briefly in this chapter and in more detail in subsequent chapters, these culture and climate profiles are associated with a variety of organizational criteria that include staff turnover, service outcomes, and innovation success. These profiles also mediate the effects of service improvement efforts at both individual service provider and organization levels.

Identifying shared beliefs through workplace norms and perceptions. The value of assessing the behavioral expectations reported by the members of a work setting and their perceptions of the work setting's impact on their well-being is well established for predicting work performance and organizational outcomes (Tucker, McCoy, & Evans, 1990). Shared behavioral expectations and perceptions in the workplace are formed as new members model coworkers within work settings through social learning (Fiske & Taylor, 2013). Based on the need to be accepted by coworkers and leaders, work behaviors can be adopted without necessarily adopting the deeper assumptions, beliefs, or values that underlie their enactment. However, we know from our research and consulting experience that the assessment of behavioral norms and staff perceptions promotes the discussion of implicit beliefs, assumptions, and priorities that support these norms and perceptions. These implicit beliefs and assumptions are often identified as the deeper elements of organizational culture (Schein, 1985; Lundberg, 1990). Because human service organizations incorporate relatively indeterminate and uncertain service technologies, appropriate decisions and approaches are often guided and supported by social interaction. Similarly, shared reasoning and assumptions often develop among organizational members who are searching for the best course of action. When inevitable failures occur, individuals review hypothetical scenarios in their minds of what may have been done differently. These scenarios are often social in nature, such as envisioning what another colleague may have done or envisioning how interactions with clients may have been different using another approach. Inferences about why successes or failures occurred are explored and shared with other organizational members. Socially influenced rationalizations, justifications, and attributions for failures are applied as organizational members attempt to gain a greater sense of predictability and certainty over what is unpredictable and uncertain work by watching or interacting with others. As explained in Chapter 8, unexpected events—particularly failures—establish shared inferences, beliefs, values, and assumptions that become implicit over time in guiding work behaviors, expectations, and perceptions.

Given these social mechanisms and their outcomes, we employ the OSC profiles of organizational culture to identify connections between expected behaviors and more implicit, deeply held assumptions and beliefs. These implicit elements of organizational culture are indirect and difficult to discern, but they play a powerful role in guiding interpretations, reasoning, decision making, and responses to events in work environments. To illustrate, during our work with one particular organization, we attended a meeting designed to evaluate staff proposals for improving services. An executive leader in the group became excited while reviewing a proposal for improvement. She interrupted the meeting, putting her hands in the air and expressing her elation about the well-thought-out solutions being suggested. She exclaimed, "These ideas are fabulous, but how are we going to get the frontline staff to do . . ." Suddenly stopping mid-sentence, she placed her hands over her mouth and said, "Oh, I am so sorry, it was your ideas" as she looked with embarrassment at the front-line team member and supervisor who had brought their team's proposal to the group. She continued, "I am so sorry. . . but I didn't realize that staff understood these issues this well and could provide such great solutions,—better than ours [referring to the executive leaders]."

That event was pivotal in helping the leaders understand what had been reported by staff in their organization's OSC profile. Leaders managed in a top-down, directive manner; they spent considerable time strategizing how to get buy-in to leaders' ideas by employing token or superficial requests for input from staff; and they failed to listen closely or trust input from front-line staff on organizational barriers. The event quickly heightened leaders' awareness of the meaning and impact of what was displayed in their OSC culture profile—a profile characterized by high scores on rigidity and resistance. The same leader indicated after her initial comment that for years leaders had been trying to figure out how to get staff to address the barrier presented in the proposal, yet they had been ineffective. The event resulted in leaders questioning their negative beliefs about staff input, its validity, and its importance for engagement. Leaders recognized that they shared a belief that obtaining input from staff was merely a strategy to develop support for the leaders' ideas, rather than an honest attempt to listen, elicit staff input, and to use that input. That is, they recognized that their pattern of behavior did not support staff input and involvement. Subsequent conversations among leaders and the organizational consultant focused on the need to develop a more flexible and open culture; underscored by beliefs in the value of staff input and participation in solving problems affecting their work. Leaders began to develop a belief that staff members are more than capable of solving problems if given the opportunity, and that staff can identify critical problems and offer innovative solutions that influence the effectiveness of their organization. Consistent with their organization's OSC profiles, leaders recognized that although they had created an agency that was functional in many ways, their elevated OSC scores on rigidity and resistance reflected an ineffective top-down approach to problem solving. Of particular importance was their awareness that their assumptions about staff input had to change. This awareness allowed them to alter their paternalistic approach to problem solving that undermined the organization's success.

Later conversations with the leaders in our example indicated the leaders' growing understanding that they had been too controlling in implementing improvement efforts and that they had modeled these behaviors to supervisors. For another executive leader, the experience challenged her belief that creating fear in staff was effective in getting good performance. She later reported recognizing that a more effective leadership approach was to be clear about goals and structures needed to accomplish work, but to listen and collaborate with staff as partners in achieving those goals. She said this realization allowed her to work with staff in identifying service barriers instead of immeasurable hours of dictating solutions and demanding they get done. Later conversations with several front-line staff confirmed that the leaders' approach to supervision and discipline changed significantly in a way that increased program effectiveness and staff engagement. As one staff member summarized the change in several leaders: "They no longer believe that they alone hold the solutions to the problems we all face."

THE OSC MEASUREMENT SYSTEM

The OSC measurement system composes three major dimensions that we have confirmed in two nationwide samples as well as several regional studies: culture, climate, and work attitudes. Although the terms "culture" and "climate" are used interchangeably by some writers, each has a unique history and we define the two constructs in distinct ways (Ashkanasy, Wilderom, & Peterson, 2000; Glisson & James, 2002; Reichers & Schneider, 1990; Verbeke, Volgering, & Hessels, 1998). We agree with those researchers who define climate as the way employees perceive the psychological impact of their work environment on their own well-being and define culture as the expectations for the way things are done in the organization (Verbeke et al., 1998). The third dimension of the OSC, work attitudes, is measured as an individual-level construct that includes job satisfaction and organizational commitment, which together reflect the morale of the members (Glisson & Durick, 1988).

We developed and refined scales of the OSC measurement system over the last four decades to assess OSC using organizational profiles. These norm-based profiles allow individual organizations to be compared against nationwide samples of similar organizations to provide a better understanding of the culture and climate described by members of an organization (Glisson, Green, & Williams, 2012; Glisson, Landsverk, et al., 2008). The profiles use standardized percentile scores for each variable to reveal what proportion of organizations providing similar services nationwide have higher or lower scores on rigidity, stress, and other culture and climate dimensions.

Our studies support the validity of the OSC, including two nationwide studies of its factor validity in mental health and social service agencies, respectively (Glisson, Green, & Williams, 2012; Glisson, Landsverk, et al., 2008). The criterion validity and predictive validity of OSC profile scores were confirmed in multiple samples of mental health and social service agencies on separate outcome criteria including clinicians' work attitudes (Glisson, Green, & Williams, 2012; Glisson & James, 2002; Williams & Glisson, 2014b), clinician turnover (Glisson & James, 2002; Glisson, Schoenwald et al., 2008; Williams & Glisson, 2013), new program sustainability (Glisson, Schoenwald et al., 2008), EBT preparation and use (Glisson et al., 2016b; Williams et al., 2016), service quality (Glisson & Green, 2006; Glisson & James, 2002; Olin et al., 2014), and clinical outcomes (Glisson, 2010; Glisson & Green, 2011; Glisson & Hemmelgarn, 1998; Glisson et al., 2013; Williams & Glisson, 2013, 2014a).

Organizational culture. Culture is a relatively new construct in the organizational literature that first appeared in the 1970s. It was influenced by sociological and anthropological views of organizations as social systems that are characterized by certain distinguishable behaviors or norms. We define culture as the behavioral norms and expectations of a work environment that determine how work is done and what is most important and rewarded by the organization. These norms are often forwarded as the primary mechanism for transmittal of organizational culture (Ashkanasy, Broadfoot, & Falcus, 2000; Hofstede, 1998; Hofstede, Neuijen, Ohayv, & Sanders, 1990). The OSC assesses three dimensions of culture: proficiency, rigidity, and resistance.

Proficient cultures. Proficient cultures are characterized by expectations that service providers will place the well-being of each client first and by expectations that individual service providers will be competent and have up-to-date skills and knowledge. Representative items completed by service providers to assess proficiency include "Members of my organizational unit are expected to be responsive to the needs of each client" and "Members of my organizational unit are expected to have up-to-date knowledge." The proficiency scale consists of both competency and responsiveness items. Competency describes the emphasis placed on training, up-to-date knowledge, and expectations of excellence in skills and abilities. Responsiveness describes the extent to which service providers are expected to meet the unique needs of individual clients.

Proficient service cultures are characterized by the expectation that the well-being of clients will be a priority and that the service provider will maintain up-to-date knowledge and skills. Emphasis is placed on training and evaluation because they contribute to effectiveness. Our research shows that service providers in proficient cultures have positive attitudes toward EBPs and are more likely to explore and prepare for using new EBPs as they become available (Aarons et al., 2012; Glisson et al., 2016b). Organizations with proficient cultures maintain formal and informal structures to promote successful service outcomes and their workers' investment in developing improved skills. Subsequently, proficient cultures are associated with higher service quality and positive service outcomes (Olin et al., 2014; Glisson et al., 2013; Williams & Glisson, 2013).

Rigid cultures. Rigid service cultures expect service providers to have less discretion and flexibility in their work; make limited input into management decisions; and work under excessive bureaucratic rules and regulations. Representative items assessing rigidity include "I have to ask a supervisor or coordinator before I do almost anything" and "The same steps must be followed in processing every piece of work." The rigidity scale includes both centralization and formalization. Centralization indicates the degree to which power and decision making are in the hands of relatively few in the organization while formalization is characterized by procedural specifications that guide work-related behavior and interactions among members of an organizational unit. Organizations that are highly centralized and highly formalized emphasize control with little individual autonomy or participative decision making.

A rigid organizational culture allows little flexibility in the way work is accomplished and services are provided. For this reason, it is difficult to tailor services to the unique needs of each individual client. Instead, services in a rigid culture resemble an assembly line with similar actions being taken for each client. Leaders in rigid organizations are committed to a narrow range of service protocols and place limited trust in staff to make independent decisions. In rigid cultures, important information is more accessible to leadership and less accessible to line-level staff. Organizational hierarchies of authority with several layers of management are associated with rigid cultures, policies are explicitly followed and micromanagement is the norm.

Resistant cultures. Resistant service cultures expect that service providers will show little interest in change or in new ways of providing service and will suppress any opportunity for innovation. Representative items include, "Members of my organizational unit are expected to not make waves" and "Members of my organizational unit are expected to avoid being different." Resistance includes items to assess both apathetic and suppressive behavioral expectations. Apathetic items assess the level of resignation and inactivity toward change while suppression items describe expectations of criticism and opposition that undermine openness and innovation.

Resistant organizational cultures are less open to new ideas, protocols, or technologies even when an innovation might be helpful to clients. Leaders are reluctant to consider change and make excuses for not adopting new ideas, citing incompatibility with current organizational practices or the lack of time or money required for the change. Resistance can take the form of passive resistance where new suggestions or ideas are simply forgotten or not implemented—or active resistance where new ideas are openly criticized in front of fellow staff members. Resistant cultures expect staff to discuss problems but never consider solutions that require doing things differently. There is a fundamental belief underlying resistant cultures that success is not something that can be controlled but is a function of external forces beyond the organization's control. In resistant cultures, staff reactions to the introduction of new ideas or programs include statements such as, "This is just one more thing that will come and go" or "Whoever designed this doesn't know the real world." Resistant organizational cultures are associated with stagnation, an inability to innovate, and difficulty with change.

Organizational climate. Organizational climate is an older construct than organizational culture and was developed by psychologists from research on leadership, teams, and workgroups in the mid-1900s. Following this work, we define climate as the psychological impact of a work environment as perceived by those who work in it. *Psychological climate* describes the individual's perception of the psychological impact (e.g., stress) of his or her work environment on his or her own functioning and well-being (James & James, 1989). When members of the same work environment agree on their perceptions (e.g., the shared perception that their work environment is stressful), their shared perceptions can be aggregated to describe the *organizational climate* of their work environment (e.g., the work environment is characterized as stressful) (Glisson, Green, & Williams, 2012; Glisson, Landsverk et al., 2008; James, Demaree, & Wolf, 1984; Jones & James, 1979; Joyce & Slocum, 1984). That is, the shared perceptions of individuals in the same work setting are used to evaluate climate (Brown & Leigh, 1996). And these perceptions are influential. Front-line staff perceptions of work settings are associated with numerous outcomes including organizational commitment, turnover, and service quality (Glisson & Durick, 1988; Glisson & James, 2002; Herman & Hulin, 1972; Morris & Sherman, 1981). Outcomes include the quality of relationships or therapeutic alliances established with clients (Blanz & Schmidt, 2000; Florsheim, Shotorbani, Guest-Warnick, Barratt & Hwang, 2000) that influence our first dimension of climate.

Engaged climates. Engaged climates are characterized by service providers reporting they accomplish worthwhile goals in their work, remain personally involved in it—and they are concerned about the welfare of their clients. Representative items include, "I feel I treat some of the clients I serve as impersonal objects (reverse coded)" and "I have accomplished many worthwhile things in this job." The items assessing engagement include both personalization and personal accomplishment items. Personalization items indicate the degree to which organizational members feel connected and involved with their clients. Personal accomplishment assesses perceptions of efficacy in dealing with clients and positive emotions related to success with clients.

Staff in engaged climates report positive interpersonal relationships with clients and a sincere concern for their well-being and success. For example, engaged staff balance requirements for timely paperwork completion and productivity with the understanding that the care and treatment of clients comprise their primary focus. Staff who are more engaged describe a high level of commitment to their clients' welfare that goes beyond the routine motions of service to include a determined effort to meet clients' individual needs. Engaged staff place the improvement of their clients' well-being as the highest priority and ensure that the services they provide are both available and responsive to each client.

Functional climates. Functional climates are characterized by employees reporting they receive the cooperation and help from their coworkers and administration that is required to do their job, have a clear understanding of how they fit into the core mission of their organization, and can be successful within their organizational unit. Representative items include, "My job responsibilities are clearly defined" and "There is a feeling of cooperation among my coworkers." The functional scale includes items for professional growth and advancement, role clarity in their job, and cooperation within their workgroup. Staff in more functional climates perceived opportunities for professional development and felt that their roles in the organization and contributions to the organization's mission were clear; they also perceived that other staff would assist and support them in their efforts.

In functional climates, staff report they receive cooperation and help from their coworkers and administration, that their job duties and work assignments are well defined, and that they can work successfully with the members of their work unit. Staff members in functional climates are familiar with organizational procedures for implementing training or introducing new ideas, and there is clear communication regarding the use of new techniques within the organization. In short, functional climates represent well-oiled machines where staff members know how to get things done in their work environment and receive the support they need to do their jobs.

Stressful climates. Stressful climates are characterized by employees reporting they are emotionally exhausted from their work, pulled in different directions, and lack the time to get the necessary things done. Representative items include, "I feel like I am at the end of my rope" and "The amount of work I have to do keeps me from doing a good job." Stress is identified by emotional exhaustion, role conflict, and role overload. Respectively, these elements include perceptions of feeling overwhelmed, of experiencing multiple conflicting demands, and of having impossible amounts of work to accomplish.

The staff members in stressful climates believe they do not have the time to do their jobs adequately and are unable to address the most important demands of their jobs. Emotional exhaustion exacerbates their declining commitment and energy to achieve positive client outcomes. Stressful climates are often seen in crisis-centered rather than client-centered work environments where reactive versus proactive approaches are a priority. For this reason, innovation and the introduction of new practices are difficult to implement in stressful climates and are more likely to represent top-down demands than a bottom-up support. The low level of enthusiasm for change occurs because staff in stressful climates experience new procedures as adding to the stress in their work.

Work attitudes. Work attitudes have been studied for many decades and are commonly represented by the constructs of *job satisfaction* and *organizational commitment* (Glisson & Durick, 1988). Job satisfaction is defined as an individual's positive appraisal of the tasks completed at work and of the responsibilities associated with those tasks. Organizational commitment is defined as an individual's attachment to the organization's goals, willingness to invest effort on behalf of the organization, and a desire to remain a member of the organization. Commitment emphasizes the employee's attachment to the organization whereas satisfaction emphasizes the employee's appraisal of the specific task environment where their own work is performed (Mowday, Porter, & Steers, 1982). Characteristics of their own tasks (e.g., role ambiguity) are the best predictors of job satisfaction while characteristics of the organization (e.g., leadership) are the best predictors of organizational commitment (Glisson & Durick, 1988). Positive culture and climate profiles are associated with both job satisfaction and organizational commitment (Glisson, Green, & Williams, 2012; Glisson, Landsverk et al., 2008).

The OSC provides an assessment of employee morale as a combination of front-line service provider's perceptions of both job satisfaction and organizational commitment. Representative items include, "How satisfied are you with the feeling of accomplishment you get from your job?" and "I really care about the fate of this organization." Morale is an attitudinal measure that is measured at the individual level. Individual-level standardized scores for morale, as well as job satisfaction and organizational commitment, are computed based on norms from the two nationwide data sets. Staff experiencing high morale feel positive about their specific jobs and positive about their organization. They are enthusiastic about their work and willing to contribute more than is required of them, contributing to positive relationships with both clients and coworkers.

ORGANIZATIONAL CULTURE AND CLIMATE PROFILES

People are unique: they have individual temperaments, predispositions, and motives. At the same time, people can share similar personality traits (e.g., extroversion, conscientiousness) and can be identified and grouped on their personality profiles. Although there is debate about the most important dimensions of personality, there is little debate on whether people share certain traits. In a similar fashion, organizations can be described and classified using their culture and climate profiles. These profiles reflect what can be viewed as an organization's personality expressed as its priorities, expectations, and impact on its members. Shared beliefs and perceptions within the same organizational unit form a social context with shared customs, norms, and perceptions that guide how members interact and what they emphasize in their work. We have identified three types of organizational profiles in our national samples of behavioral health and social service agencies that predict service quality and outcomes (Glisson, Green, & Williams, 2012; Glisson, Landsverk et al., 2008; Glisson & Williams, 2015). These profiles result from a latent profile analysis of the six culture and climate dimensions and allow us to compare new organizational profiles with these core profiles representing a "best" profile, a "worst" profile, and an "average" profile.

Members of organizations with the "worst" culture profile are embedded in social contexts with the lowest scores on proficiency. Staff in these organizations report that their work expectations do not prioritize skill development, expertise, or the use of up-to-date practices. The worst profile also includes a rigid culture in which members report having very little control over the types of service they provide and little opportunity to address service program or system barriers that interfere with client care. The service providers expect to be at risk if they surface issues or problems that might be preventing better care, and they expect that simply following the rules is the wisest course of action. Organizations with the worst profiles are also characterized by a resistant culture with expectations that no change will occur in their work environment. They expect new ideas or innovations to be criticized or not attempted (and if attempted, to fail).

The worst cultures are often associated with the worst climates. Staff in the worst climates perceive their organization to be highly dysfunctional. They report receiving minimal support from colleagues and leaders, little clarity about their roles, and little opportunity for growth in skills or professional advancement. Members of organizations with the worst climates report experiencing little personal accomplishment in their work and describe an emotional distance from their clients that creates a lack of engagement in their work. Members of organizations with the worst climates also report a high level of stress in which members report being emotionally exhausted and overloaded. We find these worst profiles in organizations where outcomes for clients are dismal. Staff are demoralized and the organization limps along, often in a bureaucratic maze of regulations, rules, and dysfunctional interactions that preclude success.

Organizations with the best culture and climate profiles look very different. Members of organizations with the best profiles describe proficient culture where staff are expected to acquire new skills and provide the best care. There is a palpable feeling of excitement and pride in being well trained. The expectation in these organizations is that organizational leaders, supervisors, and managers will respond to staff input on issues that influence services. Members have the discretion to respond to unexpected events and needs. Members also expect that new ideas will be considered, that coworkers will share responsibility in making them work, and that success will be achieved. The climates of the organizations with the best profiles include staff perceptions of being highly engaged with their clients and experiencing strong feeling of accomplishment in their work. Members report receiving the help they need to be successful and expanding their knowledge and professional skill. These members also experience lower levels of stress perceived as less exhaustion and work overload.

Our research shows that the worst and best profiles are best defined by relative differences in an organization's OSC standardized scores on each of the dimensions of culture and climate described previously. That is, in addition to higher or lower absolute values on the dimensions of culture and climate, the differences in values on each dimension within the same organization are important in identifying the best and worst profiles. For example, organizations with the worst cultures have proficiency culture scores that are at least one and a half standard deviations lower than both their rigidity and resistance scores. In other words, line-level service providers describe the worst agencies as having high expectations of resistance and rigidity relative to lower expectations for proficiency. In a similar manner, organizations with the best culture profiles are identified as having proficiency scores that are at least one and a half standard deviations higher than their rigidity and resistance scores. As described by line-level service providers, the best service organizations have expectations for proficiency that are high compared to low expectations for rigidity and resistance.

Climate profiles are categorized in a similar way. Organizations with the worst climate profiles have both engagement and functionality standardized scores that are at least one and a half standard deviations lower than their stress score. That is, line-level service providers in organizations with the worst climates report high levels of stress compared to low levels of engagement and functionality. Agencies with the best climate profile have engagement and functionality scores that are at least one and a half standard deviations higher than their stress score. Therefore, service providers in agencies with the best climate profiles describe high levels of engagement and functionality compared to low levels of stress.

THE IMPORTANCE OF OSCS TO HUMAN SERVICES

Positive OSC profiles *are important to human service outcomes* for both staff and clients (Glisson & Williams, 2015). Organizational culture and climate are associated with lower staff turnover, the sustainment of new programs, attitudes toward the use of evidence-based practices (EBPs), and preparing to use EBPs (Aarons et al., 2012; Glisson & James, 2002; Glisson, Schoenwald et al., 2008; Glisson et al., 2016b; Williams & Glisson, 2013; Williams et al., 2016). In addition, positive cultures and climates as measured by the OSC are associated with higher service quality and better outcomes (Glisson, 2010; Glisson & Green, 2006, 2011; Glisson & Hemmelgarn, 1998; Olin et al., 2014; Williams & Glisson, 2014b).

These studies show that OSC dimensions *provide insight into the nature of organizational systems and processes* that are essential to improving services. Organizations with low OSC proficiency scores, for example, have limited training capacity, especially for discretionary or volitional training guided by organizational members. This is because low proficiency expectations align with limited training opportunities for improving clinical expertise and skill development. In contrast, organizations with high-proficiency cultures emphasize and ensure effective training. Training budgets tend to be higher, training is expected, and staff members are more likely to self-select training in areas they believe will enhance their personal skill levels. In addition, formal processes often exist to support staff in reporting back to others within their programs regarding knowledge and skills gained from their training. Moreover, procedures are in place to support training and ensure training is implemented. When new techniques or approaches acquired through training show positive results, supervisors and executive leaders are more likely to disseminate information and to spread the training within other organizational programs.

In low proficiency cultures, training represents the minimum needed to meet licensing requirements, accreditation standards, or job orientation requirements and is not focused on high-level skills that ensure the highest quality of care. There are minimal processes for staff to identify clinical training needs, and procedures to acquire needed training are poorly developed. In other words, organizational members describe limited expectations for excellence in clinical skills aimed at improving client outcomes, and training systems and processes reflect these minimum expectations.

Agency A that was described previously devoted more resources to training than many other agencies we have worked with, but Agency A's proficiency scores were not high. The agency devoted resources to assessing staff training needs, providing potential training events, and maintaining clear training documents that guided staff in the steps that should be taken to acquire new skills and knowledge. However, the agency's resistant and rigid culture, along with its stressful climate and low engagement among staff thwarted success, despite functionality scores that were moderately high. The lack of discretion provided to staff accompanied with high levels of stress and a poor sense of accomplishment created little motivation or personal investment in mastering new training. For the staff in Agency A, their poor climate perceptions and negative work attitudes diminished their capacity for purposeful learning during training events. Accompanied by poor expectations for change and the belief that trying new protocols would lead to unpleasant consequences if implemented unsuccessfully, training was ineffective and the outcomes were poor.

Service providers in the previous example of Agency B reported high levels of engagement with clients and a willingness to try new things but failed in implementing training. In Agency B, however, a somewhat below-average level of functionality reported by staff on the OSC was associated with the failure of their training system. Resources for staff training were inconsistent over time, and there were no clear processes to ensure training would be implemented, although clinicians were eager to discuss training when it was offered. However, ideas for changes that emerged following training were not developed fully. It was noteworthy that simple skills that were easy to implement were more likely to be adopted and diffused within the organization because they required less planning and follow-through.

The point in comparing the two agencies, as illustrated throughout this book, is that the links between social context and organizational processes provide important targets for change in social context to support service improvement efforts. We argue that developing an effective human service organization requires a positive social context to support organizational systems affected by the shared norms, expectations, and attitudes of its members.

Secondary and broader impact of OSC. The impact of OSC goes beyond direct effects on client and staff outcomes. For example, a direct effect on high staff turnover is an outcome of poor OSC, but turnover is also costly. Estimates of turnover costs range from 70% to 200% of annual salary within human service organizations (Graef & Hills, 2000; Annie E. Casey Foundation, 2003, 2004). Moreover, turnover is linked to quality of care. Sage (2010) reviewed the repercussions of staff turnover identified in child welfare research, including its influence on longer out-of-home care for children, a loss of worker expertise, and eventual service degradation. It increases time to achieve permanency for children, repeated incidents of abuse, and produces relational problems with children, parents, and foster parents who experience high turnover among caseworkers, all of which harm client well-being. In addition, turnover is linked to system inefficiency and overload for workers who stay (e.g., Flowers et al., 2005; Strolin-Goltzman, Kollar, & Trinkle, 2010). What we know from our work with organizations and administrators is that the increased economic pressures, challenges of maintaining staff, and additional pressures of client failures associated with turnover, exacerbate the challenges of maintaining positive cultures and climates. These linkages underscore the fact that in organizational systems success breeds success and failure breeds failure in an escalating cycle.

Similar to the example of turnover, the secondary impact of OCSs is expressed in other cyclical patterns within organizations that exacerbate broader problems in achieving success. As James Thompson observed decades ago (1967, p. 99), "organizations abhor uncertainty." More accurately, organizational leaders, staff members, community stakeholders, and funders abhor uncertainty. Uncertainty is increased when organizations fail to achieve their desired outcomes. When associated with poor cultures (high rigidity, high resistance, low proficiency) and poor climates (high stress, low engagement, low functionality), reactions to poor outcomes and uncertainty result in an escalating commitment to the very approaches that have caused the failures. The example of Agency A, as described previously, struggled to allow more discretion among front-line staff but, instead, increased punitive and controlling actions. In fact, staff admitted that they were neither committed nor motivated to work as hard, but this was an outcome of their organization's social context rather than a characteristic of individual staff members. In a rigid culture that relies on detailed procedural guidelines, limited staff discretion, and no staff input into policy; increased authoritarian and directive approaches appear rational to leaders who attempt to maintain the control and order needed to achieve desired outcomes. The example of Agency A illustrates, however, that leaders' efforts to increase certainty through increased rigidity contributed to the problems they were experiencing. Similar examples are provided by government regulators, funders, judicial consent decrees, and external stakeholders who place well intended demands and additional guidelines on struggling agencies that already have unnecessarily rigid cultures. Oddly enough, efforts to avoid this mistake are often outlined in the initial improvement plans suggested in many consent decrees issued for child welfare systems nationwide. Yet, when continued problems occur, attempted solutions often lapse into the previously failed approaches characterized with control and rigidity, sacrificing the flexibility, discretion, and innovation necessary to support improved services. This conundrum appears to create an intractable problem—one that we will return to.

It is common to think about the secondary effects of OSC beyond staff turnover as economic costs or a lack of quality care. Our experience also suggests that the secondary effects of social context extend to the families of clients and the psychological health of human services staff. Our work in hospital emergency rooms (Hemmelgarn, Glisson, & Dukes, 2001), for example, found substantial variation between hospitals in behavioral norms and perceptions associated with the staff's emotional distance from patients' families during life-threatening pediatric emergencies. Staff in more stressful climates excluded patients' families in cultures that supported emotional distancing. The exclusion by staff of families of pediatric patients facing serious illness or injury affects the quality of care by reducing both the accuracy of information exchange initially and subsequent compliance with treatment protocols. It is also important that emotional distancing had direct psychological effects on the service providers as well. We found that physicians, nurses, and social workers in poor social contexts reported more emotional distancing and less attention to the emotional needs of staff as well as the patients and families. As a result, staff in cultures where excluding families was the norm in pediatric care, expressed significantly higher stress than in cultures where staff were expected to provide emotional support to families and each other.

USING THE OSC IN ORGANIZATIONAL STRATEGIES TO IMPROVE SERVICES

Our OSC measure is used to support the ARC strategies introduced in Chapter 4. The OSC profiles and percentile scores provide information that organizational leaders, managers, and program supervisors can use to identify key contextual targets for change. Multiple waves of OSC data add to its utility. Baseline assessments provide OSC profiles that establish the need for change and contribute to intervention plans, targets for change, and goals for improvement. Intermediate assessments document progress, providing feedback to the consultant and organization members during ongoing service improvement efforts. Typically spaced at one year intervals after baseline, these assessments inform adjustments, new strategies, and revised action plans. Change is assessed at the end of the formal improvement effort to assess success and identify objectives for sustainability. Post-intervention and follow-up profiles provide additional opportunities to determine whether improvements have been sustained and to guide additional actions or corrections.

Supporting initial and ongoing change in organizational efforts. Using the comparative, normative percentile scores of the OSC in conjunction with our research that links OSC scores to outcomes, we engage organizational members in discussions of their organization's scores in comparison to other providers nationwide. By design, the OSC scores provide specificity for targeted action given normed scores on multiple key dimensions of culture and climate. Using our previous work and research, we explain to organizational members why each dimension is critical and tie each of the dimensions to organizational processes and systems, expected outcomes and results, and their relevance to understanding the organization's current practices and approaches.

Introducing an organization's OSC profiles to its members begins with a review of the expectations and perceptions reported by front-line staff through their responses to the OSC, discussing associated characteristics of leader and staff behaviors and examining the organizational processes that are associated with the OSC results. The OSC profiles help organizational leaders connect OSC results to current problems, strategic objectives, and desired goals. For example, when functionality is perceived as low, organizational structures and communication may become targets for change. When proficiency scores are poor, training systems may be addressed. When rigidity is high, decision-making control or patterns of leadership behavior may be addressed. The chapters that follow explain how OSC scores are used to identify and create action plans during improvement efforts to address service barriers and needed improvements, to alter or amend strategic plans, and to clarify key priorities, mental models, and organizational components that build positive OSC profiles. Also important to long-term success is the ongoing incorporation of the OSC in these improvement efforts. This helps both organizational consultants and organizational members identify factors that sustain leadership behaviors, guide organizational approaches to problem solving, and influence interactions with staff and clients.

As explained in Chapter 8, multiple approaches are employed to help organizational members at all levels recognize how their deeply held assumptions, implicit beliefs, and shared inferences influence behavior within their organization—behaviors often reflected in their OSC scores.

A brief example. We return to our example of Agency A, which was characterized by high OSC scores on rigidity, resistance, and stress along with low engagement scores. Their OSC profile suggested shared beliefs among the leadership that effectiveness depended on close monitoring of staff behavior, limiting staff discretion, and detailed job guidelines and extensive procedural specifications for staff. These beliefs are not inherently unreasonable, but we have long known that the benefit of routinized work depends on the nature of the work and the level of workers' skills (Glisson, 1978). That is, some work settings benefit from greater guidance and structure to achieve success, such as assembly lines using technologies that produce consistent, certain outcomes. However, routinized work can have a negative impact in human service settings, especially when associated with negative assumptions about the nature of staff motivation and work attitudes. Specifically, when leaders and managers share the belief that staff are inherently unmotivated and not committed to their work, leaders lapse into a non-winning strategy of applying more control and pressure to conform while staff increasingly become less responsive and more resistant to the leaders' specified goals.

Continuing our example of Agency A, Bill was promoted to supervisor from his front-line position. Although he tended to employ participatory decision making and non-authoritarian approaches in his interactions with colleagues and clients prior to his promotion, he was mentored extensively by middle managers to become less participative and more authoritarian in his new role. Following the example of his manager, Bill adopted more of a top-down, authoritarian, and punitive approach with staff, the very staff he had worked successfully with prior to his promotion. He quickly developed a belief that his program team was not motivated to improve. In his words, "My staff are not like me. They don't want to learn or get better at what they do. They just aren't wired to want to try new things or to get better." After an initial discussion with our lead ARC consultant, he was introduced to the concept of psychologically safe environments for staff to discuss problems and errors. He then decided, without informing the consultant, to test a new approach with his staff. He confronted his staff and asked for input on things the program could do differently to improve the program's effectiveness. His staff remained silent and provided little feedback. He then informed the consultant that this experience confirmed his belief about his staff. That is, he believed his subordinates were unmotivated and had no desire to improve their work.

Bill had lapsed into a cycle of escalating commitment to continuing what was a failed approach to motivating staff. He continued to believe that he needed to push his staff harder. He even indicated he was thinking of reporting one employee for disciplinary action to motivate him, an action that in this agency was a message that the staff member was at risk of being fired. Following our analyses and discussions of his work unit's OSC profiles, and conducting work with Bill regarding the ARC principles and mental models that support staff involvement, Bill ultimately gained a better understanding of how his behavior was affecting his employees' behavior. After reviewing the OSC profile of his team and evidence that the profile contributed to poor outcomes for both staff and clients, Bill joined his staff in collaborative improvement activities to model principles of effective service organizations (see Chapter 9–13). The effort was rewarded with significant improvements in his staff members' performance and work attitudes. In his subsequent contribution to a review of the organization's discipline system that was completed as part of the ARC strategy, Bill highlighted the organization's focus on punishment versus development. Bill shared experiences using strategies we discuss in later chapters that led to a decision by several leaders within his organization to try a different approach to disciplinary procedures. The point here is that the organization's OSC profiles helped stimulate a reassessment of leaders' behaviors related to discipline and the underlying assumptions and beliefs guiding those behaviors.

As highlighted throughout this book, OSC assessment and actions to improve OSCs are critical in building work settings that support innovation, positive staff attitudes and perceptions, as well as effective services and outcomes for clients served in human services organizations. Actions to improve OSC include altering the mindsets and beliefs shared by organizational members, as illustrated in our example. It also includes introducing organization component tools to alter behaviors, systems, and processes that impact organization and service effectiveness. Finally, as outlined in the next chapter, it requires embedding and enacting core organizational principles in the mindsets, systems, processes, priorities, and behaviors of human service providers to achieve OSCs that ensure effective human services.

4

INTRODUCING THE ARC
ORGANIZATIONAL STRATEGIES

The ARC model for improving human services relies on three strategies. The three strategies provide the (a) *organizational tools* described in Chapter 7, (b) *mental models* described in Chapter 8, and (c) *principles* described in Chapters 9 to 13 for aligning organizational priorities. We view changes in organizational priorities as a central path to creating the social context and capacity required for identifying and addressing service barriers (Glisson et al., 2016a, 2016b; Hartnell, Ou, & Kinicki, 2011; Michie, Stralen, & West, 2011; Williams et al., 2016). Organizational priorities determine the allocation of resources within an organization, the focus of change efforts, and what the organization values most.

A variety of strategic goals and demands compete for emphasis in organizations as they struggle to survive and succeed (Quinn & Rohrbaugh, 1983; Schneider & Bowen, 1995). Organizations that do similar work differ in their priorities and in the extent to which they align priorities in a way that complements their efforts to be effective. An organization's priorities reflect what is most important to that organization and signal to members and stakeholders what it hopes to accomplish, but it is not a simple process. In practice, an organization's espoused and enacted priorities can be different. Organizations can say one thing and do another (Argyris & Schon, 1996; Pate-Cornell, 1990; Simons, 2002). Moreover, an organization can enact inconsistent and even conflicting priorities (Weick, 1979). The relative priorities placed on competing demands that specify what is most important to the organization, the alignment of enacted and espoused priorities ensuring the organization's actions reflect what it says is most important, and the extent to which the organization's priorities complement rather than conflict with each other distinguish effective from ineffective organizations (Zohar & Hoffman, 2012).

We have learned from our consulting experience and research that organizational priorities become misaligned for several reasons. First, mental health, social service, and other human service organizations face multiple *competing demands*. Common examples of competing demands are the demand for service quality versus the demand for service quantity, the demand for resources to develop staff versus the demand for fiscal restraint, or the demand for addressing regulatory and accreditation demands versus the demand for adequate provider time with clients. Organizations also face the *difficulty of enacting espoused priorities*. For example, an organization must ensure that a priority on improving client wellbeing is reflected in organizational practices to ensure that the needs of the identified target population are actually being addressed. Invariably, organizations must also resolve the *conflicts created by inconsistent priorities*. Examples include organizations enacting strict guidelines to ensure service providers avoid mistakes while decreasing their ability to use discretion and judgment in providing individualized services. What we know is that inconsistent priorities or the failure to enact espoused priorities can increase staff turnover, decrease staff morale, harm service relationships, limit commitment to improving care, and reduce the continuity of services. Misaligned priorities can create inappropriate referral procedures or delay access to care and reduce service availability and responsiveness. Organizations can fail to enact priorities that promote effective services for clients even when service providers have the knowledge and skills to provide high-quality care. Of most importance, however, is that these challenges can be addressed. Organizational strategies that build the capacity for aligning priorities—enacting consistent priorities that focus on improving client wellbeing and eliminating conflicting priorities within and across organizational levels—improve service effectiveness.

The ARC model is based on deploying organizational strategies for aligning priorities or addressing inconsistent priorities at all levels of the organization. We find that direct service providers (rather than middle managers or upper administration) in an organization are best able to identify the conflicting priorities that are associated with service barriers to high-quality care. At the same time, service providers are unable to align organizational priorities to address those barriers without the participation and support of upper management in an organization-wide strategy. Therefore, an organization's capacity for identifying and addressing its misaligned priorities requires a structured, collaborative process that includes participation at all levels and employs clear guiding principles that drive organizational priorities.

The ARC organizational strategies are designed to improve service systems using a participatory process to align priorities with ARC's five principles of organizational effectiveness. The five ARC principles were developed specifically for mental health and social service agencies based on previous work with strategies for improving effectiveness in other types of organizations (Osborne & Gaebler, 1992). Each ARC principle describes a distinct dichotomy of conflicting priorities for human service providers. The ARC intervention uses the principles to guide the enactment and alignment of priorities for the organization's improvement efforts. To do so, ARC provides a structured, multi-level, team-based process that is more comprehensive than related models for improving organizational effectiveness. ARC is the first intervention of this type to be designed specifically for human service organizations and to bring all three of its strategies together in an integrated process. It incorporates specific components at each stage of the intervention process (as described below under *Stages*) that have been developed from the broader organizational literature.

This chapter provides an introduction to the ARC model for improving social context and services using the three strategies of (1) guiding principles, (2) organizational component tools, and (3) mental models, respectively. The strategies are introduced here to provide an overview of the ARC intervention process and its effects on human services through improvements in social context. Detailed in later chapters, ARC has been shown in multiple randomized controlled trials to improve OSC, service quality, and service outcomes in behavioral health, child welfare, and juvenile justice systems (Glisson, Dukes & Green, 2006; Glisson et al., 2010, 2012, 2013, 2016a, 2016b; Williams et al., 2016).

ARC

The ARC acronym stands for availability, responsiveness, and continuity. These characteristics describe positive service relationships between service providers and their clients. Availability exists when clients are ensured prompt and efficient access to the service providers and the services they provide. Responsiveness indicates that clients believe their needs and concerns are understood and addressed by the service providers. When providers are available and responsive, clients experience providers who make themselves accessible, listen, and respond in a way that meet their needs. Continuity is established when service providers are consistent with their behaviors, expectations, and approaches and foster this consistency with others in the client's network. In other words, continuity describes service provider behavior that is consistent over time toward the client and the individuals that compose the client's social environment (e.g., members of client's family, other service providers).

Early on in our work with human service organizations, we recognized that availability, responsiveness, and continuity also characterize functional relationships among staff that work in organizations with positive social contexts. That is, service providers in organizations with cultures and climates promoting effective services are more likely to be available, responsive, and consistent in their responses to each other, as well as their clients. Successful service providers consistently share information, knowledge, and resources with relevant organization members. They work collaboratively and openly to ensure they are available and responsive to others within and outside their organization. They also ensure that they share goals and agree on consistent approaches to support continuity of care.

The ARC organizational strategies encourage service availability, responsiveness, and continuity by creating OSCs (e.g., proficient cultures, engaged climates) that promote service relationships that garner positive outcomes. These strategies create both the context and capacity for clinicians and administrators to collaboratively improve services through successful innovation. That is, ARC provides the structure and process for service providers to identify and address organizational barriers that impede service and treatment outcomes. In addition, the three ARC strategies foster the organizational norms, perceptions, reasoning, and attitudes necessary for organizational members to identify and implement innovations successfully. Thus, the positive cultures and climates developed by the ARC strategies contribute to desired organizational outcomes through behavioral norms, staff perceptions, and staff attitudes, each of which have long been associated with organizational performance in a variety of areas (Denison & Mishra, 1995; Glisson, 2007, 2010; Glisson & Green, 2006; Glisson & Hemmelgarn, 1998; Glisson & James, 2002; Glisson, Schoenwald et al., 2008; Glisson et al., 2016a, 2016b; Glisson & Williams, 2015; Hoy, 1990; Joyce & Slocum, 1984; Petty et al., 1995; Schneider et al. 1994; Wilkins & Ouchi, 1983).

The first ARC strategy embeds five key principles of service system effectiveness into all aspects of organizational functioning, including decision making, priorities, behavioral norms, and processes that guide innovation and change. The second ARC strategy trains teams of clinicians and administrators to use organizational component tools and processes (e.g., feedback, teamwork, participative decision making) to improve services following the five ARC principles. The third ARC strategy introduces the concept of mental models and explains how specific models (e.g., openness to change, psychological safety) influence reasoning and beliefs among organizational members to support or inhibit the successful application of ARC principles and components. Taken together, the three strategies are designed to (1) alter the priorities enacted by organizational members in their work; (2) develop and enhance the beliefs and cognitive models organizational members hold to reason, understand, and react to their work; (3) develop positive work perceptions and attitudes; and (4) improve the organizational systems and processes that affect service quality and outcomes (Glisson, Dukes, & Green, 2006; Glisson et al., 2010, 2012, 2013, 2016a, 2016b; Williams et al., 2016).

Chapters 6 and 7 explain in greater detail how ARC implements the three strategies using manuals and structured activities guided by an external ARC specialist. The ARC specialist works closely with leaders, middle managers, and line-level service providers to support organizational improvement efforts. In addition, the ARC specialist helps organizational leaders identify an internal ARC liaison that guides internal efforts to apply the ARC principles, tools, and mental models. Training, consultation, and support are provided by the specialist and liaison to organizational members at all levels. Support from the ARC specialist and liaison includes providing ongoing feedback on improvements and opportunities for additional improvements. They identify practices, behaviors, enacted beliefs, and attitudes that either enhance or inhibit priorities reflected in the ARC principles.

The need for ARC in human service organizations. The impact of ARC on human services is linked to the role OSC plays in determining service-related behavior and attitudes. As previously explained, human services are relatively indeterminate and uncertain with unpredictable outcomes, even when using evidence-based practices (Kazdin, 2015; NIMH, 2015; Weisz, Doss, & Hawley, 2005; Weisz et al., 2013, 2015). Given this uncertainty and unpredictability, social processes and social learning play a significant role in guiding behavior and priorities among organizational members (Glisson et al., 2016a). Unpredictable events, such as client failures or negative outcomes, stimulate information seeking and social learning among service providers as they share beliefs, inferences, and assumptions to decipher and understand these events. In turn, these beliefs, inferences, and assumptions contribute to mental representations (mental models) that are used to understand, interpret, and reason about subsequent work events.

As a result of these processes, social contexts play a substantial role in guiding the attitudes, reasoning, decision making, and behavior of organizational members. These effects apply to administrative decisions and actions as well as clinical practices and interactions with clients. Workplace perceptions and attitudes develop as staff interact and learn from each other's reactions to work events. These workplace perceptions and attitudes, in turn, influence provider behavior such as turnover, innovation adoption, and most importantly, the quality of care they provide. The effects of social context on performance are acknowledged in a wide array of organizations, including behavior in financial, engineering, manufacturing, pharmaceutical, and other types of organizations. We argue, however, that the effects of social context are especially pronounced in human services. While a burned-out, disgruntled assembly-line worker assembling automobiles in a poor OSC may slow production or harm product quality in numerous ways, the nature of the core technology allows their work behavior to be defined and constrained by well-established patterns that are relatively easy to monitor. Similar processes can occur in human services. However, service providers affect client outcomes in less easily observed ways due to the inherently indeterminate and uncertain nature of the work. We argue from our research and experience that the effects of social context are in fact more pronounced in human service organizations because social interaction, perceptions, and attitudes not only affect the choice or approaches employed in an organization's core technology; they actually compose the core technology. That is, the implementation of a new clinical treatment practice will be affected and defined by norms and attitudes that influence the quality and nature of interactions occurring between the provider and client.

Internal and external challenges. The value of organizational intervention strategies such as ARC is further explained by the internal and external challenges that human service organizations face. These challenges affect organizational cultures and climates as service providers construct shared expectations, beliefs, and practices to negotiate these internal and external demands (Fiske & Taylor, 2013; Schein, 1985). First, the demands from policymakers, regulators, funders, and constituent communities can push the leaders of these organizations toward practices that can undermine the development of effective

OSCs. Well-intentioned efforts to improve an organization's performance such as the decision to assess service outcomes provide an example. Routine outcome monitoring and feedback help clarify the direction of work activities and foster motivation for action, improvement, and enhanced performance. But as shown in our case study of Agency A presented previously, members of human service organizations often perceive outcome measurement, new data management systems, and use of client data feedback as negative and disruptive to their ability to accomplish work.

The reasons for these negative reactions are a function of the practical realities human services face and the existing social contexts. We have worked with mental health agencies that receive funding from multiple funding sources, each with different requirements for sustained financial support. We worked with one agency that gathered and reported separate, unique client outcomes in one program for six separate funders. A time study found that staff members were spending almost half of their time completing paperwork, client assessments, and data entry to document outcomes in this program. The beliefs and perceptions of front-line staff that accompanied these demands were that data and outcome measurement interfere substantially with their ability to provide high-quality service. These beliefs were reinforced by comments from supervisors and leaders who suggested the following: "We have to do this if we are going to get paid" and "Just do the best you can to make sure the funders get what they want." Behavioral expectations developed that supported completing assessments and paperwork for funders as quickly as possible while ignoring the results of the assessments. The staff members' negative attitudes toward monitoring outcomes were associated with poor climate perceptions in general, as increased workloads, frustrations regarding assessment requirements, and resentment over control of data collection transformed the intended purpose of the effort (i.e., service improvement). Interpretations of monitoring outcomes as a barrier to success—rather than a tool for improving quality of care—dominated and led to negative reactions to data usage, assessments, and data system innovations.

Demands vary across different human service arenas. In child welfare, internal pressure stemming from limited resources, high caseloads, and excessive staff turnover is common and accompanied by external pressures from media, regulators, and court systems (e.g., judicial decisions regarding individual cases, consent decrees regarding classes of cases). Human service providers face challenges associated with extensive documentation demands from funders and regulators, inadequate reimbursement for services, and the difficult and complex presenting problems of clients. Educators experience overwhelming demands on teachers' time and resources that accompany educational reform (e.g., No Child Left Behind), while health-care providers face the challenges of implementing legal mandates such as HIPPA or, more recently, the Affordable Care Act.

Although unintended, these internal and external pressures contribute to perceptions, beliefs, attitudes, and practices that are associated with OSCs and can undermine an organization's improvement efforts. Many efforts to improve the quality of services in mental health, schools, or health-care facilities are aimed at internal challenges that all organizations face, such as developing sufficient expertise and skill levels among staff. For example, skill-based training with practices that are supported by research evidence is critical for improving the quality of services for clients. Moreover, associated perceptions of self-efficacy, personal accomplishment, and motivation should improve as staff members apply new training skills to achieve success with clients. Yet, the very act of providing this training can be perceived negatively by staff members in poor social contexts, no matter how well intentioned.

Ensuring innovation success. The potential impact of efforts to improve organizations is reduced in work environments characterized by the types of negative culture and climate profiles we have described. In the worst social contexts, staff doubts that their leaders are committed to improving service quality or client outcomes and organizational norms of resistance to change impede any attempted innovations. In punitive or psychologically unsafe contexts, front-line staff believe they would be at risk of being demeaned or criticized if they adopted new practices and failed, or if they openly discussed barriers to their success. We find that staff in organizations with the most negative profiles are stressed and unengaged to the point that their motivation to improve is minimal. Moreover, shared beliefs among leaders and staff can be incompatible with the fundamental underlying assumptions that accompany innovation or improvement efforts before efforts begin. For example, our experience with pediatric emergency rooms described earlier illustrated how rigid cultures and less engaged climates that supported norms of emotional distancing from clients thwarted the implementation of family-centered practices—practices that are essential to the best outcomes in pediatric care.

Existing cultures and climates consist of shared norms, expectations, and perceptions among staff that have evolved over time in response to internal and external demands. Whether they lead to optimal organizational effectiveness is not always certain, particularly when leaders and organizational members develop priorities that are incompatible with success. In our study of pediatric emergency rooms, we worked with some ERs that developed practices and norms to ensure emotional support for colleagues and families during serious pediatric trauma. In these ERs, staff relied on colleagues for comfort and support to address the emotional toll of the work. In other ERs, emotional distancing from patients and families, as well as colleagues, while focusing on medical demands provided some immediate, temporary protection from the emotional toll. But in both cases, norms had developed to address the internal challenge of treating seriously ill or injured children with life-threatening emergencies. The difference, however, was that one social context created an emotionally supportive environment that kept staff highly engaged in their work. As a result, they were able to be family-centered and facilitate communication and trust between parents and providers, resulting in improved care.

Staff in the emotionally distanced settings, while enduring the trauma of their work with stoicism, reported suffering much higher levels of personal stress and minimal engagement with patients and families, resulting in poor communication and low levels of trust between providers and families, all of which undermined the type of family-centered care necessary for responsiveness and continuity in care.

We argue that improvement efforts do not necessarily fail because innovations are poorly selected or poorly designed but because they are introduced into social contexts that are incapable of supporting change. Organizations develop and sustain cultures, climates, and worker attitudes (OSC) that define their receptiveness to innovation and support for efforts to improve care. OSCs include shared expectations, beliefs, and assumptions that guide the interpretation and meaning of innovation by the members and the reactions (emotionally and behaviorally) that organizational members have toward innovation and change in their work environment. It is important to understand that the practices, beliefs, and behavioral norms that develop within any organization serve a purpose and evolve to address internal and external demands. This occurs even when those practices, beliefs, and norms prevent improvements in care.

Regardless of the history or intentions that created a social context, poor contexts lower service quality and hamper efforts to improve services. Our work has found that mental health, child welfare, juvenile justice, and other human service systems can depend on bureaucracies that require extensive documentation, supervisory control, and conformity as protection against service provider error, public criticism, administrative sanctions, and litigation. Such bureaucracies affect service quality and outcomes by routinizing core technologies using checklists, decision matrices, and cookie-cutter services that ignore the individual needs of each client. These bureaucracies also impede efforts to improve services with norms that emphasize rigidity and resistance to change while ignoring the importance of proficiency.

CONCEPTUAL AND EMPIRICAL FOUNDATIONS FOR ARC

ARC is based on a long history of organizational research beyond our own work. Much of this research extends over many decades beginning with early efforts to understand why some organizations were more effective at innovation and implementing new technologies than others. The well-known socio-technical model describes organizations as core technologies embedded within social contexts that influence organizational effectiveness as much as the organization's core technology (Burns & Stalker, 1961; Porras & Robertson, 1992; Rousseau, 1977; Trist, Higgin, Murray, & Pollock, 1963). The model views organizational effectiveness as a function of the fit between its social context and core technology. For example, routinized technologies of production assembly lines may be more successful when implemented in rigid cultures characterized by formalized divisions of labor and centralized decision making. However, more flexible social contexts allow discretion and adaptation to unique demands. These contexts are required for success in using less determinate core technologies that are characterized by variable raw materials (e.g., clients in human service systems), incomplete knowledge, and unpredictable outcomes. To be successful, these latter types of work settings require collaboration in identifying and addressing problems, continual adjustments in procedures, and the ongoing update of technical knowledge and skills. These are the types of characteristics that describe behavioral health, social service, and other human service organizations.

Our work has shown that human service organizations do not necessarily adjust their social contexts to support their core technologies. Instead, the opposite happens. That is, the malleable core technologies (such as a new evidence-based approach) used within human service organizations are adapted to fit their organization's social contexts (Glisson, 1978, 1992). We described this reverse fit process in Chapter 1 where our introduction of a child assessment tool designed to improve service and placement decisions in child welfare evolved into a bureaucratic process. This resulted from cultural norms for routine decision making and an emphasis on paperwork, as opposed to individualizing and improving care. This example highlights the assumption of the socio-technical model that altering social contexts to support new technologies is required to ensure successful implementation of treatment models, assessment tools, or any new practices (Cooke & Rousseau, 1988; Hartnell, Ou, & Kinicki, 2011; Hofstede, Neuijen, Ohayv, & Sanders, 1990; Olin et al., 2014).

The norms and expectations of an organization's culture influence service providers' behaviors by providing social cues to the behaviors that are most valued, rewarded, and consistent with work priorities (Glisson et al., 2016a; Schein, 2004; Trice & Beyer, 1993). Social processes create shared norms and beliefs that influence individuals' intentions to engage in selected behaviors (Jaccard, Litardo, & Wan, 1999; Sheeran, 2002). The ARC strategy supports service improvement by changing OCSs to affect clinicians' intentions to engage in innovative behavior (Williams & Glisson, 2014b; Williams et al., 2016).

A meta-analysis of 84 studies supports the association between organizational culture and innovation in the workplace (Hartnell, Ou & Kinicki, 2011). Hartnell and colleagues (2011) estimated a population correlation of $\rho = .59$ between organizational culture and innovation behavior across a range of business, industrial, and healthcare settings. In human service settings, several studies confirm strong associations between organizational culture and clinicians' practice attitudes, behaviors, and clinical outcomes (Aarons et al., 2012; Glisson, Schoenwald et al., 2008, 2016b; Olin et al., 2014; Williams & Glisson, 2013; Williams & Glisson, 2014a; Williams et al., 2016). Clinicians who work in agencies characterized by proficient cultures report they are expected to prioritize improvement in client well-being and to be competent in the use of up-to-date treatment practices such as EBPs (Glisson, Landverk et al., 2008). Proficient organizational cultures are linked to positive clinician attitudes toward EBPs, higher quality services, and superior client outcomes (Aarons et al., 2012; Olin et al., 2014; Glisson et al., 2013; Williams & Glisson, 2013, 2014a; Williams et al., 2016). Organizational norms and expectations that emphasize proficiency increase clinicians' intentions to adopt EBPs and explain ARC's effects on clinicians' EBP intentions, adoption, and use.

In addition to creating a context for service improvement, ARC develops an organization's capacity for innovation through processes and infrastructure for identifying and addressing service barriers. Numerous studies of EBP adoption in mental health settings suggest job-related barriers are among the most widely cited impediments to clinicians' EBP adoption, even when EBP use is mandated and clinicians receive EBP training and consultation (Aarons et al., 2009; Baer et al., 2009; Gioia & Dziadosz, 2008; Jensen-Doss et al., 2009). Examples of job-related barriers include an agency's refusal to modify policies or workflow to accommodate EBPs, failure to provide materials necessary for implementing EBPs, and the lack of clinical supervision that supports EBPs (Bartholomew et al., 2007; Raghavan et al., 2007). These data are consistent with implementation theories such as the capacity, opportunity, and motivation (COM-B) model (Michie, van Stralen, & West, 2011) which predict that barriers in the work setting limit individuals' EBP adoption. The ARC strategies develop the organizational infrastructure and capacity to identify and remove these barriers to innovation and effectiveness.

Altering reasoning and beliefs. ARC's three strategies address the norms and shared behaviors practiced within an organization in part by changing the assumptions, beliefs, and reasoning used by organizational members. Research on mental models and social cognition help guide this work as explained in Chapter 8. The ARC process, materials, and activities encourage organizational members to examine, understand, and modify the beliefs, assumptions, and inferences that comprise their mental models and affect their behavior. Although definitions of mental models vary, mental models can be described as internal representations that individuals use to understand and form reactions to experiences and events. Developed on the basis of previous experiences and social learning, mental models form from interrelated beliefs and assumptions that help us reason and make inferences. A contentious history among researchers points out multiple measurement issues with mental models. Among these are the unlimited number of mental models that exist and the nature of what constitutes mental models. Nonetheless, researchers also acknowledge the usefulness of mental models for many applications, such as the design of more effective training efforts, the redesign of systems (Rouse & Morris, 1986), and organizational development (see Senge, 2006). Moreover, research on social cognition affirms that individuals in the same social context develop shared mental representations that provide meaning and motivation for behavioral change. For the purposes of our work, mental models provide a useful heuristic framework for identifying and altering beliefs, expectations, and assumptions that support optimal OSCs, ARC principles, and effective organizational functioning.

Several core tenants of mental models identified by Johnson-Laird (1983) are particularly useful. These tenants suggest that our internal mental representations are (1) often based on an individual's or a group's beliefs, rather than veridical truth, (2) heuristic in nature to support the processing and interpretation of overwhelming environmental stimuli, and (3) often formed to provide certainty and structure to the world or contexts we live in. The variation between organizations in their leaders' mental representations of poor staff performance provides an example. In some organizations, leaders use mental models or internal representations of staff's inability to achieve outcomes that suggest laziness, a lack of motivation, or dispositional weaknesses that are the fault of the staff, even where failure is a function of factors beyond the staff's control. That is, the leaders' mental representations of failure include shortcomings of the staff and that appropriate actions to correct failure include close monitoring and control. Underlying this mental model are implicit assumptions and inferences of which the leaders may not be aware. These might include, for example, implicit beliefs that staff members are lazy, unmotivated, or unwilling to work hard.

In other organizations, leaders share mental models that link staff failures to factors external to staff, such as the need for additional training, resources, or access to information. That is, leaders assume that staff desire and strive to do a good job but are unable to succeed due to factors that staff cannot easily change. Although these alternative assumptions and associated mental models differ and lead to different solutions—sanctions versus support—both mental models serve a purpose by allowing organizational leaders to understand and respond to the immediate challenge of poor performance. In both cases, mental models are shared and supported by social processes. And, both lead to results that reinforce their accuracy as defined by those holding the respective models. Leaders cite success in improving outcomes by threatening disciplinary action or firing key individuals. Likewise, additional training efforts or increased focus in supporting staff by leadership can lead to improved performance as well.

The mental model examples may appear overly simplistic. Yet, social cognition and neuroscience research provide evidence that supports the basic tenants outlined by Johnson-Laird (1983). That is, these literatures confirm that our brains are designed to address the complexity of our environments by establishing and using categories, schemas, prototypes, and other mental representations that help organize and simplify cognitive demands over time. Our brains create and often automate (implicitly, without our explicit awareness) categorizations, inferences, and patterns of responses over time that help us manage our day-to-day lives. This is mainly due to limitations in our working memories that limit our capacity to hold exhaustive information during purposeful, conscious thought and processing. All of us experience this automation. For example, we successfully drive our vehicles from point A to point B with varying levels of consciousness while our brain processes react to thousands of stimuli on the way. Similarly, leaders who share assumptions that the staff is lazy often attribute failure automatically to innate flaws in their staff while ignoring other determining factors.

Second, social cognition research reaffirms that our mental representations, inferences, memories, among other things, are influenced by social interactions and social contexts. For example, we often learn to value core traits, such as being responsible, given our parents' emphasis and reactions that highlight this trait during childhood. Moreover, as we adopt this trait into our cognitive systems, we attend closely to stimuli associated with this trait with minimal conscious awareness. (Fiske & Taylor, 2013). We then tend to perceive others in relation to this trait versus using other potential traits for interpretation. And we incorporate inferences that connect behaviors, and the trait in question, based on previous experiences such as inferring a lack of conscientiousness when one performs poorly. Within work settings, the social nature of these processes is expressed in our tendency to pay close attention to social cues and to acquire social information during novel, salient, and anxiety-provoking events. That is, when we switch to more active reasoning and examination of events that cannot be processed automatically, we depend on information from our social context. Thus, when a newly appointed supervisor is distraught and faced with their first crisis of addressing a staff member who has made a major mistake, the supervisor pays close attention to their own boss's interpretations of causality for these mistakes, not to mention their behaviors. When the interpretation is that the staff member lacks motivation or a desire to work hard, he or she suggests punishment as the appropriate consequence. For a young supervisor without experience, the boss sets and shares a precedent for beliefs, expectations, and inferences that are appropriate for the new supervisor. Over multiple experiences, these types of expectations and inferences are stored in our long-term cognitive systems and begin to operate automatically, or without consciousness, priming both what we attend to and our reactions that follow.

As explained in Chapter 8, our brains are not perfect information processors that make attributions, inferences, and decisions based solely on empirical truth. Limitations in our ability to consciously process the vast amount of information entering through our senses require stored beliefs, inferences, and assumptions that we draw upon in our conscious mental representations. Furthermore, our cognitive systems are not designed to be capricious in this work. That is, the mental representations we hold as well as the more implicit beliefs, assumptions, and inferences we develop and have stored in our cognitive systems are aimed at meeting our needs and goals, including those fostered within our social contexts.

Given our need for survival, however, our cognitive systems are also designed to trigger conscious awareness for adapting what have become relatively automatic internal representations. This occurs when incongruent information, experiences, or events force us to reestablish understanding and control over our environment. Taken together, these facets allow us to better understand the internal cognitive processes and mental representations that are influencing our decisions and actions. It also allows us to better understand how to trigger change. Within organizational improvement efforts, this means we need to trigger conscious processing to challenge our existing implicit beliefs, assumptions, and inferences. We use this process in the ARC model by having organizational members examine their conscious mental models and reasoning to gain a better understanding of their more implicit beliefs, assumptions, and inferences.

A HEURISTIC MODEL OF ARC'S THREE STRATEGIES

A simple, heuristic model is presented in Figure 4.1 to illustrate how the three strategies of ARC are brought together to improve OSCs. As the model illustrates, the three ARC strategies affect organizational norms (culture), shared perceptions (climate), and staff attitudes as a way of improving the availability, responsiveness, and continuity of services.

ARC's five core principles, detailed in Chapters 9 through 13, were adapted specifically for mental health, social service, and other human service organizations. Employed in randomized controlled trials of the ARC model, the principles are essential in creating social contexts that support organizational innovation, capacity for change, and effectiveness (Glisson et al., 2016a). The principles evolved from strategies that have improved a variety of public service organizations (Osborne & Gaebler, 1992). The three ARC strategies are designed to complement and support an organization's efforts to select and enact

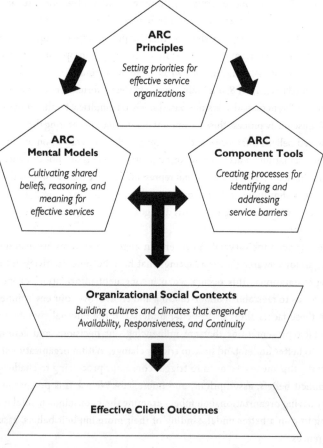

FIGURE 4.1 ARC Conceptual Model

priorities consistent with the five principles. To be successful, organizational members must share reasoning and beliefs that support the selected priorities. ARC introduces the mental models that help establish this reasoning, which includes beliefs and assumptions that align with these priorities. Second, organizational members must have the tools to select and enact priorities. ARC's organizational component tools are designed to help members identify and address service barriers within their organizations so that behavioral expectations (norms), perceptions, and attitudes are developed that reflect the principles. What we have learned is that the creation of positive social contexts depends on all three strategies (principles, mental models, and component tools) working together in an orchestrated manner to enact organizational priorities that improve services.

Each of the five ARC principles describes a dichotomy of conflicting priorities for human service organizations. The ARC principles describe effective organizations as (1) mission driven versus rule driven, (2) results oriented versus process oriented, (3) improvement directed versus status quo directed, (4) participatory based versus authority based, and (5) relationship centered versus individual centered. We present the principles in the form of dichotomies to illustrate conflicting priorities. In practice, organizations can be characterized on a continuum that represents the organization as being closer to one or the other extreme of the continuum. To illustrate, ARC's principle of mission driven requires that all members' decisions and behavior improve client well-being. This principle addresses the threat of organizations becoming rule-driven bureaucracies that place a priority on regulations and red tape versus a mission-driven organization that relies on service provider discretion to provide individualized care that addresses the unique needs and best interests of each client, regardless of the bureaucracy. Organizations can obviously have a mix of the two, but the presentation of the dichotomy underscores that rule-driven organizations are less mission driven, and vice versa. Each of the five ARC principles as described in Chapters 9 to 13, respectively, presents a similar dichotomy to guide the implementation of ARC component tools and associated mental models.

ARC operationalizes the five principles with the ARC component tools that are described in Chapter 7. For example, the introduction of ARC's *continuous quality improvement* component requires new or altered work behavior of organizational members at all levels to embed ARC's principle of being improvement directed. The continuous improvement process identifies and addresses service barriers with proposals developed by line-level ARC teams of direct service providers. These proposals are reviewed and enacted by an Organizational Action Team (OAT) composed of representatives from all organizational levels, including top leadership. Front-line staff and leaders' experiences with addressing service barriers alter a variety of expectations and norms, including expectations about the potential for removing barriers to improve services, expectations about who can identify and address barriers, and assumptions about front-line staff motivation and commitment. Staff perceptions and attitudes are altered as leaders support staff proposals and expectations are changed about openness to change and whether change can even occur. Guided by the five principles and supported by altered mental models, applying the component tools influence behaviors, alter expectations about what can be done, and affect members' perceptions and attitudes about improvement, leadership support, and commitment.

To continue this example, organizational members learn new skills and behaviors in the identification and elimination of a service barrier using *participative decision-making* and *continuous improvement* component tools. The behaviors are reinforced when they experience positive results from *feedback*, another ARC component. Sustained long-term change is not guaranteed, however, due to the work associated with the new approaches and behaviors and the ease of going back to old patterns and reasoning. Sustained change requires leaders and middle managers to alter their own behaviors, put in place new processes and procedures, restructure priorities on how staff time is spent, and allocate resources for training and ongoing support. In other words, sustained organizational change requires leaders' investment of time and resources. Beyond these costs, our experience is that sustained change is a function of the congruence between reasoning, beliefs, and assumptions held by organizational members and those needed to successfully embed ARC components and ARC principles into everyday functioning. This requires altering existing beliefs and reasoning to align with new approaches and behaviors to sustain new practices that evolve from the implementation of ARC principles and components (Hemmelgarn et al., 2001; Olin, Hemmelgarn, Madenwald, & Hoagwood, 2016). Perhaps most importantly, altering beliefs, assumptions, and mental models concerning innovation and change alters the perceptions held by organizational members regarding the cost versus benefits of innovation and change.

Mental models are integral to changes in beliefs and reasoning consistent with ARC principles and component tools. For example, an organizational priority on collaborative participation necessary for continuous improvement processes requires that leaders' beliefs and reasoning support this priority. Support of front-line staff participation in continuous improvement requires leaders to believe that staff input is critical to successful change. It requires a belief that staff are inherently capable and motivated to improve services, and that staff have the ability to assist in identifying and addressing service barriers. Equally important is a work environment where staff is comfortable discussing problems or barriers created by the organizational bureaucracy. ARC introduces concepts such as psychological safety to explore with organizational members the beliefs, reasoning, and assumptions necessary to promote behaviors that support safe work environments that invite improvement (Edmondson, Bohmer & Pisano, 2001). These efforts include an explanation of how authoritarian, rigid, and punitive behaviors influence organizational members' motivation for openly discussing and addressing organizational barriers. It also includes leaders identifying external pressures that drive more directive and authoritarian approaches, beliefs, and assumptions that support punitive or authoritarian behavior and examination of the repercussions that may result from these behaviors. That is, ARC tools, priorities, and mental models help leaders and other organizational members connect the dots between external and internal demands, their beliefs and assumptions, their subsequent behaviors, and the resulting outcomes.

In summary, the three ARC strategies of principles, component tools, and mental models, establish work norms, perceptions, and attitudes that are associated with successful innovation and service improvement efforts. The strategies create consistency in organizational priorities that guide organizational decision making, congruence between an organization's espoused priorities and its enacted priorities, as well as the alignment in priorities as organizational members face competing demands (Glisson et al., 2016a; Zohar & Hofmann, 2012). The three strategies provide the tools and thinking that guide behaviors and processes for aligning these priorities and developing shared beliefs, assumptions, and mental representations among organizational members that ensure consistency in decisions, processes, and practices that contribute to improved service quality and outcomes.

5

THE IMPACT OF ARC IN HUMAN SERVICE ORGANIZATIONS

The need to improve the effectiveness of organizations that deliver mental health, social services, and other human services has been widely documented, but organizational leaders, policymakers, and other stakeholders have had few options that are supported by evidence. Although many organizational strategies to improve the effectiveness of human services have been promoted, few have a solid foundation in research. A major reason for this deficit is the difficulty in conducting experimental studies of organizational interventions in actual service systems. Experimental studies in the field require that programs, organizational units, or entire organizations be randomly assigned to different organizational interventions and that the outcomes of those interventions are assessed with valid measurement strategies. This type of randomized controlled trial of organizational interventions is rare because of the cost and complexity of such studies. For example, a systematic review of organizational change studies found only 11% of the 563 studies used an experimental design (Barends et al., 2013).

Although non-experimental data are informative and can contribute to existing knowledge, non-experimental studies of organizational interventions provide a weak basis for making *causal* claims. These designs cannot control for the numerous alternative explanations that may account for the observed results. Understandably, the lack of controlled studies and the promotion of strategies with little evidence to support their effectiveness have contributed to healthy skepticism among organizational leaders regarding organizational interventions to improve service system outcomes.

The reality is that organizational change efforts involve considerable time, resources, and energy from agency leaders, managers, and front-line staff. Using strategies based on experimental evidence of what works is critical to the efficient use of resources. In contrast to many approaches for organizational change, the ARC model is supported by randomized controlled trials that demonstrate its effects on organizational culture and climate, organizational priorities, clinicians' work attitudes, clinicians' evidence-based practice behaviors, and most importantly, client outcomes. Both the ARC model and the validity of the OSC measurement system are also supported by a number of non-experimental and quasi-experimental studies. These studies examine linkages with OSC and related criteria using regional and nationwide samples that are fundamental to our work. Much of this work is referenced throughout the book. In this chapter, we summarize findings from our randomized controlled trials. These findings highlight what we learned from these studies to support causal inferences about the effects of ARC. They also highlight the implications for using ARC strategies in planned efforts to improve service effectiveness.

ARC EFFECTS ON CLIENT OUTCOMES

The most important criterion for evaluating any intervention in behavioral health and social services is improved client outcomes. Interventions, whether at the individual service provider, program, or organizational levels—ones that fail to contribute to improved client well-being—waste limited resources that could otherwise be allocated to care. Improved client well-being is the primary outcome of interest in both the ARC process and in randomized trials evaluating ARC's effectiveness.

Studies of ARC include three large, randomized controlled trials that examined ARC's effects on client outcomes and all three trials confirmed that ARC improved service outcomes (Glisson et al., 2010, 2013, 2016a). In a study supported by the National Institute of Mental Health (NIMH), 615 youth with mental health problems who were referred to juvenile court in 14 rural Appalachian counties and were at-risk of out-of-home placement were served in one of four conditions. The four conditions involved all possible combinations of ARC and an evidence-based family therapy treatment model called Multi-Systemic Therapy or MST (Glisson et al., 2010). Random assignment to ARC occurred at the county level so that all youth in the same county were assigned to receive juvenile justice services under the ARC condition or not. Random assignment to MST occurred at the youth level so that youth within counties were randomly assigned to either participate in MST or usual services. Outcome criteria included caregiver-reported youth psychosocial functioning measured using the well-established Child Behavior Checklist and out-of-home placements.

The study was designed to assess the extent to which ARC would enhance the outcomes of MST so that youth who received MST in organizations that implemented ARC would achieve the best outcomes. Results provided support for this hypothesis. Youth treated with MST in the ARC condition improved significantly faster. During the first six months of treatment on caregiver-reported psychosocial functioning, measured using the

Child Behavior Checklist (CBCL), youth improvement was greater compared to youth who received MST only. These results suggest a synergistic effect in which ARC and MST enhanced each other's effects. Results for youth out-of-home placements indicated that youth in the ARC condition and youth who received MST were significantly less likely to enter out-of-home placements 18 months after entering care. Those that received both ARC and MST had the lowest out-of-home placements. The two analyses suggested that ARC improved both the clinical and placement outcomes of youth.

ARC's effects on the outcomes of mental health services were assessed in a second randomized trial. In this trial, supported by the W.T. Grant Foundation, 18 youth mental health programs from a large multi-county, non-profit, mental health, and social service system were randomly assigned to one of two conditions, ARC or control (Glisson et al., 2013). Programs in the ARC condition participated in a 36-month ARC intervention. Client outcomes in the ARC and control conditions were compared using caregiver-rated youth psychosocial functioning using the Short Form Assessment for Children (SAC; Glisson, Hemmelgarn, & Post, 2002; Hemmelgarn, Glisson, & Sharp, 2003; Tyson & Glisson, 2005).

Results confirmed ARC's positive effects on youth clinical outcomes for the 393 youth served by the programs in the study. Youth served by programs that participated in ARC improved significantly faster and to a significantly greater degree after six months of services than youth served by programs in the control group. Notably, the effect of ARC on client outcomes was identical to the average effect observed when mental health agencies adopt a specific evidence-based treatment (EBT) protocol. There was a .29 standard deviation difference ($d = .29$) in outcome scores between the ARC versus control groups. It was also important that the programs that achieved the greatest improvement in culture were the most successful in improving clinical outcomes. However, there is one important difference between the use of ARC and the use of specific EBT protocols—ARC's effects apply to clients across all diagnostic groups and all program types whereas specific evidence-based treatment protocols are usually designed to influence specific client subgroups (e.g., depressed) in one type of program (i.e., office-based psychotherapy). These results further support ARC's effects for improving the clinical outcomes of mental health and social services.

A third large randomized trial to assess ARC's effects on youth outcomes was completed in a major Midwestern metropolis with agencies that provide community-based mental health services (Glisson et al., 2016a). In this study, supported by the NIMH, 14 organizations that provide mental health services to youth were randomly assigned to an ARC or control condition. The goals of the study were to replicate ARC's effects on clinical outcomes in a unique sample. The outcome was again caregiver-reported youth psychosocial functioning based on the SAC. A total of 475 clinicians and 605 youth participated in the study. Youth were followed for six months after initiation of treatment. Results indicated that although youth assigned to ARC and control did not differ at baseline in terms of psychosocial impairment, youth in the ARC condition improved significantly faster and to a greater degree than youth served by control agencies during the first six months of treatment. Effects in this study were similar to those reported in the previous study ($d = .31$). Most importantly, the severity of psychosocial impairment in the control condition continued to remain in a clinical range after six months of services. This was not the case in the ARC condition. Moreover, the agencies that were most successful in implementing the ARC principles achieved the most improvement in outcomes. These results replicated the positive effects of ARC on the clinical outcomes of mental health services.

ARC EFFECTS ON DIRECT CARE STAFF TURNOVER

High turnover among clinicians, caseworkers, and other service providers represents a significant threat to the quality and outcomes of human services. It is difficult to ensure services are available, responsive, continuous, and effective when staff are changing and clients are re-assigned on a recurring basis. Moreover, the process of recruiting, screening, selecting, and training employees is costly. The negative impact of turnover has been an important focus of our research and development work, especially in areas such as child welfare that have high turnover rates (Williams & Glisson, 2013).

An early randomized controlled trial of ARC focused on reducing caseworker turnover in child welfare case management teams (Glisson et al., 2006). In this study, 26 case management teams were randomly assigned from rural and urban areas to participate in a 12-month ARC intervention or to a control condition. Turnover was assessed objectively and prospectively as the loss of caseworkers who were members of the participating case management teams at the beginning of the study. Specifically, 65% of the caseworkers in the control condition quit their jobs versus 39% in the intervention condition in the one-year follow-up period. Although this zero-order effect was significant, Hierarchical Linear Models estimates of the impact of ARC on team turnover rates indicated an even larger main effect of ARC after controlling for team random effects, location, and individual-level covariates such as age, education, and gender. The odds of turnover in the ARC intervention group teams were only 5% of the odds of turnover in the control group teams. These results indicated that ARC reduced the probability of turnover among caseworkers by two-thirds (probability of turnover in ARC = .23 versus probability of turnover in control condition = .89)

ARC EFFECTS ON CLINICIANS' USE OF EVIDENCE-BASED TREATMENTS

As noted in prior chapters, the ARC intervention strategies focus on changing leaders' and clinicians' mental models and behaviors regarding their organization's innovation and service improvement efforts. Consistent with emerging models of implementation science, the ARC strategies are designed to improve service outcomes by supporting the adoption and integration of scientifically validated, effective treatment practices (i.e., evidence-based treatments or EBTs) into routine care (Proctor et al., 2009; Williams & Glisson, 2014a). An important part of our research has been on understanding how ARC influences clinicians' EBT-related practice behaviors. Three randomized trials have examined ARC's relationship to EBT exploration/preparation, adoption, and implementation. The results of these trials suggest the ARC strategies contribute to improved services by supporting the use of EBTs.

Results from the ARC and MST study described earlier provide evidence of the effect of ARC on EBT implementation efforts (Glisson et al., 2010). In that study, youth in the combined ARC plus MST condition improved significantly faster than youth who received MST without ARC. The investigators reasoned that the youths' served by counties assigned to the ARC condition experienced higher-quality services and therefore better outcomes because of ARC's role in facilitating the integration of MST into each counties' juvenile justice system. However, clinicians' fidelity to the MST intervention was no different in ARC versus control counties as measured by parent-, youth-, and caregiver-reported surveys and by observer-rated audio tapes. These data suggest factors other than EBT fidelity accounted for ARC's effects on youth clinical outcomes. Other studies have examined several potential factors.

The randomized trial of mental health service organizations in the Midwest described above examined ARC's effects on clinicians' EBT exploration, preparation, and adoption behaviors (Glisson et al., 2016b; Williams et al., 2016). Diffusion of innovation theory and theories of EBT implementation in mental health and social services describe the adoption and integration of EBTs into routine services as a non-linear multiphase process that proceeds through stages of (a) exploring potential EBTs and preparing to adopt them, (b) adopting the EBT, (c) implementing the EBT, and (d) sustaining EBT use. This study was designed to test ARC's effects on the first two stages of exploration/preparation and adoption. Results from this trial supported ARC's effects on these initial stages of integrating EBT use into routine care.

First, findings from the study showed that over a three-year period during and after the ARC intervention, clinicians in ARC agencies became significantly and increasingly more likely to attend self-selected EBT workshops provided in the community than their peers in non-ARC agencies. A series of nine different community-based EBT workshops (each focused on a different treatment) were available to all clinicians in both conditions (as well as to clinicians in the community). At the beginning of the study, clinicians in ARC agencies were no more likely to attend the first EBT workshop than their peers in control agencies (3.6%). However, clinicians participating in ARC became significantly more likely to attend workshops and clinicians in the control group became significantly *less* likely to attend the EBT workshops over time. Approximately 12% of clinicians in ARC agencies attended the final EBT workshop whereas less than 1% of control clinicians attended the workshop. Importantly, the findings confirmed that ARC encouraged clinicians to explore new EBTs and prepare for their use by improving the organizational cultures of the agencies.

Second, findings from the study showed that the ARC intervention significantly increased clinicians' motivation to adopt EBTs ($d = .49$) while simultaneously lowering policy and procedure barriers to EBT adoption ($d = -.56$). These effects are significant given that motivation and organizational barriers are primary determinants of clinicians' practice-related behaviors. Furthermore, the study showed that improvements in organizational culture increased motivation and reduced policy and procedure barriers, which in turn contributed to significantly greater adoption of EBTs and use of EBTs with clients in the ARC group. Twelve months after completion of the ARC intervention, clinicians in ARC agencies had almost four times greater odds of adopting an EBT than clinicians in control agencies. Furthermore, clinicians in ARC agencies used EBTs with a significantly higher percentage of their clients (81%) than clinicians in control agencies (57%). Taken together, these results suggest the ARC intervention affects clinicians' motivation to adopt EBTs, their EBT exploration and preparation behavior, the barriers to EBT adoption within their agency, and ultimately, their EBT adoption and use of EBTs with clients (Glisson et al., 2016b; Williams et al., 2016).

ARC EFFECTS ON ORGANIZATIONAL CULTURE AND CLIMATE

A central premise of the ARC model is that positive changes in organizational culture and climate influence service provider behavior to improve service outcomes. Thus, an important criterion in testing ARC's effects and understanding how it works involves assessing whether and how ARC influences OSC (i.e., culture and climate). Systematic reviews of organizational interventions in health and behavioral health indicate that although many interventions target culture and climate for change, almost no studies test whether the interventions change social context even when they report positive effects on other outcomes. This is an important knowledge gap because understanding exactly how interventions work is necessary for improving their efficiency and effectiveness. Understanding how interventions work is also important for potential adopters so that they know which parts of an intervention may be essential versus non-essential given their specific objectives and resources.

Three randomized controlled trials tested ARC's effects on OSC in addition to other outcomes (Glisson et al., 2006, 2012, 2016b). As expected, the three studies reported positive effects of ARC on organizational culture and/or climate, depending on the length of the intervention. Our findings show that climate can be improved in a one-year period, but changes in culture can require up to three years. In the first trial of ARC, a 12-month ARC intervention significantly improved the organizational climates of the case management teams. This was expressed in service providers' perceptions of less role conflict, role overload, depersonalization, and emotional exhaustion at work. The 12-month intervention failed to influence organizational culture as measured by clinicians' survey responses due to the shorter length of the ARC intervention (i.e., 12 months versus 36 months). In a second trial, a longer ARC intervention (36 months) improved both the organizational climates and cultures of 15 mental health and social service programs randomly assigned to ARC versus control conditions (Glisson et al., 2012). Finally, in a third trial, a 36-month ARC intervention improved the proficiency culture of behavioral health organizations randomly assigned to the ARC condition (Glisson et al., 2016b; Williams et al., 2016).

A few conclusions can be drawn from these results. First, because the ARC intervention is flexible and customized based on agency-identified needs and goals during the assessment process, the specific dimensions of culture and climate dimensions that are changed can differ from organization to organization. Second, consistent with theories of organizational culture and climate, organizational climate can be improved within a 12-month intervention period, but changes in organizational culture require more time. Third, given the well-established empirical links between OSC and service quality and outcomes described above, the findings support the ARC program theory that positive changes in organizational culture and climate link ARC intervention strategies to improved service system quality and outcomes.

MECHANISMS OF CHANGE IN ARC

The randomized controlled trials that have evaluated ARC are unique in assessing (a) an organizational intervention using true experimental designs, (b) the intervention's effects on both social context and services outcomes, and (c) a range of programs, organizations, and services. The trials also address important questions regarding ARC's program theory concerning the mechanisms of change that explain ARC's effects on service outcomes. Tests of hypothesized mechanisms offer useful information to stakeholders interested in improving service effectiveness. This information is important because interventions do not always work for the reasons we believe and therefore testing our assumptions regarding how an intervention works is an important step in developing a better understanding of how to improve service effectiveness. Our recent ARC trials focus on this issue by simultaneously examining ARC's effects on targeted outcome criteria as well as the mechanisms through which these effects occur.

Preliminary data on the potential mechanisms of the ARC intervention came from the trial of 15 mental health programs described above (Glisson et al., 2012, 2013). In this trial, agencies that exhibited more improvement in their total culture and climate profiles from baseline to 18-month follow-up also demonstrated the most positive outcomes for youth. Results of this study demonstrated a significant association between improvement in the social contexts of ARC agencies and improved youth outcomes.

The trial including 16 organizations in the Midwest that was described previously provided additional data regarding ARC's mechanisms of change. Using data collected over five years, this study incorporated three mediation analyses that tested the mechanisms through which ARC contributed to targeted outcomes. These mediation analyses hypothesized that ARC increased clinicians' EBT adoption and use through two primary mechanisms (Williams et al., 2016). First, ARC created proficient organizational cultures and engaged organizational climates that increased individual clinicians' motivation to adopt and use EBTs. Second, the study hypothesized that ARC facilitated clinicians' follow-through to adopt and use EBTs by reducing job-related policy and procedural barriers. Findings confirmed that ARC increased proficiency culture in participating agencies, that increased proficiency culture contributed to increased motivation to adopt EBTs, and that increased motivation explained clinicians' increased EBT adoption and EBT use. Furthermore, ARC reduced policy and procedural barriers to EBPs and the reduced barriers enhanced the effect of clinicians' motivation on their subsequent behavior. When barriers were lower, clinicians were more successful in following-through on positive EBT intentions. Clinicians adopted more EBTs and used them more frequently with clients during the follow-up period. These findings for the multiple levels involved (i.e., organizational level, individual clinician level) paint a comprehensive picture of the motivational and opportunity-related mechanisms through which ARC influences clinicians' practice behaviors.

Another study from the trial examined how a long-term change in proficiency culture influenced clinicians' likelihood of attending community-based EBT workshops over a three-year period (Glisson et al., 2016b). Results from this study showed that improved proficiency cultures that resulted from the ARC intervention explained ARC's effects on service providers' EBT workshop attendance. That is, ARC's positive effect on clinicians' increased probability of workshop attendance over the three-year period was fully explained by the improvement in proficiency culture during the study period. These results support the importance of proficiency culture as an intervention target in shaping clinicians' EBT-related practice behaviors.

The final analysis of ARC's change mechanisms focused on the role of ARC's five principles in explaining its effects on clinical outcomes for youth (Glisson et al., 2016a). This study demonstrated that ARC's effects on improved clinical outcomes were fully explained by adherence to the ARC principles. That is, ARC improved outcomes for youth by increasing agencies' enactment of the five ARC principles. The more the agencies enacted the ARC principles, the better the youth outcomes. These findings provide robust support for the effect of ARC's principles on clinical outcomes for youth and suggest that agencies can improve their effectiveness by enacting the five principles described in Chapters 9–13. As explained in those chapters, the five principles guide the use of organizational tools in creating positive social contexts and removing organizational barriers to promote innovation and implementation success.

6

ARC INFRASTRUCTURE, PREPARATION, AND KEY STRATEGIES FOR CREATING EFFECTIVE HUMAN SERVICE ORGANIZATIONS

A successful effort to improve the effectiveness of a health-care, behavioral health, social service, or other human service organization must begin with the understanding that organizations are first and foremost social systems. Human service systems address a bewildering array of social issues through the behavior, priorities, and thinking of the people who compose both the service providers and the clients they serve. We have argued in the previous chapters that the inherent characteristics of human service work, including high levels of uncertainty, unpredictability, and heterogeneity, magnify the importance of OSC (i.e., norms, perspectives, and attitudes) for service quality and outcomes. These characteristics also increase the complexity of efforts to improve services.

We have learned that success in improving organizations demands time, resources, and a level of commitment that not all organizations or members share. This is reinforced by our experience with the randomized controlled trials summarized in Chapter 5 and from our consultation in a large number of other projects nationwide. It is clear that organizations can improve their social contexts and services by participating in ARC. Yet, we also know that the level of success varies with some organizations being more successful than others. This variation is a function, in part, of their ability to commit the necessary time and resources toward improvement efforts. Given the complexity of the tasks and the commitment of resources necessary for success, we have recognized the need for more efficient improvement strategies and have continued to streamline the ARC implementation process. However, we also understand that success in changing a large, complex social system cannot be achieved with oversimplified processes. As we describe here, a carefully planned infrastructure and orchestrated process is necessary to achieve success. First, ARC implementation requires a team-based structure of ARC teams composed of direct service providers, an Organizational Action Team (OAT) with representatives from all levels of the organization, and an executive leadership team that actively monitors and provides ongoing support for ARC implementation. Additionally, an internal ARC liaison selected from top management and an external ARC specialist guide the ARC process using ARC materials. These include manuals for ARC teams and leaders, facilitator's guides, and associated ARC materials for OAT members and executives.

In this chapter we share additional information about the structures and materials needed to implement ARC and review in more detail the core strategies of ARC that help us achieve success.

THREE ARC STRATEGIES: PRINCIPLES, COMPONENT TOOLS, AND MENTAL MODELS

As presented in Chapter 4, ARC employs five core principles to guide the implementation of ARC's organizational component tools that support service system improvement. ARC also targets mental models to foster the reasoning and beliefs among organizational members that support ARC principles and the effective use of the component tools. The external ARC specialist works with organizational leaders to ensure they understand each of the strategies, the underlying rationale, and the structure and process for improving services.

ARC principles. ARC's five core principles were developed and expanded for human services from Osborne and Gaebler's (1992) descriptions of effective organizations across a variety of public services. The five principles are described in Chapters 9–13, respectively, and include being (1) mission-driven versus rule-driven (ensuring all actions and decisions contribute to improving the well-being of clients) (2) results-oriented versus process oriented (measuring individual, team, and organizational performance by improvements in the well-being of clients) (3) improvement-directed versus status quo-directed (continually seeking to be more effective in improving the well-being of clients), (4) participation-based versus authority-based (including service providers and other stakeholders in policy and service decisions for improving client well-being), and (5) relationship-centered versus individual-centered (focusing service and improvement efforts on the network of relationships, e.g., service providers, family, community) that contribute to improving client well-being.

These principles are first explained to organizational leaders who are considering ARC as a service improvement strategy. Upon the decision to adopt ARC, these principles are fully explained in initial engagement meetings with leaders to clarify the meaning, impact, and central roles of the principles in improving organizational effectiveness. Throughout ARC implementation, we embed these principles as we align organizational priorities that support the ARC tools, processes, and shared reasoning necessary to improve services.

The first objective is to help organizational leaders examine the fit between the ARC principles and their organizations' existing practices. This process helps leaders identify the barriers that detract from these principles and those they would like to address. After the decision to implement the ARC strategy is made, the ARC specialist uses ARC manuals to explain how the five principles are embedded within an organization. ARC materials and exercises explore how the principles align with the organization's broader mission, strategic plans, objectives, and priorities. And, leaders' behaviors and decisions, as well as the design of organizational systems are examined to illustrate leaders' influence on enacting these principles. As explained in Chapter 3, baseline OSC measures are completed by direct service providers and results are shared with leaders. This allows leaders to examine the OSC profiles described by direct service providers and explore the connection between ARC principles, the key dimensions of OSC and service quality and outcomes.

These initial discussions and activities prepare leaders for their roles in supporting ARC, as they work with the ARC specialist to articulate goals and objectives of the service improvement effort and develop plans to explain ARC strategies to organizational members. Leaders are taught to monitor ARC activities, communicate ARC's purpose and objectives, and model behaviors and actions consistent with the ARC principles. ARC materials are designed to support leaders in specific tasks, such as implementing effective ARC orientation meetings for staff. By design, these orientation meetings model and reinforce behaviors and approaches consistent with the ARC principles. For example, orientation meetings are designed to expand front-line staff discretion and input (participation based), demonstrate a clear rationale of how ARC strategies will contribute to improvements in client well-being (mission driven), and provide the opportunity to discuss the use of data for monitoring desired outcomes (results oriented). Leaders are actively involved in identifying and addressing organizational barriers that are expected to interfere with implementation (improvement directed), and in building stronger relationships with staff through their availability and responsiveness to staff (relationship-centered).

ARC component tools. The design and implementation of ARC's 12 organizational component tools are guided by the ARC principles. Initial efforts support leaders and staff in identifying potential issues as the ARC components are put into place. Described in more detail in Chapter 7, these components range from increasing leaders' understanding of embedding ARC principles, an example of ARC's *leadership development* component, to key service improvement processes such as *continuous improvement* and *job redesign*.

The introduction of the 12 ARC components is based on the belief that effective organizational change requires the coordinated use of multiple organizational tools to address the behavior, priorities, and thinking of its members. We also know that identifying which of the multiple components will contribute most to success in a particular organization, whether addressing social, technical, or strategic factors, is difficult to predict *a priori* (Robertson, Roberts, & Porras,1993; Worren, Ruddle, & Moore, 1999). For this reason, ARC presents multiple components gathered from the organizational literature that have a record of success in improving organizational effectiveness. In initial meetings with organizational leaders, we describe these components, the strategies for implementing the components, and identify which of the components are likely to be most important for the specific organization based on the organization's OSC profile and feedback from service providers. This process includes helping leaders identify existing organizational strengths and approaches that complement ARC's components and principles, as well as organizational deficits that can be addressed by the components and principles.

ARC mental models. Identifying and explaining the roles of mental models in efforts to improve services provide the third ARC strategy for creating effective organizations (see Chapter 8). Preliminary work during the initial ARC meetings with leaders define and describe mental models, beginning with exercises that explain the concept of mental models and their association with leaders' perceptions, interpretations, and reactions to organizational events. Case studies are used to identify patterns of reasoning and underlying assumptions and beliefs that are supported by different mental models such as psychological safety. Psychological safety is a well-known construct in the organizational literature. It is employed to promote leadership that encourages exploration of new techniques or approaches without increasing the fear of criticism or threat among employees. It supports work environments where unintentional errors, mistakes, or problems are openly discussed and addressed to support learning and improvement efforts (Edmondson, Bohmer, & Pisano, 2001). Leaders are assisted in recognizing the beliefs and assumptions that promote behaviors consistent with psychologically safe environments. The goal is for leaders to understand linkages between psychologically safety and key outcomes that they desire. Providing evidence of these linkages and practical examples of their contribution to critical outcomes encourages the development of mental models that support and sustain psychological safety.

ARC materials and exercises illustrate underlying assumption of mental models. The underlying assumptions and beliefs of each model are used to explain how leaders and organizational members can support or undermine ARC principles and the priorities that are being enacted through actual practices. Organizational processes for discipline, training, and feedback are examined, for example, to identify how leaders' approaches are driven by shared assumptions, beliefs, and mental models. Leaders and staff explore how their shared beliefs, mindsets, and assumptions are used to reason, make decisions, and act in congruence with the ARC principles. These examples of mental models exploration and use provide a framework for embedding key principles within one's reasoning, decisions, organizational processes, and leadership behavior. The objective is to emphasize how improving services in an organization requires changes in the shared mental models associated with the organization's processes and leadership practices. Similarly, it makes explicit how members' mental models and underlying assumptions affect the way members perceive and react to the behavior of leaders, coworkers, and organizational events.

ARC'S PARTICIPANTS AND CHANGE AGENTS

Altering OSC requires multiple strategies and working with organizational members at all levels, from front-line service providers to executive leaders. That is, altering an organization's social context (i.e., culture and climate) requires changes in beliefs, practices, norms, expectations, and perceptions at all levels of the organization. These changes are supported by both internal and external ARC change agents to ensure sustainable improvement and change.

ARC's external change agent: The ARC specialist. An ARC specialist who is trained in the three ARC strategies functions as an external consultant to support an organization's improvement effort. The ARC specialist is instrumental in developing the need and direction for change in the organization. As the ARC process continues, the specialist provides training, consultation, and coaching for the ARC teams and members. The ARC specialist establishes relationships with leaders and members at each level to maintain effective, ongoing information exchange. In turn, the specialist employs these relationships to develop and translate the need for change into action by guiding the ARC strategies and associated processes with ARC participants. Following the role prescribed over a long history of organizational literature on external change agents, the ARC specialist works with service teams, administrators, key opinion leaders, and community stakeholders to address service barriers created by bureaucratic red tape, turf wars, misinformation, ineffective procedures, poor communication, and mistrust (Beer, 1980; Bennis, 1966; Blake, Shepard, & Mouton, 1964; Callister & Wall, 2001; French & Bell, 1984; Porras & Robertson, 1992; Robey & Altman, 1982; Rogers, 1995). The specialist provides training, tools, and coaching for organizational members to address barriers by adopting new technologies and practices, developing new service strategies, or designing improved work processes (Burke, 1993; French & Bell, 1984; Pasmore, Francis, Haldeman, & Shani, 1982; Porras & Robertson, 1992; Steel & Shane, 1986; Walton, 1987). The ARC specialist uses organizational events and practices as a stimulus for sharing additional information and processes among leaders, service providers, and external stakeholders to support service improvement. Critical information that is shared includes feedback regarding observed organizational events, organizational member behaviors and decisions, as well as outcomes that result from altered processes, behavioral patterns, or approaches. Reflections regarding these changes and subsequent outcomes are facilitated by the ARC

Specialist to reinforce positive changes in behaviors, thinking, and priorities that align with ARC components and principles.

ARC's internal change agents. There are also multiple internal change agents that contribute to the implementation of the three ARC strategies. Several teams and individuals are actively involved in shaping the relationships, communication structures, organizational systems, shared beliefs, and shared behavioral norms that define the work environment. Most importantly, we have learned that successful organizational improvement efforts require the commitment and active involvement of the organization's top leaders as well as the direct service providers. As explained in the following paragraphs, the ARC strategies rely on and support this involvement at all levels.

Upper leadership. It is necessary but not sufficient for an organization's leaders to support their staff's use of the ARC strategies to improve services. Leaders must take an active role in (1) establishing and maintaining clarity of purpose for engaging in ARC for all members; (2) championing ARC and its desired goals; (3) providing support, resources, and direct action, if needed, to eliminate barriers to implementation; (4) selecting and monitoring outcomes and ensuring recognition of outcome successes internally and externally (5) modeling and enacting ARC principles in their own decisions and actions; and (6) developing and enacting their own action plans for behavioral, procedural, structural, and strategic changes that support implementation of the ARC principles within their organization when needed.

Organization Action Team (OAT). The OAT is a multilevel team consisting of representatives from executive leadership (e.g., CEO or COO), midlevel managers, ARC team supervisors, and front-line ARC team members. In larger agencies, it is important that managers from human resources and quality improvement divisions be included. Additional members, such as representatives from information technology (IT), finances, or community relations often serve as members when addressing improvement efforts relevant to their expertise.

The OAT team supports and assists front-line ARC teams in identifying and addressing service barriers that inhibit effectiveness. The OAT provides reviews, recommendations, and assistance in implementing the proposed plans generated by the ARC teams for addressing service barriers. The role of the OAT is to ensure the success of these proposals with active support. Active support includes assistance in engaging additional staff and resources needed to eliminate service barriers identified by the ARC teams while facilitating networking, information sharing, and communication necessary for change to occur. The OAT also assists in planning and providing the necessary training and support for sustaining ARC tools, processes, and activities within the organization on an ongoing basis. The OAT works with the ARC specialist, ARC liaison, and front-line teams to develop specific organizational processes such as data monitoring systems to provide front-line staff with client feedback that can be used for improving services. These efforts include coordinating with front-line staff to put measures and processes in place that are safe, desired, and effective in driving front-line staff improvement efforts. Finally,

OAT members use ARC component tools to eliminate broader organizational barriers they identify throughout ARC implementation as they help front-line staff address service barriers.

ARC front-line teams and team supervisors. ARC teams of front-line service providers use the ARC component tools described in Chapter 7 to identify service barriers. The teams generate proposals for addressing the identified barriers, guided by the five ARC principles described in Chapters 9–13. The ARC teams comprise members of preexisting front-line service units in the organization that may or may not already be functioning as teams. The ARC team supervisors are the service units' front-line supervisors who are trained by the ARC specialist and internal ARC liaison to deploy ARC materials and exercises with front-line team members. ARC team supervisors train, facilitate, and guide staff in the use of ARC processes throughout ARC implementation. With the support of the OAT, the ARC teams monitor the successes and failures in addressing service barriers, report progress to the liaison and specialist, and assist in troubleshooting and making corrections to achieve further improvement. Some ARC supervisors serve as members of the OAT, and others provide temporary assistance within OAT meetings on specific topics in which they have expertise.

Under the structured guidance of the ARC team supervisors, front-line ARC team members identify, analyze, and address service barriers with proposals for improving services that are presented to the OAT. The proposals include action plans for eliminating barriers based on collaborative work with the ARC specialist, ARC liaison, and OAT to implement changes in policies and practices. Using the ARC component tools such as *feedback, participative decision making,* and *teamwork* (see Chapter 7), the teams of front-line staff members monitor data on client outcomes and employ the data to guide continuous improvement efforts. Among other tasks, these teams identify and enact changes in the organization's service models, practices, procedural requirements, and training to improve services.

The ARC liaison. The ARC liaison is selected from mid- to upper-level leaders to serve as the key internal change agent, boundary spanner, and opinion leader for implementing ARC strategies. The external ARC specialist mentors the ARC liaison's efforts as the internal ARC expert who guides ongoing ARC activities to ensure successful change and sustainability. The ARC liaison works closely with the external ARC specialist to implement all aspects of the ARC process. Over time, the internal ARC liaison transitions from a co-facilitator of upper leadership and OAT meetings to the sole facilitator of these meetings. The ARC liaison facilitates communication between and among all organizational levels, sharing information across groups, and developing linkages among organization members. The liaison's efforts are supported by the external ARC specialist in using the ARC component tools to promote practices consistent with the ARC principles. The liaison's work extends to areas of the organization beyond the ARC teams and includes the identification of additional improvements that are needed to further embed ARC principles across the entire organization. Given their substantial responsibilities and role demands, organizational leaders are asked to allocate 20% to 50% of the ARC liaison's weekly workload to ARC activities, depending on the size and complexity of the organization.

Other stakeholders. As indicated earlier, additional external stakeholders are identified by OAT and ARC teams to improve services and included in efforts to identify and address targeted barriers. Reflecting ARC's principle of maintaining a relationship-centered focus, the relationships with external stakeholders are often critical when addressing barriers to effective care. These stakeholders are included in action planning and the implementation of strategies to improve service quality and coordination with other service systems. For example, we have worked to help establish collaborative efforts between mental health providers and external stakeholders such as school personnel, court personnel, and other community service providers who collaborate to address service barriers to improve care.

SELECTING AND PREPARING CHANGE AGENTS FOR ARC

To be successful, initial preparation is necessary to assure that the primary change agents are trained and prepared to implement ARC. This includes both external ARC specialists who conduct ARC and the internal ARC liaisons who transition over time to assume the responsibilities of the external ARC specialists.

ARC specialists. Our experience in selecting and training ARC specialists suggests that several characteristics are associated with their success as change agents. To support an organization's efforts to improve services using ARC, the specialist must understand the organizational components and strategies employed in ARC as well as have experience in working with human service improvement efforts. To do so, ARC specialists require training in organizational change, organizational culture and climate, and technical expertise for ARC's organizational components (e.g., team development, conflict management, feedback systems, etc.). In their role as boundary spanners (Trist, 1985), they need to interact effectively with multiple groups, be excellent communicators, and be able to effectively interpret and translate information across groups (e.g., leaders, direct service providers, OAT, ARC teams, external stakeholders). ARC specialists require analytic skills to identify, understand, and communicate OSC profiles to promote and support positive change. The ARC specialist's ability to establish and maintain effective interpersonal relationships is critical in gaining the confidence and commitment of organizational leaders, middle managers, and line staff. Candidates with these qualifications are typically selected with doctoral or master's-level degrees in areas such as social work, organizational psychology, health management science, clinical psychology, or other professional fields linked to organizational development or human services.

To enhance their skills for facilitating ARC, training for ARC specialists begins with readings on organizational culture and climate, the practice literature on the ARC organizational component tools, and research on the concepts of mental models and the ARC principles. Specialists are provided preliminary training and coaching to support their re-view of all ARC training materials, videos, and accompanying resource materials. Active role-playing, enactment, and modeling are used under the guidance of a trained ARC specialist to assure efficacy and expertise in employing the ARC materials and processes. Most importantly, a trained ARC specialist mentors and guides trainees by first modeling the ARC strategy within an agency and then providing support if necessary while the trainee supports activities and meetings with ARC team supervisors and members.

ARC Liaison. The internal ARC liaison is selected from top management and is supported in their work to improve services by the ARC specialist. The importance of selecting a competent ARC liaison cannot be overstated. In our experience the liaison is pivotal in the success of the organization's efforts to implement ARC, to improve OSC, and to successfully address service barriers. We have found several personal character-istics are important to the liaison's success, and we encourage leaders to select the ARC liaison on that basis. The key characteristics include (1) a strong interest and desire to influence organizational change, (2) experience with improvement efforts within the or-ganization, (3) credibility among leaders and staff at all levels of the participating organi-zation, (4) sufficient formal and informal power in the agency to encourage and support change efforts, (5) the ability to foster psychologically safe relationships with leaders and members that allow constructive criticism of ideas and practices, (6) demonstrated effec-tiveness in planning and task completion, (7) consistently improvement-directed attitude, and (8) expected longevity in the organization. Arranging the necessary commitment of time is critical but can be particularly difficult: this is because individuals who meet the previously listed criteria tend to be valued and over-utilized within organizations, yet most desirable as the liaison. That is to say that the best person for liaison is often the person who already has too much to do. A considerable amount of restructuring assignments is often required for the liaison to have the time to commit to the improvement effort.

The selection of the ARC liaison is completed by organizational leaders in early meetings with the ARC specialist. Once identified, the liaison attends all leadership meetings and begins initial tasks with the support of the ARC specialist. The liaison is oriented to the position's responsibilities and their role in facilitating the implemen-tation of the three ARC strategies. ARC materials and workbooks for ARC participant groups are provided to the liaison for review with the ARC specialist. The ARC specialist provides the liaison with additional references and sources throughout the process to fur-ther expand their knowledge of ARC strategies and concepts. The ARC liaison attends all ARC training events and meetings with upper leaders, the OAT, and front-line ARC team supervisors. One-on-one sessions with the ARC specialist occur monthly along with ongoing consults through e-mail and phone. The ongoing sessions allow the ARC specialist and liaison to review progress, troubleshoot, and establish action plans for con-tinuing progress. The liaison is expected to assume an increasing level of responsibility in supporting leaders, guiding OAT meetings, and facilitating ARC activities across all ARC teams throughout the ARC process.

PRELIMINARY TRAINING

Organizational leaders, OAT members, and ARC team supervisors receive initial training using ARC materials tailored for each group. Common elements include establishing clarity on ARC logistics (overall strategy, timelines, scheduling, involvement, responsibilities, etc.), ARC purpose and objectives, ARC principles, and introduction to component tools and processes for changing OSC and addressing service barriers. Unique to each group's training are the elements and foci of their respective roles. For example, leaders are included in activities to understand OSC scores, ARC principles, and their role in championing ARC; front-line ARC team supervisors are trained in team leadership, facilitating meetings, and strategies to address problems in teamwork. The OAT team is trained in effective team practices and meeting tools to ensure a participative team of members from various organizational levels. An emphasis on key concepts such as fostering psychological safety, openness to change, and dialogue are introduced. Further exploration of their roles and responsibilities prepares the OAT team for evaluating, discussing, providing feedback, and communicating with front-line ARC teams when addressing their proposals for change and improvement.

ONGOING TRAINING AND PREPARATION

The internal ARC liaison and ARC team supervisors receive monthly training from the external ARC specialist to prepare for meetings with front-line ARC teams. These monthly sessions introduce new leadership skills, address previous ARC meeting successes and failures, and prepare ARC team leaders to facilitate the use of ARC materials and processes in the upcoming weekly ARC meetings with team members. Team supervisors are provided with their own manuals to guide front-line staff through skill development, activities, and processes outlined in front-line staff workbooks. Initial front-line training includes areas ranging from applying ARC principles to establishing effective meeting and team practices. These initial training efforts transition to identifying, analyzing, and eliminating barriers to effective care and to improving key organizational processes.

The ARC liaison and ARC specialist collaborate on an ongoing basis, identifying additional training needs for upper leadership and OAT members throughout the ARC process. The specialist and liaison monitor and collect observations, critical incidents, identified service barriers, and related work issues that trigger further development, including additional application of ARC tools, processes, or concepts that aid leaders or OAT members in developing their capacity to improve services. Front-line service providers, for example, may identify leadership directives that interfere with a focus on improving client wellbeing, promoting the need for further exploration and development with leaders. Or, critical incidents of clients not receiving quality care can prompt the need for additional training, development, or application of ARC tools to eliminate service barriers. Additional training for management groups or other support personal are also identified and provided as needed by the ARC liaison and specialist.

CREATING AN ARCHITECTURE FOR CHANGE

ARC incorporates multiple groups and individuals in a purposeful fashion to create organizational change focused on improving services. Although there are separate responsibilities and roles for individuals and groups, ARC's approach and activities are designed to develop interdependence. Thus, the activities of upper leaders, the OAT, the ARC liaison, and the ARC teams support parallel improvement efforts. For example, while front-line staff are developing team skills and experience with continuous improvement processes to identify and eliminate service barriers, OAT members establish their own team skills and work on the most effective process for supporting improvements proposed by front-line ARC teams. The organization's leaders learn to foster the ARC principles and specific practices that support a learning environment in the organization, practices that will ensure front-line ARC teams are comfortable in identifying and addressing service barriers within their organization.

ARC's use of structured materials to guide and facilitate a planned progression of activities for all ARC groups is critical to this architecture. Upper leaders, the OAT team, and the ARC team facilitators receive support manuals, workbooks, and guides that help them implement ARC activities, but the materials are not designed to lock activities into rigid, bureaucratic steps. Instead, they provide the framework, tools, and processes to identify and address real problems and barriers identified by the respective groups. Some groups identify more problems than others, or more difficult problems according to the unique experience and character of each work environment. Although similar tools and practices are taught to all members, they are applied and learned while addressing real problems and issues that the leaders and staff currently face. Explicit in this architecture is a focus on building effective teams at all levels, applying tools from several of the ARC components reviewed in Chapter 7. The process includes training on social contexts, team behaviors, meeting management, and mental models that support effective team interactions and practices that promote a learning environment. Training also includes activities for team members to enact ARC principles and embed these principles in a work environment where addressing problems and errors is psychologically safe at all levels (see Chapter 8).

BUILDING IN SUSTAINABILITY

Although an essential part of the last stage of ARC (see Chapter 7), sustainability is built into the process from the beginning of ARC to ensure that ongoing improvement continues. Sustainability is encouraged with three approaches. First, we know from

Rogers's (2003) work on the diffusion of innovations that information carried through social communication among community or organizational members is critical to the success or failure of implementation efforts. ARC is designed to create and maintain communication among all participants regarding the value of ARC processes and goals. The ARC specialist and liaison focus on identifying, elaborating, and promoting positive experiences and outcomes achieved across all organizational members. In the monthly meeting of ARC team supervisors, for example, an ARC supervisor's excitement in facilitating an effective meeting using ARC meeting tools can encourage other members to share their excitement and experience. These interactions lead to discussions of ARC component tools associated with that success with other program leaders and informal mentoring by ARC supervisors in using the tools. Upper leaders and OAT members are made aware of these successes and plan with the ARC liaison further steps to spread the successes within the agency. Both the ARC specialist and liaison monitor successes and failures within the ARC teams to address problems before social information processes adversely impact commitment and sustainability.

Second, multiple assessment and feedback mechanisms are built into ARC, ranging from formal and informal meeting evaluations with front-line ARC teams to monthly reports from ARC team leaders on successes and failures in their previous activities. Broader measures, such as OSC measurement once a year and monthly assessments from ARC participants regarding the use of the ARC principles, reinforce ongoing implementation. These activities provide an opportunity for the ARC specialist and liaison to model the use of data in a positive, psychologically safe, and constructive way that encourages the use of data in monitoring performance. Outcomes identified by leaders (e.g., staff turnover, client retention, improvement in client well-being), as well as indicators of success in front-line ARC teams such as the elimination of service barriers are assessed over time and shared to celebrate successes.

Finally, implementation science is clear on the importance of ongoing support and guidance for individuals trying new approaches, processes, or technologies they are not familiar with. That is, simply explaining how to apply a new approach or technology is often not enough to ensure fidelity to protocols and effective deployment of the new practices. ARC is designed to go beyond assessment and feedback to include ongoing social support that develops confidence that the new expectations can be met. For ARC team supervisors who are struggling to implement ARC, we find that collaborative reviews of videotaped meetings can generate specific recommendations for strategies to support and improve their efforts. Individual consultation with leaders, OAT members, or other ARC team supervisors can address problems or difficulties they are experiencing in implementation. These individuals benefit from identifying specific events, mental models, or situational cues that lead to behaviors that interfere with their ability to create a team environment that supports problem solving among members.

CARVING-OUT TIME FOR EFFECTIVENESS

Our studies suggest that meaningful changes in organizational climate (e.g., lower stress, higher engagement) and worker attitudes (e.g., higher commitment and job satisfaction) within human service agencies can begin within 12 months while improvements in culture (e.g., higher proficiency, lower rigidity) require up to 36 months. Consistent with our research and recognizing the practical challenges of multi-year implementation efforts, our experience is that ARC should be implemented for at least 24 months to create a sustainable trend towards improvement.

The ARC specialist works closely with organizational leaders in the first quarter of the ARC intervention to address logistical concerns, clarify purpose, strategic fit, desired outcomes, and to begin orientation sessions for all ARC participants. In this first quarter, the ARC specialist provides a two-day leadership workshop to engage leaders in embedding ARC principles within their organization. Subsequently, leaders meet once a month with their ARC liaison and tri-annually with the ARC specialist and ARC liaison to monitor progress, address needed actions, and plan for additional leadership support.

As described above, success requires that the ARC liaison commit 20% to 50% of their time to ARC depending on the size and complexity of the organization. The ARC liaison spends this time learning about, supporting, and guiding the ARC process. The liaison attends all ARC orientation and training events, transitions over time to facilitating all upper leadership and OAT meetings, and accompanies ARC team supervisors when needed in facilitating front-line ARC meetings. The liaison meets by phone with the ARC specialist at a minimum of once a month, or more often when needed, for support and consultation.

OAT members begin to meet in the second quarter of ARC for two hours per month. These meetings focus on training in the second quarter of ARC before beginning their role of supporting ARC team proposals to address service barriers identified by the front-line ARC team members. The OAT focuses on ensuring the long-term sustainability of ARC, including creating necessary infrastructure (e.g., training, tracking of outcome data) in latter stages of ARC.

The ARC team supervisors receive in the second quarter of ARC 8 to 12 hours of initial skill training. They then begin to participate in three-hour monthly meetings of their fellow supervisors to review progress and prepare them to lead three ARC team meetings per month. ARC team supervisors invest 30 minutes to plan for each team meeting and several hours a week coordinating work and actions agreed upon within their teams. As indicated, front-line team members meet with their ARC supervisor for three meetings per month in the second quarter of ARC. Additional time is required outside of meetings to collect information and enact their service improvement plans.

Initial meetings with key personnel from support departments (e.g., IT, HR) are conducted in the first six months of ARC to explain the ARC process. As teams identify and propose improvements beginning in month seven of ARC, organizational members from these non-client service areas can be called upon by front-line teams and the OAT to help address organizational issues relevant to identified service barriers.

Given the diversity in design and structure of human service organizations and programs, adjustments are often required in meeting schedules and length of meetings. This is particularly true in the latter stages of ARC where sustainability encourages adaptations to ARC processes, timelines, and meeting schedules to enable organizations to effectively adapt ARC to their specific needs, schedules, and planned strategic activities and goals.

ADDITIONAL CONSIDERATIONS

Although ARC provides a structured sequence of activities and processes, adaptations are always a necessary part of success. The ARC specialist must be careful to listen closely to the pressing demands that exist within organizations both by leadership as well as front-line providers and mid-level managers. That is, ARC implementation requires flexibility and adaptation for unique organizational needs and challenges. Although core elements are always applied, each organization has different strengths, weaknesses, and areas of concern. Efforts must be made to accommodate and address these differences. And these weaknesses or pressing concerns are often carefully assessed to make accommodations for addressing them in the ARC process. A particular challenge, for example, is high staff turnover that is often associated with organizational units characterized by poor climates and cultures. It is difficult to embed new practices or approaches when the workforce is constantly evolving, so high turnover may require procedures to train multiple individuals for leading front-line teams, or first using ARC strategies with a team of supervisors to address the issue of turnover. Applying ARC processes to these problems, such as including front-line staff in efforts to solve them, can be effective in creating change. In either case, ARC remains a structured strategy, yet adaptation and flexibility are required to not only foster change but to model and promote normative behaviors, expectations, and beliefs that support innovation, adaptation, and improvement.

7

ARC STAGES AND COMPONENT
TOOLS

This chapter describes the three ARC stages of collaboration, participation, and innovation in service improvement efforts and introduces 12 ARC component tools that
organizational leaders, managers, and front-line staff use in those stages to identify and
eliminate service barriers. The use of the 12 tools is guided by ARC's five principles
of effective organizations described in Chapters 9–13. The use of multiple component
tools has long been recognized in the organizational literature as a need for effective
organizational responses to identified problems (Barraud-Didier & Guerrero, 2002;
Burke, 1993; Guzzo, Jette, & Katzell, 1985; Neuman, Edwards, & Raju, 1989; Porras
& Robertson, 1992; Robertson et al., 1993; Rogers, 2003; Trist, 1985; Worren et al.,
1999). This need is generated by multiple factors that affect the success of an organizational change effort because the relative importance of each factor in a specific effort
is difficult to predict *a priori* (Robertson et al., 1993; Worren et al., 1999). The 12
components, therefore, comprise a repertoire of tools that can be used in developing
an organization's capacity for improvement, depending on the organization's strengths
and needs.

Although the ARC components and the associated stages are presented here in linear
fashion, the process of building an OSC that supports service improvements and the
capacity to identify and eliminate service barriers is often nonlinear and characterized
by starts and stops, feedback loops, and multiple iterations. At the same time, the three
ARC stages provide an overarching guideline or heuristic for understanding how this process unfolds and for organizing the steps that are taken along the way. The component
tools represent an array of empirically supported organizational change techniques that
we have drawn from the organizational research literature, adapted and tested with social

service, mental health, and other human service organizations over the last three decades. In reviewing these components, we provide examples from our experiences that go beyond the mechanics of applying the components. These include efforts to address mental models and establish beliefs and practices that support the alignment of an organization's priorities with the five ARC principles.

STAGES OF THE ARC PROCESS

The first ARC stage, *collaboration*, focuses on establishing the necessary foundation for subsequent change efforts that include: (a) forming relationships between the external ARC specialist and the organization's leaders, managers, and front-line staff, (b) providing information and expectations about the roles and responsibilities of participating members of the organization, and (c) the development of social networks and communication among key stakeholders. During the collaboration stage, the ARC specialist works with leaders and middle managers to disseminate the five ARC principles among all staff. An emphasis is placed on building commitment for the enactment of the principles, and information is shared about how the ARC organizational tools will be used to assist the organization in enacting the principles.

During the first stage, the ARC specialist works with leaders to understand strategic goals, objectives, and immediate challenges organizational leaders perceive as critical to their functioning and effectiveness. Careful attention is given to the ARC principles during this work accompanied by specific ARC activities to identify leadership mental models and shared beliefs that are reflected in the organization's existing processes, systems, and approaches. The ARC specialist and leaders review the ARC process, principles, and component tools to establish objectives and goals that are shared by the leaders and the ARC specialist. Leaders work with the ARC specialist to identify outcomes for assessing improvements critical to both the organization and staff. Collaborative efforts continue as the ARC specialist and organizational leaders design orientation meetings for ARC participants jointly. The orientation sessions include collaborative efforts that address the questions, concerns, and needs of front-line staff, initiating adjustments or modifications to the ARC process that ensure its success. The ARC specialist assists leaders in forming multilevel Organizational Action Team (OAT) OAT and line-level ARC teams described in the previous chapter. Members of the OAT include the CEO and representatives from top administration, middle managers, and clinicians. These individuals are selected on the basis of their potential to successfully champion and guide service improvement efforts within the organization. ARC teams are formed from existing direct service teams or units with members that share functional goals and supervisors. The organization's existing front-line supervisors lead the ARC teams. Completion of the activities during the collaboration stage typically requires three to six months. In all these activities, the ARC specialist is available and responsive to participating members with the goal of establishing trust and collaborative work norms that will guide subsequent work.

The second ARC stage, *participation*, focuses on (a) building teamwork and openness to change within the newly formed OAT and ARC teams, (b) increasing effectiveness in using meeting and planning tools, and (c) developing the teams' knowledge and skills to effectively identify, analyze, and address service barriers that impede effectiveness. During this stage, the ARC teams are provided tools for participatory decision making, information sharing, and creating mutual support among team members. ARC specialists engage participants in activities that help team members use the ARC principles and train ARC team supervisors to guide ARC team in using component tools to identify and address service barriers. Key concepts and mental models are introduced, such as psychological safety and service availability, responsiveness, and continuity to build social contexts that support safe, effective participation and behaviors that support ongoing learning and improvement. ARC teams use structured manuals to complete a series of activities that develop their capacity and skills for effective teamwork, effective action planning and participative decision making while identifying service barriers. Completion of the participation stage takes 8 to 12 months.

During the third ARC stage, *innovation*, ARC teams use the skills and processes developed during the prior two stages to address barriers to effective service. Such barriers include, for example, inappropriate referral procedures, unnecessary red tape for intake and assignment, process-oriented evaluative criteria, ineffective practice models, and any other barriers documented by the ARC teams. The innovation stage can include implementing new treatment models or information technologies, redesigning work processes or structures, redefining job responsibilities, planning for ongoing training for sustained improvement, or processes for ongoing evaluation of change. This stage incorporates information developed and gained by frontline service providers during the previous ARC stage. The ARC teams propose innovations and solutions to the identified service barriers and forward action plans to the OAT. The OAT is responsible for assessing the proposals, providing feedback to the ARC teams regarding feasibility or the need for additional information, and then guiding the implementation of proposed changes. Including top leaders as members of the OAT provides the authority to enact changes in organization-wide practices, protocols, and procedures that are necessary to embed the ARC principles. This process ensures that recommended improvements originate from line-level service teams and address the service barriers identified by front-line service providers.

The third ARC stage of innovation evolves into an ongoing process of improvement through which ARC teams and the OAT monitor client outcomes, identify barriers to service effectiveness, and address service barriers. Research on the ARC intervention suggests organizations typically move into the innovation stage 12 to 18 months after initiation of the ARC process and can see service-related improvements in client outcomes beginning 18 to 24 months after starting ARC.

TWELVE COMPONENTS OF THE ARC INTERVENTION

This section describes the 12 ARC component tools that organizations use to align organizational priorities with the five ARC principles of effective services. Components include: (a) leadership development, (b) personal relationships, (c) network development, (d) team building, (e) information and training, (f) feedback, (g) participatory decision making, (h) conflict management, (i) goal setting, (j) continuous improvement, (k) job redesign, and (l) stabilization.

Leadership development. *Leadership development* prepares leaders in the use of the ARC principles to communicate a clear vision for change, sets high-performance standards related to that vision, and creates a healthy climate for implementing new practices and innovations. Initial work includes sharing information with staff, forming a participative structure to implement the ARC model that includes the Organization Action Team, and guiding the collaborative efforts needed to initiate and maintain ARC (Edmondson et al., 2001; Green, 1998; Gustafson, Sainfort, Eichler, Adams, & Bisognano, 2003; Meyers, Sivakumar, & Nakata, 1999; Murphy & Southey, 2003; Young, 2000).

Efforts include developing leaders' understanding of the ARC principles and their impact, including the reasoning and beliefs leaders need to sustain enactment of the principles. Leaders are guided in examining the behaviors and actions needed to support the principles, the influence and practice of the principles in their organizational systems and processes, and their implications for client, staff, and organizational outcomes. These efforts continue throughout the ARC process. Failures and successes in decision making, behavioral actions, and approaches to improving organizational systems are examined with leaders to ensure consistency with ARC principles. These efforts can precipitate additional activities with leaders, including training of alternative leadership behaviors, a closer examination of existing organizational systems, and scrutiny of organizational processes.

Personal relationships. Relationships and social processes are essential to improving organizational culture and climate. Therefore, a central component of the ARC intervention involves cultivating personal relationships among members of the organization across levels and departments, developing strategically important linkages with stakeholders outside the organization, and identifying and engaging opinion leaders. These relationships provide a basis for communication, sharing information, and solving problems that emerge during the change effort. Relationships are formed through one-on-one meetings, quid pro quo activities that are valued by stakeholders and organizational members, and arranging group meetings that focus on service issues and barriers that are a priority for all parties. These relationships are critical to negotiating and reframing the meaning of problems, reaching solutions, and achieving innovations—and for supporting the adoption of best practices (Backer & Rogers, 1998; Ferlie, Gabbay, Fitzgerald, Locock, & Dopson, 2001; Gray, 1990; Rogers, 1995).

Efforts to establish or strengthen organizational member relationships include expanded information sharing and cross-training between organizational programs. The use of OAT teams enhances collaboration, joint efforts, and trust among organizational members as they work across multiple levels. The ARC specialist supports leaders and managers in promoting information sharing with staff, increasing the frequency and quality of their interactions, and reinforcing enhanced recognition among all organizational members of individual and team successes, all of which help to foster trust. With ARC participants at all levels, ARC specialists work on building stronger relationships by explicitly training on and promoting interactions characterized by availability, responsiveness, and continuity. Explicitly addresses in training activities and explored to build a mental model of effective working relationships, we work with ARC participants to enact these characteristics in their relationships and interactions with coworkers and clients (see Chapter 13). Efforts in building strong relationships extend to the use of other component tools as well. For example, team building and conflict management contribute collectively to the quality of relationships needed for successful innovation.

Network development. This ARC component incorporates boundary spanning among ARC specialists, leaders, service providers, opinion leaders, and other stakeholders. Developing intra- and inter-organizational networks of organizational members provides opportunities for information and idea exchange, service provider access to experts, and stakeholder participation. Success in implementing innovations is influenced by the structure and quality of social networks because of their influence on members' perceptions, their facilitation of information sharing, and their provision of support. Organizations that promote boundary-spanning networks through participation with other collaborating organizations, by accessing existing internal and external networks, and by engaging in newly formed OAT and ARC teams are more likely to assimilate innovations and resolve service barriers (Barnsley, Lemieux-Charles, & McKinney, 1998; Edmondson et al., 2001; Goes & Park, 1997; Rogers, 2003; Tushman, 1977).

The ARC process is designed to establish and strengthen relationships internally within organizations through information sharing, the use of the OAT team to enhance collaboration, trust and shared work efforts across organizational levels; and by promoting leaders' efforts to build networks within their organization. Network development with external stakeholders includes the ARC specialist's and liaison's efforts to identify and foster linkages between ARC organizations and key external service providers, community leaders, and key opinion leaders such as judges, school superintendents, principles, and religious leaders. Supporting the development of these networks allow ARC participants and external stakeholders to collaboratively address barriers, problems, or enhancements that can improve services. This work includes identifying and establishing key contacts, meeting with individuals to share information, and building collaborative action plans to accomplish shared goals and objectives that support service improvements.

Team building. Effective teamwork within the newly formed OAT and ARC teams is necessary to facilitate participation, information sharing, and support among members.

The emphasis of this ARC component is on helping new or existing teams use their collective expertise and resources. Efforts for team building include increasing participation and social support to reduce the perceived risks associated with sharing ideas, identifying problems, learning new techniques, and implementing innovations. Teamwork is developed in ARC teams by first providing direct training to team supervisors for effective team leadership and facilitation. Second, these same supervisors are supported by the ARC specialists to guide members in team development activities and apply ARC team tools and team problem solving to service barriers identified by team members (Baer & Frese, 2003; Dyer, 1977; Edmondson et al., 2001; Ensley & Pearce, 2001; Higgins & Routhieaux, 1999; Patten, 1981; Rentsch, 1990; Rentsch & Klimoski, 2001).

Team development includes activities that contribute to effective communication practices, maintaining effective team behaviors, and deploying effective team mental models that support growth and learning. Team strategies and tools range from the use of simple meeting support activities such as note taking or brainstorming to more complex work such as establishing psychological safety within teams. Team members explore the use of mental models that enhance their own learning from each other and that improve shared efforts to identify service barriers, build effectively on others' ideas, and create sustainable solutions. Team building also requires the use of additional component tools such as continuous improvement, effective feedback, and goal setting that depend on effective team interaction and engagement.

Information and training. Identifying and addressing service barriers require the infusion of new information and training into service organizations. This component of ARC focuses on providing information and training about the ARC model, resources on best practices and service models relevant to the organization's clients, and technical training such as data management strategies that teams can use to assess barriers and innovations that improve services. For example, ARC team leaders are trained to guide their teams in how to use outcome data to establish baselines and monitor progress in addressing identified service barriers. The information and training provided by this component address members' technical needs as well as alter perceptions of innovations and proposed improvement efforts, such as best practices, new assessment tools, or information systems that are essential to adoption and successful implementation of new innovations. Training and information focus on demonstrating the relative advantage of an innovation, explaining ARC principles that support innovation, offering opportunities to experiment with a new practice, reducing uncertainty associated with innovation, and providing technical support (Barraud-Didier & Guerrero, 2002; Dearing & And, 1994; Dirkson, Ament, & Go, 1996; Ferlie et al., 2001; Green, 1998; Gustafson et al., 2003; Meyers, Sivakumar, & Nakata, 1999; Meyer & Goes, 1988; Pasmore et al., 1982; Rogers, 2003; Tasi, 2001).

The ARC specialist routinely provides additional resources, information, and training in the use of alternative approaches and processes to improve organizational functioning. These include new approaches to organizational processes such as disciplinary actions, strategies for improving communication to enhance team functioning, and strategies to uncover hidden assumptions that interfere with effective change. Information can include examples of leadership practices that endorse participatory approaches or guides that help team supervisors address specific problems with difficult team challenges. Specialists work closely with individuals in creating plans of action based on new ideas or training that evolve from reviewing training materials provided. Information and training are integral to supporting innovation and increasing flexibility and attention to the individual needs of each organization. Ideally, this leads to organizations building their own unique training processes across a variety of areas to improve their effectiveness.

Feedback. Feedback about performance and outcomes contributes to the successful adoption of new practices and other improvements by first creating the recognition that change is needed. It provides both clarity about where attention and efforts need to be focused and impetus for action by identifying needed change. In addition, feedback is necessary for the continuous quality improvement activities described in this chapter that guide innovation and change within the organization. Consequently, a central component of the ARC intervention is the establishment of a feedback process of assessment and monitoring data that provides performance information to direct service providers, ARC teams, programs, and leaders. Following ARC principles, performance feedback is aggregated at different levels and used by ARC teams and the OAT to guide and monitor improvement efforts (Burke, 1993; Green, 1998; Grimshaw et al., 2004; Merlani et al., 2001; Meyer & Goes, 1988; Porras, 1986; Rogers, 2003; Scanlon, Darby, Rolph, & Doty, 2001).

Activities for this component include a data feedback cycle that includes data collection, analyses, reporting, and application to guide improvement plans. Organizational members at multiple levels participate in establishing the collection of high-quality data (valid, feasible, and practical) on meaningful client outcomes that service providers can use to monitor improvement. Most importantly, efforts are focused on creating social contexts that support the effective use of data. These efforts include improving the level of psychological safety experienced by service providers in receiving performance feedback and the effectiveness of leader and supervisory approaches being applied in applying the data. These approaches are influenced by the shared belief systems and mental models discussed in Chapter 8 and elsewhere that determine how leaders address poor performance and view their role in improving performance.

Participatory decision making. Participatory decision making in the newly formed OAT and ARC line-level teams creates support for innovation and provides members the opportunity for input into problem-solving efforts that affect the way services are delivered (e.g., referral procedures, service areas, adoption of best practices). Participatory decision-making is central to conflict resolution, goal setting, continuous quality improvement, teamwork, and other components of the intervention. The use of participatory decision making in the identification of a best practice or other innovation is central to developing social support for its subsequent implementation (Bennis, 1966; McGregor, 1960; Meyers et al., 1999; Porras, 1986; Terziovski, 2002; Yousef, 2000).

Participatory decision making is enhanced by introducing tools such as team problem solving and consensus formation that help guide group decision processes. More importantly, the ARC process targets the mental models, reasoning, beliefs, and practices that support participatory decision making. The ARC specialist works with participants at multiple levels to examine ARC's principle of being participation based (see Chapter 10) and its impact on improving services. The behavioral practices of those who effectively deploy participatory decision making are embedded to guide team process and the shared beliefs, assumptions, and mindsets associated with successful participatory decision making are reviewed and supported. Workbook guided activities enable teams to identify the pressures, practical realities, and external forces that inhibit participatory decision making and address ways to support its use.

Conflict management. Processes of change within an organization inevitably lead to conflict as members grapple with new ways of interacting, realign organizational priorities, and change business as usual. Conflicts occur at the interpersonal, intra-organizational, and inter-organizational levels. The ARC strategies proactively address these differences in opinions and competing interests that threaten service effectiveness. Using information sharing, clarification of issues, prioritizing, and procedures for identifying implicit schema that drives behavior, the ARC specialist assists the OAT and ARC teams in resolving conflicts that are identified in the improvement effort. Additionally, tools, behavioral examples, and training on dialogue and inquiry as well as tools to de-escalate conflict are provided. This component of the ARC model provides direct training to staff in conflict resolution skills as a means of creating sustainable innovation within the organization (Alper, Tjosvold, & Law, 2000; Caldwell & O'Reilly, 1982; Callister & Wall, 2001; Rentsch & Klimoski, 2001; Walton, 1987).

Goal setting. Goal-setting procedures use feedback from client assessment and monitoring information systems to identify goals and set performance criteria that are shared and form the basis for the evaluation of improvement. Selection of goals occurs in a participatory manner and is guided by the five ARC principles, such as focusing on client well-being data to be mission driven (see Chapter 9). The ARC teams and OAT establish short-term and long-term performance goals to address difficult and complex goals that represent challenges for the ARC teams and OAT related to service improvement, learning, and innovation (Durham, Knight, & Locke, 1997; Gibson, 2001; Knight, Durham, & Locke, 2001; Sue-Chan & Ong, 2002; Weldon & Yun, 2000). Accompanying these goals are clear action plans, timelines, and realistic outcomes to track success. Participants are taught how to set effective goals, how to monitor them, and how to manage them.

Continuous improvement. This component teaches ARC team members techniques for continuous improvement as a means for changing organizational practices and identifying potential innovations that facilitate and support the work of frontline service providers. Continuous improvement procedures and subsequent recommendations for improvements originate from the ARC teams. These teams rely on data to identify barriers to effective care and monitor the results of improvement activities. It is expected that the ARC teams will recommend innovations and changes that address identified service deficits and that service improvement plans will include the identification of best practices that can be implemented by service teams, as well as other changes in existing organizational rules and procedures (Berlowitz et al., 2003; Lemieux-Charles et al., 2002; Shortell, Bennett, & Byck, 1998; Shortell et al., 1995; Steel & Shane, 1986).

ARC provides training for front-line service provider teams by their ARC team supervisor and accompanying ARC materials and tools used for continuous improvement. This training enables the front-line service provider teams to identify and address service barriers using continuous improvement processes. Monthly ARC specialist training and preparation to ARC team leaders, as well as ongoing weekly monitoring and assistance, supports the ARC teams' work by the ARC liaison. Continuous improvement is also supported by ARC's OAT team members that employ established procedures for collaboratively working to address identified barriers. The ARC specialist and ARC liaison guide continuous improvement steps with OAT members to address broader organizational barriers identified by these groups.

Job redesign. The implementation of continuous improvement and other ARC components described above identify ways in which jobs can be redesigned to improve service outcomes measured as improvements in client well-being. Job redesign focuses on eliminating service barriers by revising job characteristics that redefine responsibilities, alter tasks, and require new skills for specific positions. Within ARC, line-level service teams suggest improvements in how their members approach their work and what responsibilities should be added or deleted as a function of the identification of service barriers. This input informs the redesign of existing jobs to facilitate greater availability, responsiveness, and continuity of services to clients (French & Bell, 1984; Hackman & Oldham, 1980; Terziovski, 2002).

Stabilization. The ARC model supports the stabilization of the innovation stage by providing information and training to facilitate the independent use of the previous components so that the innovation process continues after the ARC specialist discontinues the formal organizational intervention. ARC team leaders trained in the ARC components and principles are given progressively more responsibility for implementing these components with their service teams. Training service team leaders to implement ARC strategies and integrating the work of the OAT to support the ARC teams' efforts contribute to the ongoing use of these tools following the completion of the innovation stage (Porras, 1986; Porras & Robertson, 1992; Rogers, 2003).

During ARC's innovation stage, the ARC specialist and ARC liaison collaborate with OAT members to embed the necessary training for sustaining ARC. Training includes all elements of ARC necessary to prepare new organizational program supervisors or team members in the use of ARC approaches, knowledge, and tools. OAT members and the ARC liaison identify additional areas of training from ARC that are required for on-going success and stability. For example, many organizations maintain training for new employees on ARC principles, psychological safety, and ensuring service availability, responsiveness, and continuity. In addition to training, action plans are established for on-going work in improving systems, processes, and approaches by leaders, the OAT, and service providers to sustain continued change. These efforts include creating plans for disseminating innovations and improvements developed by specific service teams to additional programs in the organization.

COMPONENTS AS A PLATFORM FOR PRINCIPLES

Each of the component tools described above is familiar to organizational consultants, well publicized in organizational research, and often used individually in organizational change efforts. It is less common for all 12 components to be introduced in the same organizational improvement effort. As we have explained, the ARC intervention model includes all 12 component tools along with the other two strategies of mental models and principles of effective service, with specific components more prominent during different stages. Relationship development, for example, is closely targeted in the first ARC stage of collaboration. And despite its importance throughout, it becomes less explicit as a focus of intervention in later stages. It is important to emphasize that the use of the ARC components is also customized based on the unique strengths and needs of each organization. Because organizational needs cannot be assessed fully *a priori*, the ARC intervention incorporates all 12 elements in a customized fashion for each agency so that the relative importance of the individual components varies by organization.

It is important to note that organizational change efforts in the field and our own experience suggest that it would be difficult, if not impossible to identify any of these 12 components as the most important single key to generating service improvements. Reports from service providers in the field suggest that planned organizational change efforts incorporating a single component such as continuous improvement, job redesign, and other organizational strategy have a high failure rate due to lack of attention to the other issues and the broader OSC within the participating agency. We argue that the use of the component tools listed above in the absence of guiding principles of effectiveness, an emphasis on mental models, and associated improvements in organizational culture and climate are unlikely to be successful in improving services to clients. Instead, we view the 12 components as a *means* for identifying and addressing service barriers, guided by ARC's five core principles and supported by changes in mental models that affect the leaders' and members' understanding of the change effort. It is the transformation of an organization's underlying core principles, values, beliefs, and the associated behavioral norms, expectations, and psychological impact on employees that ultimately improves services in a way that positively affects client well-being. For this reason, the five ARC principles reviewed in Chapters 9–13 comprise the core of this book and are the focus of the ARC intervention. Our most recent research provides evidence that without a fundamental realignment of the agencies core norms, expectations, and principles that align with key priorities, improvement in client outcomes is unlikely to occur (Glisson et al., 2013, 2016a, 2016b; Williams et al., 2016).

8

THE ROLE OF MENTAL MODELS
IN ORGANIZATIONAL CHANGE

The term *mental model* captures the idea that our interpretation and perceptions of our world, such as work experiences, are held in the internal mental representations we hold of the environment and others' behavior in that environment. In other words, the lens we see work events through influence what we see and how we interpret and react to it. The lens can vary from person to person, but we often share similar mental representations with coworkers who share the same work environment. These mental models shared with our coworkers reflect our understanding and interpretation of what we observe in our work environments and the actions we take in response. ARC's third strategy focuses on identifying, interpreting, and altering the shared mental models among service providers in a way that complements their efforts to improve services. Explicitly addressing these shared mental models provides a way of altering the beliefs, reasoning, and mindsets of organizational members to support and sustain service improvement efforts. This strategy is based on the idea that reasoning and thinking reinforce the use of ARC's organizational components (Chapter 7) and ARC's five principles (Chapters 9–13). If aligned correctly, reasoning and thinking should support decision making tool usage, and actions that reflect priorities consistent with the ARC principles.

Without aligning mental models and the priorities we follow to support effective services, the efforts of service providers to address service barriers are unlikely to be successful. The introduction of organizational component tools such as continuous improvement, for example, can promote behavior that has the potential to improve services. However, these behaviors can dissipate if underlying shared beliefs and assumptions inconsistent with change return one's thinking and actions to the well-worn paths of status quo. For example, the shared leadership belief that effectiveness depends on establishing strict hierarchical structures and processes to be followed by direct service providers impedes improvement efforts that require line-level decision-making and discretion. In other words, bringing tools and processes for improving services into settings where deeply held beliefs and mindsets aren't congruent with their optimal use cannot produce sustainable improvements. The following illustrates the importance of addressing the beliefs, mindsets, and mental models held by organizational members in service improvement efforts.

A CHILD WELFARE EXAMPLE

A regional director of a state child welfare system we have previously worked with expressed his discomfort with our suggestion that participative decision making and flexibility be increased among caseworkers. The suggestion was made to increase caseworker input and commitment to improving the services they provided. Specifically, this change required that front-line caseworkers be given more discretion in using ARC tools to identify and address regulation, paperwork, and bureaucratic red tape that interfered with service quality. The director, who was sincerely committed to improving services, stated emphatically, "I have to tell you . . . this suggestion goes against everything in my nature. Everything in me wants to exert more control and reduce flexibility in what caseworkers are doing." To his credit, he agreed and backed up his commitment by allowing front-line ARC teams to identify unnecessary paperwork that was overwhelming them. When multiple proposals for a reduction in paperwork and other bureaucratic processes were forwarded to him, he—with difficulty—agreed to the proposed changes. The experience affected both the director and the members of the front-line team. The director was reassured that chaos did not result from the reduced paperwork and red tape as changes took place. The front-line team members' engagement in the service improvement effort significantly increased when their initial proposals were supported. Approval of their proposed changes reduced the burden of paperwork and changed caseworker and leaders' beliefs about their capacity to improve the services they provided.

In a related example, the same director supported training for his program supervisors and managers on the use of a new client assessment to support placement and treatment referrals. During the training, attended by the director, a new supervisor repeatedly challenged the trainer on a psychometric issue after being reassured twice that documentation would be provided. Several days after the training, the regional director told the trainer, "I took care of the problem you experienced the other day." When asked what he meant, he said, "I fired him," referring to the new supervisor. "I won't tolerate my staff being disrespectful to an external trainer." The trainer was deeply concerned that the supervisors' comments resulted in the loss of his job. Although the supervisor was persistent in questioning the training, being fired made little sense to our colleague who conducted the training.

The regional director, however, held a much different mental model of the event than the trainer. The trainer described the supervisor to his colleagues as a bright, ambitious young man who wanted to prove his worth. The director perceived the supervisor as a disrespectful staff member who had stepped out of line and needed to be punished as an example to others. While the trainer believed that the supervisor's behavior was commendable for not blindly laying down and following the informal rules of not questioning things, the director saw him as a rule breaker who didn't respect authority; one who would interfere with success and needed to be fired to send a clear message to others in the organization to toe the line.

As we got to know the director after working with him and others across that state's child welfare system, we gained a better understanding of the basis of his reasoning and interpretation of events. Not surprisingly, we learned that the core assumptions and beliefs the director held appeared to be shared by other leaders and managers within his region that he had promoted. As we listened to the director and other leaders discuss how they addressed problems in the day-to-day management of staff, their mental model of effective leadership became evident. They viewed effective leadership as strictly directing and controlling decision making and staff behavior, reinforcing a clear chain of command and establishing rigid procedures and guidelines for all staff activities. Their mental model regarding effective leadership was supported from their observations. That is, staff became more focused on tasks when they were forcibly directed by leaders as well as more compliant in completing paperwork in a timely manner when closely monitored. What was lacking in their mental model was the link between their leadership approach and criteria such as staff turnover, job dissatisfaction, and disengagement of staff in their work with clients. This link didn't exist in their mindset because they shared a deeper, more implicit assumption—one that easily explained turnover, job dissatisfaction, and disengagement.

We learned that the leaders in this system shared the fundamental assumption that front-line service providers were inherently lacking either the ability or drive to do their work. Our own work with the direct service providers, however, illustrated organizational barriers and engrained constraints that were legitimately impeding their success. When leaders were asked about turnover of their staff, they agreed that high turnover was expected as part of their business because staff were hired who were lazy or not capable of doing the work. Failures were met with automatic assumptions that the staff didn't want to do their jobs well. Their shared mental model supported leadership behaviors that were excessively controlling and autocratic. Moreover, their underlying beliefs and the mental models shared by the leaders were evidenced in their approaches to a variety of organizational activities. Training was focused on control issues to establish clarity about procedures and guidelines that standardized decision making. Discipline was harsh and often without examination of factors outside of the individual that influenced performance.

In practical terms, there was an incongruity between the practices we were introducing and the core mental models of events held by the organizational leaders. We wanted to build a social context that supported learning and improvement where the staff was engaged in the idea of improving the services they provided and in improving the skills and abilities of each other. The leaders wanted our efforts to lead to more guidelines and standardized procedures to support their control of staff behavior. For example, the director asked if a decision-making matrix based on standardized client assessments could be designed to direct placement and referral to avoid front-line staff discretion. Our efforts at improving services by fostering staff participation and engagement in addressing service barriers were constrained by the beliefs and mindset that staff needed to be closely monitored and controlled, as well as given limited discretion and flexibility.

MENTAL MODELS AND SUPPORTING EVIDENCE

Mental models are routinely defined as internal cognitive representations or models that individuals hold in conscious awareness to guide understanding and reasoning about work and other life experiences (Johnson-Laird, 1983). Just as models support technical applications such as understanding how electricity works by creating analogous models to the flow of water in a plumbing system, mental models help us establish the meaning of complex events and phenomena we experience. Such models can help us organize the myriad variables we experience, capture perceived causes for observed events, and determine appropriate actions to respond to events (Rasmussen, 1979). In this way, mental models can help us predict future events and test alternative assumptions and beliefs by envisioning modifications or alternatives to the models we currently use. In turn, the models influence our decisions, behaviors, and the social institutions we create. For example, if one holds a mental model of effective leadership as maintaining centralized and rigid control of staff behavior, allowing staff discretion to work together in improving services is less likely to occur. Creating structures to encourage input are left unconsidered.

Early research (Craik, 1943) described mental models as the mind's construction of "small scale models" of reality to anticipate events, to reason, and to form explanations and predictions. Early conceptualizations of mental models ranged from visual representations of mechanical systems (e.g., a bicycle's drive system envisioned in one's mind) to deductive reasoning models based on symbolic representations of premises and accompanying rules of logic for conducting formal reasoning—with many variations in between (Craik, 1943; Johnson-Laird, 1983; Johnson-Laird, 1994; Khemlani, Barbey, & Johnson-Laird, 2014; Leung & Bond, 2004; Oakhill & Garnham, 1996).

Johnson-Laird (1983) advanced the idea that mental models weren't as formal, rigid, or structured as some researchers were suggesting. Early logicians, for example, believed it was innate to hold mental models of reasoning that relied on symbolic representations of logic propositions and formal calculated logic. Although one can hold a logic problem in mind using symbols for premises and formal propositional rules of formal logic (e.g., if A, then B), research suggests our informal, everyday reasoning and our presumed formal logic are based on mental models of a different nature. Johnson-Laird suggested that common, everyday mental models more closely resemble real-life examples or counterexamples we form in our minds. That is, we simply envision or maintain mental representations of what is described by premises and propositions and then test them by envisioning examples and counter examples that disqualify the conclusions being presented.

The important point is that we hold in awareness mental representations in a variety of forms and levels of abstraction that we use to make sense out our worlds. We formulate and use these models to help us reason and interact with our environments, including hypothetical or alternative scenarios to predict and gain control over our environments and the events within them. Individuals after car accidents, for example, will often replay the accident in their minds as they reason about what exactly happened and why? They often begin to envision alternative scenarios of what might have happened under different sets of conditions, such as if they had arrived only 10 seconds later or if the other car hadn't turned so quickly. They hold in their consciousness mental models of what occurred and adjust the mental models as they process other outcomes or possibilities.

As suggested by Johnson-Laird, mental models are influenced by previous experiences, learning, and social interactions with others. For example, a young organizational leader who disciplines an employee for the first time actively processes this uncertain and new event, trying to understand in her mind what happened and what needs to be done. In the process, she may depend on more seasoned colleagues to understand the problem and how to proceed. Other experienced leaders might provide interpretations of unacceptable staff behavior by, for example, asserting that it is seldom intentional. They may contend it is not due to a staff member not caring or not trying to do the best they can. They could also interpret and approach the disciplinary process as a learning experience that helps a struggling staff member improve, while also building an open and trusting supervisory relationship. In this way, the inexperienced supervisor might adopt the shared beliefs and inferences held by her colleagues about staff failures while learning a mental model that supports effective supervision. Over time, repeated exposure to staff mistakes and associated interpretations and actions by colleagues solidify shared beliefs, creating easily accessible mental models shared by her and other leaders. These beliefs and mental models, however, become relatively implicit (without awareness) in guiding future interpretations, and reactions when addressing staff errors or mistakes, often with little conscious effort or thought.

Both social cognition research and more recent neuroscience studies, as described below, suggest that individuals establish and maintain implicitly held assumptions, attributions, inferences, and knowledge structures over time as their conscious efforts to understand and reason about events leave behind more automated (implicit) structures. Mental models are associated with developing meaning and the cognitive maps and schemas that help us perceive and make sense out of experiences as we interact with others in our daily work and life experiences (Rentsch & Mot, 2012).

Applying mental models in our work lives. Although the characteristics of mental models are debated, the utility of mental models is clearly recognized (Rouse & Morris,

1986). Their utility is illustrated in application across a variety of areas, ranging from causal reasoning to control systems, from effective repair strategies of refrigeration technicians to effective mental models for organizational teamwork; and from establishing more effective learning paradigms to the examination of psychopathology (Druskat & Pescosolido, 2002; Jonassen & Henning, 1996; Levesque, Wilson, Wholey, 2001; Marks, Sabella, Burke, & Zaccaro, 2002; Rasmussen, 1979; Senge, Kleiner, Roberts, Ross, & Smith, 1994).

Mental models have substantial utility in improving and supporting training efforts (Rouse & Morris, 1986). That is, instruction can focus on amending or altering weaknesses of learner's mental models so that more effective models can contribute to success. Alternative models, including new causal links between key variables can be presented to build stronger, more accurate models. For example, helping a leader recognize that screaming at a subordinate is linked to more than just increased activity, such as turnover or hiding mistakes, can help the leader develop a more complex mental model to apply in leadership. In child welfare, caseworkers must understand abusive parents' mental models during their disciplinary actions to target underlying assumptions, beliefs, or causal links that influence parental actions and outcomes. Within organizational improvement efforts, exploring mental models of effective leadership can help foster alternative mindsets and beliefs associated with improved organizational functioning.

Peter Senge's bestseller, *The Fifth Discipline*, illustrates multiple strategies and activities for exploring and altering mental models that can help support learning organizations. Essential to these strategies and activities is helping organizational members recognize and address assumptions that hinder their own organizational learning. In other areas, organizational research on team functioning finds that shared mental models among team members enhance coordination, effectiveness, and performance. Applications within teams include establishing shared team mental models for successfully accomplishing tasks and for improving communication and interaction, both of which enhance team effectiveness (Marks et al., 2002; Mathieu, Heffner, Goodwin, Salas, & Cannon-Bowers, 2000). Related work focuses on developing shared team models around psychological ownership, continuous learning, and heedful interacting (Druskat & Pescosolido, 2002).

Support for the importance of mental models is also found in leading trade publications for organizations, such as the 10th edition of the leading publication *Organization Development and Change* (Cummings & Worley, 2014). Organizational change theorists and practitioners present the development of internal mental models as mechanisms that can help organizations learn how to learn. Double loop learning models, for example, prepare organizational leaders to push their organizations beyond superficial solutions that repeat work patterns that support the status quo (Argyris, 2004), to think deeper about one's reasoning and how it affects success.

Mental models are also used in broader applications, such as efforts to foster positive development in the economic health of economically deprived communities. The World Bank's publication, *World Development Report: Mind, Society, and Behavior* (Bank, 2014), introduces mental models as a framework for understanding and influencing economic development across cultures. Changing mental models held by community members in poverty-stricken villages, such as supporting an underlying belief that saving money can lead to more money, has been effective in supporting community members' efforts to build and invest in their own small business ventures. That is, working to alter basic beliefs can alter the mental models community members hold regarding the merits of saving money. Just as important, over time, new assumptions, norms, and ways of thinking are reinforced through the social diffusion of the mental models, creating additional economic development throughout the members' communities.

Our ARC strategy works with service providers to identify existing mental models and to describe alternative models that enhance beliefs, assumptions, and reasoning consistent with the five ARC principles. Organizational members learn to envision alternative models and underlying assumptions that support deployment of ARC's organizational component tools. And they explore how existing mental models and alternative models, along with accompanying reasoning and beliefs, can influence norms and attitudes. Mental models also include constructs such as psychological safety that promote new shared mental representations that are supportive of more effective behaviors within optimal social contexts. The ARC mental models' strategy is based on the practical applications described above and informed by social cognition and neuroscience research.

Supporting evidence from social cognition and neuroscience. Several characteristics of mental models are particularly important to organizational efforts focused on improving services (Johnson-Laird, 1983). First, mental models reflect an individual's or a group's belief of the truth as they learn and share those beliefs and explain their world. Second, mental models are heuristic in nature in that they enable individuals to handle and control overwhelming amounts of environmental stimuli when attempting to meet complex needs and goals. Third, our cognitive systems automate our application of mental models via stored memories, inferences, and schemas. These cognitive structures are often implicit in guiding decisions, reasoning, and actions as they influence our conscious mental models when processing new information and events. Both social cognition and neural science provide insight into these characteristics of mental models and inform how mental models can be used to support organizational change and service improvement.

Cognitive and neuroscience research confirms our social nature. We know that social exclusion stimulates neural systems associated with physical pain (Eisenberger, Lieberman, & Williams, 2003) and neurological studies suggest that social cognition may be our brain's natural baseline. That is, social cognition continues as our spontaneous resting state when our cognitive resources are not being used otherwise (Iacoboni et al., 2004). Daydreaming, for example, is often social in nature. Numerous social motives are posited as the source of human motivation and neuroscience supports their presence and impact in our cognitive processes and neural systems (Fiske & Taylor, 2013, p. 48; Rock, 2008). Fiske and Taylor (2013) explain that social context matters in understanding cognition. We are predisposed to adopt cultural norms and expectations via socialization and social learning, including shared mental representations or mental models that are passed on through social interaction, shared experiences with others, and through vicarious learning and modeling (Bandura, 1977; Hysong, Best, Pugh, & Moore, 2005).

Culture-based socialization processes associated with mental models are illustrated with differences in causal attributions between cultures. Ascribing cause to either individuals or to social circumstances has been demonstrated to vary across western and Asian cultures, respectively (Morling & Masuda, 2012). Patterns of casual attributions also vary across organizational cultures, such as attributing poor performance to individual-level traits versus contextual characteristics such as insufficient resources or lack of support. These shared attributions that vary across cultures are reflected in the mental representations individuals hold regarding poor performance. They also drive the solutions that will address poor performance, such as ensuring that the required support and resources are available to organizational members to achieve success or, in targeting and assessing individuals who perform poorly to address individual-level deficits. Research also shows that different patterns of beliefs at the individual level are a function of their respective cultures, whether the cultures are defined as societal or organizational (Fu et al., 2004; Leung & Bond, 2004, Martin & Glisson, 1989).

Lastly, mental models are both heuristic and purposeful. They provide simplified representations of reality that address innate cognitive limitations of human brains, such as limited short-term memory for conducting active, conscious processing. The simplified versions of reality provided by mental models are effective in helping us gain control and prediction over our environments and in obtaining desired needs, goals, and outcomes without excess effort. A critical benefit of heuristics and cognitive simplification is that it facilitates our brain's ability to automate (below awareness) much of our conscious processing (Fiske & Taylor, 2013). Our neural systems automate and engrain elements of more conscious thought processes such as inferences, attributions, or knowledge into longer-term cognitive structures that reduce the demands on our ongoing, active processing. For example, driving a car for the first time can be overwhelming as we attend to a blinding number of stimuli from the car itself, the road, and the surrounding environment. After years of driving, the effort becomes automated with minimal effort until a unique problem or unexpected condition arises that we have not encountered previously. We can do this because our neural systems store essential elements of previous, conscious processing and mental representations that contribute to automatic and less resource intensive processing.

Automaticity applies to many of the components that make up mental models, such as our inferences regarding causal relations, attributions that are made, and basic categorizations of objects, people, and events to which we are repeatedly exposed. *Proceduralization* is a term used to describe what occurs as repeated inferences in cognitive processing become quicker and more automated (less conscious) over time (Smith & Branscombe, 1987). In OSCs, for example, inferring that poor staff performance is linked to an individual's ability or motivation becomes quicker, less effortful, and automatic with repetition. These repeated inferences—often influenced or supported by information provided by other members of a shared social context—become implicit and are stored in our longer-term cognitive systems as part of schemas, prototypes, or knowledge structures that guide ongoing processing without consciousness awareness (Bargh, Chen, & Burrows, 1996). Again, however, these inferences and stored schema or knowledge structures can be retrieved into more conscious awareness, especially when new inferences or altered mental representations must be drawn. For example, when a punitive, autocratic leader is told that their approach has led to low staff productivity and that she is at risk of losing her position, the leader is likely to become highly engaged in active, conscious processing. The leader might look to others for input as she reevaluates her assumptions regarding effective leadership, the causal links between her leadership behavior and staff performance, and the beliefs she holds regarding staff that may influence behavior and their performance. Without having received the performance feedback, however, she might have continued to rely on inferences and implicit theories about staff performance that had become automatic in guiding her decisions and behaviors.

From a cultural perspective, these are the mechanisms that guide behavior and actions without conscious recognition of the shared inferences, schemas, or patterns of thinking and behavior that guide our processing. Moreover, these processes are in part hardwired and linked to our social motives. As described by Fiske and Taylor (2013), conscious processing is a function of internal motives, needs, and goals that human beings seek to meet or fulfill. Thus, neurological studies show that internal motives for control can serve as an impetus for conscious processing (Rock, 2008; Taylor, 1991; Eysenck, 1992). That is, if we are experiencing uncertainty or crises that threaten our sense of control and understanding—or more simply, create significant inconsistencies with our mental models—we switch to more active, conscious processing to regain control and understanding. In fact, we can learn to engage in inconsistency monitoring that can trigger more top-down, directed processing when desired outputs aren't being met (Miller & Cohen, 2001). When faced with inconsistencies, uncertainty, or crisis, we reexamine our existing models to understand our world and build new models to regain a sense of understanding and control. If we lack information to regain understanding and control, we actively seek additional information from others (Kelly, 1972). During this rebuilding, we retrieve information from our previous experiences, our implicit beliefs, and our mental models to examine additional causes, variables, and relationships that need to be considered to reduce uncertainty.

To summarize, our cognitive and neural systems use mental models to help us simplify and make sense of work events and our social environments. These mental models are associated with inferences, assumptions, and causal links for explaining and predicting future events. These mental representations are influenced by others through socialization and acculturation and are driven by social motives, such as our desire to belong, to experience relatedness, to achieve status among others, or simply to gain control and understanding. And, our mental models and underlying inferences and beliefs often become, through repeated use, implicit or automatic in guiding the meaning of events and reactions to those events going forward. For our inferences to change, we need to experience uncertainty, discrepancies, or inconsistencies that trigger conscious examination of our implicit beliefs and the mental models we hold. Often looking to others, we consciously consider alternative beliefs or views of the world to regain a sense of understanding and certainty after encountering contradictory evidence or experiences. This process is the basis of the value of cross-cultural experiences for broadening one's worldviews and for altering attitudes, perceptions, and behavior as conflicting worldviews are experienced. Guided by the five ARC principles, this process underscores our use of mental models. We challenge organizational members to envision, explore, and test new mental models that support the use of ARC component tools in identifying and addressing service barriers sustained by an organization's culture. This often means recognizing existing mental models driven by implicit assumptions and beliefs that may need to be challenged.

THE IMPORTANCE OF MENTAL MODELS FOR CHANGE AND SUSTAINABLE IMPROVEMENT

What we know about mental models, social cognition, and the neurological basis for our cognitive processing suggests that the introduction of ARC's organizational component tools may not be sufficient to create the OSCs and the realignment of organizational priorities necessary for sustained improvements in services. The mixed success of EBPs across different organizational settings highlights the challenge of implementation and sustainment of new technologies. Despite implementation efforts that include substantial training, repeated practice of behaviors with actual clients, and ongoing behavioral support and consultation, EBPs are not consistently effective in actual, real world settings. EBPs, or any new practices that are inconsistent with existing cultures and practices, including the underlying beliefs, assumptions, and mental models held by organizational members, are less likely to be implemented and sustained.

The role that mental models play in EBP implementation and sustainment is associated with our brains automatic inferences and assumptions that guide our interpretations and reactions to events. As we have explained, however, we do have a window into our more implicit cognitive beliefs, assumptions, and inferences as well as knowledge structures (e.g., schemas) that are guiding our behaviors. In the same way that automatic processes give way to conscious processing, such as perceived threats to safety or feelings of uncertainty, we can influence implicit assumptions, beliefs, inferences, and schemas that help guide reasoning and action.

Again, this is particularly important within human service organizations given work environments that are by nature uncertain, unpredictable, and often complex. In these settings, selecting the right practice behaviors and interventions is influenced by social cognition and reliance on colleagues for information, guidance, and modeling of appropriate behaviors and practices. Service environments that create inconsistencies between what is desired and what is achieved generate repeated crises and provide ample experiences of conscious reasoning to regain certainty, understanding, and control. By its nature, human services are based on relationships and interactions among individuals who continually seek information and understanding of uncertain events. It is this information, via social interaction and social learning among service providers, that builds shared mental representations.

ARC creates explicit expectations among service providers to explore mental models and associated beliefs to understand what is guiding service provider's decisions and actions. Service providers are helped to establish alternative mental models for effectiveness, including the use of ARC component tools and principles that drive highly successful human service organizations.

Revisiting Agencies A and B. In the example of Agency B from Chapter 2, participating service providers shared beliefs and attitudes about the value of employing a participatory leadership approach. However, they lacked the specific behaviors and processes to follow up on decisions and plans developed within their participatory environment. Thus, they benefited from training and practice on simple behaviors such as note taking, assigning work tasks, and being careful to monitor and follow through with plans. Agency A, in contrast, had training in participatory practices but was unable to engage in participatory behaviors on the job because of shared mental models among leaders. Introducing the concept of psychological safety allowed leaders and staff to identify and address beliefs and assumptions that contributed to their inability to be more participatory. Their mental models regarding participation were associated with beliefs, assumptions, and attitudes that inhibited participatory approaches that provided safety in discussing errors and mistakes.

Our experience from studying and working with organizations over several decades is that the long-term sustainability of behavior change is linked to these mental models. That is, the implementation of new practices within organizations hinges on whether the new practices and behaviors are consistent with the mental models and associated beliefs and assumptions that organizational members share within their organization.

ARC STRATEGIES TO INFLUENCE MENTAL MODELS

Mental models are introduced at ARC's introductory meetings, initial workshops, and training sessions with executive leaders as one of three complementary strategies for altering OSCs. Second, ARC manualized activities engage participants in planned activities that guide the identification of assumptions and beliefs that underlie their decision-making and actions. These initial activities establish expectations for assessing and altering mental models to support the use of ARC component tools (Chapter 7) in aligning organizational priorities with the five ARC principles (Chapters 9–13). We describe below the multiple activities that compose ARC's approach to identifying and altering mental models.

Creating a new vocabulary for mental models to support ARC's principles. Materials are presented early in the ARC process to provide participants with a conceptual understanding of mental models, including a description of how these models develop and influence reasoning, decision making, and reactions to work events. The materials provide examples of mental models, including their susceptibility to social learning and their implications for effectiveness within human services organizations. The materials provide examples of implicit assumptions that underlie individuals' reasoning and decision-making that affects services provision. Participants discuss examples of simple causal beliefs that influence critical activities, such as performance appraisals or services coordination efforts. And, participants learn how to explore the mental models they hold when experiencing work events to identify their own shared beliefs and assumptions. As a part of the ARC process, the ARC specialist engages participants in activities to examine their beliefs in relationship to enacting each of the ARC principles and component tools.

Second, ARC activities explicitly build mental models around core concepts that help create OSCs that support the ARC principles. For example, the concept of psychological safety is introduced as a mental model with associated attitudes, assumptions, and cause-effect inferences that support behaviors necessary for creating a context for identifying and addressing service barriers to improve service quality and outcomes. The concept of psychological safety provides a substantive concept for staff and leaders to promote the beliefs, assumptions, and attitudes required for constructive criticism of current services and practices.

The importance of a new vocabulary and new conceptual framework around mental models from which to understand work events is fundamental to organizational change. The use of mental models helps participants articulate a rationale for new behaviors and discuss improvements and changes with other colleagues and organizational members. Success in the adoption of a new mental model is expressed in the language that emerges in the improvement effort, such as staff members referring to psychological safety in their team activities or discussions when the focus requires a critique of existing protocols or practices.

Socratic questioning. Sometimes described as disciplined questioning, Socratic questioning (Paul & Elder, 2007) is used in the ARC process to guide the discussion of fundamental concepts, assumptions, and implications of organizational members' reasoning and behavior. Employed throughout the ARC process for improving services, the ARC specialist and liaison question participants to identify the underlying beliefs and mental models they may hold that are consistent or inconsistent with ARC principles and practices. Socratic questioning allows ARC specialists to help organizational members recognize inconsistencies between the use of suggested mental models such as psychological safety and their current behaviors, assumptions, inferences, and reasoning. In other words, Socratic questioning provides a strategy for identifying what lies beneath the expressed ideas and behaviors of organizational members to identify the mental representations that guide their behavior.

Socratic questioning is particularly useful when organizational members are presented with scenarios or actual events occurring in their organization that are linked to the five ARC principles. Organizational members assist the ARC specialist in understanding the reasoning behind these events to actively process their implicit beliefs and existing mental models. Socratic questioning includes (1) asking participants to *clarify their thinking* to help the specialist understand what occurred (e.g., "Could you explain further or explain your rationale for why the decisions and actions taken occurred?"), (2) *asking about assumptions or beliefs* expressed in participants" explanations (e.g., "Why do you think that this assumption or inference holds here?"), (3) asking for *supporting experiences or evidence* that suggest the assumptions or beliefs are accurate (e.g., "Talk to me about other experiences or evidence that supports the reasoning and approach taken?"), (4) asking for *counter arguments or viewpoints* (e.g., "Could this be seen another way?" or "Is there a different way others might approach what occurred?"), and (5) addressing *implications and consequences* (e.g., "But if . . . happened, what else would result?" and "What's the effect of thinking or believing this? What could be the effect of thinking differently and no longer holding onto this belief?").

These questions allow individuals to identify reasoning, inferences, and assumptions that are implicit but important factors in their decisions and actions. It allows participants the opportunity to reflect on the repercussions of the way they perceive work events and their actions, as well as to consider other approaches and beliefs that may more fully support ARC principles.

Developing more complex cognitive models for disparate beliefs and practices. Organizational members often apply strategies based on beliefs that in certain situations could be valid but when applied in others may interfere with their success. The ARC specialist's objective is not to erase these beliefs or assumptions or associated mental models but to build more complex and differentiated mental models where alternative approaches, behaviors, and beliefs can be encouraged and tested when appropriate. For example, being authoritarian and directive in a crisis that demands quick decisions and action could be precisely what is needed. At the same time, applying a more participatory approach that includes staff input and participation could be required for success when adopting and implementing a new practice. Thus, organizational leaders and members are guided in identifying specific conditions under which different models may be applicable to expand or alter their models, supported by practical examples or case studies that document successful alternative paths.

This approach provides a way of introducing alternative beliefs and mental representations to participants who may hold rigid, oversimplified models that are not effective in all situations. The introduction of more complexity in this case is aligned with the inherent nature and development of our cognitive systems. That is, social cognition research suggests that mental representations become more complex and diversified as our life experiences unfold. For example, it is common for less experienced leaders to apply simpler, one-dimensional models of leadership across a variety of situations while more experienced leaders combine multiple approaches depending on the situation and those involved. The ARC strategy is to build complexity by moving toward multiple practices that support the ARC principles.

Motivational interviewing. Consistent with the spirit of motivational interviewing, it is often necessary to address the motivation to change as something to be evoked, not something that can or should be imposed (for review, see Britt, Blampied, & Hudson, 2003). Motivational interviewing is itself a mental model for effective change underscored by a core assumption that imposing change is likely to create resistance. A responsibility of the ARC specialist is to identify organizational participants' ambivalence to the improvement effort and promote an examination and resolution of the ambivalence they feel. This is particularly important when behavior change is truly volitional or at the discretion of the individual and requires altering mental models that are supported by strongly held assumptions. Examples include moving authoritarian leadership cultures toward more participatory approaches or, by contrast, helping highly participative cultures establish clear boundaries to participation and discretion.

Skills included in motivational interviewing include empathic listening and questioning for factors, beliefs, and rationales held by organizational members that support their current behaviors. This requires neutrality when exploring with organizational members the potential implications of their beliefs, assumptions, and subsequent behaviors on desired goals. Using these skills, the ARC specialist, along with leaders and staff, identifies the key outcomes they seek to achieve and the linkages to behaviors and practices. Leaders and staff benefit by improving their understanding of how their behaviors and assumptions impact, negatively or positively, their desired goals. The ARC materials also guide participants' efforts in creating specific targets for change, behavior change plans, and approaches for tracking success.

Information sharing. ARC specialists collect and share personal experiences, stories, and materials that support organizational members' learning. This information can be particularly helpful to organizational members who identify specific service barriers but are unable to identify alternative mental models and associated practices, procedures, or policies that can address the barriers. The ARC specialist, in collaboration with the ARC liaison, share information and learned experiences to influence the use of shared mental models. For example, ARC specialists provide information to leaders and staff who are concerned about the effects of high staff turnover. The information includes their own experiences with helping organizations reduce turnover, including the mental models leaders hold that diminish turnover or that support culture and climate characteristics associated with low staff turnover. The information can also include published articles that describe organizations' successes in altering key factors such as performance evaluation systems or clinical supervision by altering the mental models that guide the use of these systems. Common to these examples is the social nature of the information, whether it is stories of experiences of other individuals in similar positions, written descriptions of examples of others, or helping others to interact and hear from others who have made changes. The information often questions core assumptions that leaders or staff hold as well as associated behaviors, illustrating alternative paths and describing case examples where improved services are achieved.

Magnifying consequences and successes of practicing new beliefs. Studies of social cognition explain that thinking and reasoning influence behavior, even when conscious reasoning has been replaced by automated inferences and assumptions established through repeated experience. These cognitive processes explain the resistance to efforts by ARC specialists and liaisons to change mental models, assumptions, or behaviors that contribute to results while creating other unintended issues that may be costly. For example, a leader threatening an employee can produce success in getting certain tasks accomplished but at the same time create problems by diminishing psychological safety, engagement, or flexibility that lead to more serious problems. Whether it is a result of conscious or automated processing, our cognitive systems cling to well-worn paths. However, mental models may need alteration yet be difficult to alter given the user's inability to see signs of needed repair—particularly when results appear to be occurring. That is, mental models can be difficult to fix because the models achieve goals, even while preventing attention to other goals that may be important. Members of organizations with rigid cultures can fail to understand the implications of their culture for turnover or performance, or they maintain assumptions and mental models that reduce its importance, such as the often-heard idea, "In this business there will always be high turnover and people are replaceable." As another example, participative-oriented leaders can fail to see the need for more structure and less flexibility in uncertain situations. As one leader said in response to learning that employees were requesting more structure, "I didn't understand they wanted more guidance. I wanted to make sure they felt like they made the decision on their own."

ARC specialists ensure that organization members recognize the ripples that occur when organizational members implement new practices that are consistent with the ARC principles. The ARC process encourages organizational members to attend closely to service outcomes as desired changes are occurring and to reflect on subtle qualitative changes. For example, organizational members are prompted to recognize positive indicators such as overlooked improvements in how staff members are interacting. The ARC process also incorporates participants' views of changes that have occurred (including shared expectations, perceptions, and attitudes) and makes explicit the ripples of change that participants may not be seeing. This includes questions around critical outcomes that can be missed by those implementing new practices or procedures, such as, "Are you seeing differences in staff's responsiveness and motivation to improve their work?" Additionally, the ARC specialist works with the ARC liaison to establish formal mechanisms of social recognition and information sharing among ARC participants that promote sharing of success for improving services. These activities include explicit recognition of how beliefs, assumptions, or inferences are changing as well as how motivation levels, attitudes, and desired outcomes are improving. These efforts allow members to share change experiences and service improvements they have experienced with other staff. It also allows members to explain how they are framing their work differently, how they are engaging in new behaviors, and how these efforts are leading to improved outcomes.

Participant advocacy of mental models. This strategy focuses on helping participants to increase their conscious processing of the mental representations of events—including the associated beliefs and attitudes that guide their decisions and behavior. Our brains engage in similar processes when faced with a crisis or, in general, when we encounter inconsistencies or discrepancies that threaten our wellbeing. At these times, our brains switch to more conscious processing of our behaviors and actions with top-down monitoring of inconsistencies. For example, having an explicit goal of creating a more psychologically safe work environment can trigger automatic monitoring within our brain to initiate additional conscious processing when we experience or create less psychological safety (Miller & Cohen, 2001).

Participant advocacy capitalizes on this partly by establishing monitoring mechanisms. That is, participant advocacy promotes self-monitoring for reasoning or behaviors that are inconsistent with ARC principles, components, or mental models. Explicit monitoring entails having a selected team participant (1) consciously monitor and provide feedback to team members or colleagues on the observed use of behaviors, decision making, or approaches linked with ARC principles or key mental models, (2) actively inject leading questions or comments to help direct team members attend more closely to the ARC principles or desired mental models, and (3) facilitate quick reflection with colleagues and team members on their application of ARC principles or key mental models. In other words, it forces the observer to attend closely to a selected principle or mental model such as psychological safety when observing the behavior or decision making of others. Reflection with the advocate and team members promotes discussion of the advocate's experience and often helps all members set up self-monitoring.

To illustrate, an ARC team member is asked to monitor examples of the presence or absence of psychological safety during a team meeting. The participant advocate is instructed to interject a simple cue or question that orients organizational members to recognize behaviors or reasoning that may have detracted from or promoted psychological safety during the meeting. At the meeting's end, a few minutes are provided for the participant advocate to share their observations of the group and allow the group to respond, including discussion of their beliefs that contributed to behaviors around psychological safety.

Participant advocacy creates an explicit focus for the individual who takes on the role while increasing sensitivity among team members to the inconsistencies between their actions and thinking as they are monitored. This is illustrated with members' awareness that they engaged in reasoning or behavior that supported or countered the selected concept or principle being monitored. As one leader exclaimed, "What have you done to me? I can't stop thinking about whether I'm being participatory-based when I work with my staff."

Testing new mental models and approaches. When there is resistance to improvement efforts, an explicit experiment or test can be agreed upon to increase participants' consideration of different approaches in their work. The ARC specialist works with organizational members to identify an approach or strategy that the staff members agree to alter. They work together to establish the importance of the new approach and jointly select a third party to monitor fidelity to the behavior. The ARC specialist helps the organizational members explore assumptions, beliefs, and attitudes associated with the new behavior. For example, a leader might agree to approach employee errors or mistakes without framing the employee as an opponent or use the errors or mistakes as opportunities for leaning. The specialist discusses underlying assumptions and behaviors that support the new approach, such as the assumption that people do not purposively want to fail and errors often have causes that are misunderstood or not recognized. This is reinforced with teaching leaders to approach mistakes by inquiring what circumstances led to the mistake and to self-monitor their thinking that triggers thoughts of blame.

Participants first reported that the new framework and behavior feels artificial or foreign, but this changes with its use. The alternative framing or representation of events such as effective approaches to errors lead to discussions that help connect leader attitudes, underlying beliefs, and the application of the suggested behaviors. The process provides the organizational members opportunities to safely discuss their views, assumptions, and experiences with the ARC specialist present and to envision the framing necessary for practicing the new behavior.

AN EXAMPLE OF BUILDING A MENTAL MODEL ASSOCIATED WITH PSYCHOLOGICAL SAFETY

The concept of psychological safety helps build mental models in organizational members' minds that support behavior and perceptions that align with the ARC principles. Psychological safety refers to a belief that one's work environment is safe for members to offer suggestions for improving practices or for avoiding errors with little interpersonal risk of being viewed negatively by leaders or coworkers. The notion of psychological safety in a work environment is connected most recently to the work of Amy Edmondson (2002), who revived the concept of psychological safety from Schein (1985). She is known best for her research on the association of psychological safety to effective health care outcomes for teams. She found that a lack of psychological safety prevented surgical teams from identifying and correcting problems that harmed the teams' performance and produced poor outcomes for patients.

ARC materials and activities help organizational members explore factors associated with a lack of psychological safety, such as a fear of appearing naïve, disruptive, or incompetent in discussing errors, mistakes, or problems. The ARC strategy identifies the characteristics of OSC that increase psychological safety; such as leaders who treat errors as opportunities for improvement, team behaviors that supports improvement efforts, and staff beliefs that the examination of errors are beneficial for learning. ARC activities help participants identify existing assumptions that either inhibit or enhance behavior that supports psychological safety. For example, an implicit belief that errors are predominately due to a lack of effort versus a belief that individuals typically want to do their jobs well. Participants are asked to envision examples from their own experiences, such as when they felt safe to take personal risks to openly address service problems and, on the other hand, when they did not feel safe in identifying and addressing problems.

Additional activities are used to help participants identify the repercussions of psychological safety or its absence within their organization or their teams. As explained in our introductory example in Chapter 2, staff members in Agency A felt that the death of a client could have been prevented if it had been safer to discuss a recurrent problem associated with a client's death. ARC participants are encouraged to examine current beliefs and assumptions associated with psychological safety in their work environment. The mental representation they hold includes causal links between their beliefs, their behaviors, and their assumptions about errors and mistakes to critical outcomes. These include outcomes such as their ability to learn and improve, their ability to eliminate problems within their organization or teams, and their ability to provide high-quality care. Additional efforts to reinforce these mental representations throughout the ARC process include an examination of participants' behaviors and beliefs related to being psychologically safe and examining the repercussions of their new beliefs and behaviors.

In the example of Agency A from Chapter 2, low psychological safety explained why front-line staff was reluctant to use a new system that allowed them to access data on client wellbeing to monitor their success. That is, they were afraid of being targeted for mistakes, errors, or problems that they believed would be associated with data indicating a failure, a belief that led to avoidance of evaluating whether or not they were making a difference. After learning more about the role of psychological safety and practicing behaviors to support it, leaders requested additional training from the ARC specialist to develop their ability to use the data to improve services in in a psychologically safe manner. This training occurred at the top leadership and management levels, as well as for front-line staff teams and supervisors so that the approaches around data ensured psychological safety. We worked long enough with the agency to see leaders, mid-level managers, and line-level service providers develop an understanding of psychological safety and its application not only in using data, but also in disciplinary actions, in continuous improvement processes, and in performance appraisals. That is, they altered their thinking, reasoning, and beliefs about the causes or errors and the most effective approaches to take when errors occur.

They brought these changes to bear on multiple organizational systems and processes, including their own leadership and management behaviors. The application of new mental models and the examination of underlying beliefs, assumptions, and inferences fostered sustainable change across a variety of systems and processes. Most importantly, these changes were consistent with the ARC principles and ARC component tools in a way that assured success for staff and clients.

9

MISSION-DRIVEN VERSUS
RULE-DRIVEN HUMAN SERVICE
ORGANIZATIONS

The ARC organizational model is designed to improve behavioral health services, social services, and other human services by aligning organizational priorities with five principles of effective human service organizations. These include being mission driven, results oriented, improvement directed, participation based, and relationship centered. Chapter 9 is the first of five chapters (Chapters 9–13) that each describe one of ARC's five principles. We developed and tested the five principles of effective human services by building on the work of Osborne and Gaebler (1992) and others who have described the characteristics that distinguish effective and ineffective organizations. The ARC model is based, in part, on the theory that priorities develop from competing demands that mental health, social service, and other human service organizations face as they attempt to survive and succeed. The relative priorities placed on competing demands specify what is most important to the organization. The alignment of enacted and espoused priorities ensures actions reflect what organizations say is important. And the consistency in an organization's enacted priorities complement rather than contradict organizational priorities, each of which distinguish effective from ineffective organizations (Zohar & Hoffman, 2012). Our recent studies confirm that the priorities enacted by these organizations can be aligned by the ARC strategies with the five principles to improve service outcomes (Glisson et al., 2016a).

ARC's first principle, being mission driven rather than rule driven, specifies that all administrative, managerial, and service provider behavior and decisions must contribute to improving the well-being of clients, and that the appropriateness of any work behavior or decision within the organization is assessed on that basis (Glisson et al., 2016a). This principle addresses the threat posed by the conflicting organizational priority of relying on bureaucratic processes and rules to guide policy and practice decisions. This conflicting priority restricts service providers' discretion through rules and red tape that ignore the varying needs of individual clients and inhibit service providers' responsiveness to specific client circumstances and characteristics. Placing an explicit priority on being mission driven requires that service providers' decisions and actions be guided by what improves the well-being of clients and counters the reliance on bureaucratic rules and procedural red tape that reduces responsiveness to the unique needs of each client (Nugent & Glisson, 1999).

In our work with organizations, leaders readily acknowledge and espouse the importance of being mission driven and are usually quick to commit to the idea of creating a mission-driven work environment. We find, however, that it is more difficult for leaders to put the principle into practice. Leaders are likely to reaffirm during ARC orientation meetings the importance of their organization's focus on client well-being, but staff members will frequently share subtle glances and raised eyebrows as they listen to leaders' comments. We have heard on multiple occasions executive leaders make statements such as, "If we remain focused on our mission of client-wellbeing, the money will follow," but contradicting their statements are practices such as monitoring productivity with headcounts without any parallel focus on assessing improvements in client well-being. These contradictions leave staff questioning the authenticity of the framed mission statements hanging on the wall that proudly emphasize the importance of improving client well-being.

BEING MISSION DRIVEN

The idea of being mission driven is attractive to leaders and staff, but a mission-driven organization is much easier to envision than to create. As explained throughout this book, a range of factors impinge on human service providers' efforts, factors that challenge leaders and staff in their efforts to focus on the mission of improving client well-being. For example, economic downturns can reduce funding and pressure mental health leaders to attend more closely to their organization's financial bottom line. Measures of productivity become the priority, such as client headcounts or billable hours that are directly related to funding. When the demand for funding shifts an organization's priorities to client headcounts, the emphasis on improving clients' well-being fades. Creating and maintaining a mission-driven focus requires the management of internal and external demands as well as careful attention to associated expectations and perceptions of front-line staff. In human service organizations, regulatory demands often create extensive paperwork and associated time demands that when combined with high caseloads and productivity concerns, influence front-line staff perceptions of organizational priorities and the purpose of their work. The mission cannot be a priority when spending adequate time to ensure service availability, responsiveness, or continuity is put at risk because of conflicting demands.

Other factors that detract from an organizational priority on mission include the need to avoid external litigation, community criticism, or government sanctions. This avoidance leads to organization-imposed rules, red tape, standardized procedures, and overly restrictive supervisory approval processes that erode staff perceptions of having adequate time and support for improving client well-being. Administrative efforts to improve services by increasing rules and procedural specifications represents a managerial approach more suited to assembly lines and generally degrades services with cookie-cutter, routinized approaches to care. In the public education arena, similar problems are created with educational reforms and the continuous redesign of curricula that leave teachers feeling a loss of personal control and little discretion in determining the path to student success. Such approaches can increase staff burnout, emotional exhaustion, and disengagement. ARC addresses these issues by introducing alternate approaches to increasing accountability and maintaining a clear focus on mission that guides behavior and decision making through a shared sense of purpose among organizational members.

We have learned that many organizations respond to internal and external demands in a way that directs their priorities away from a clear focus on client well-being. The example of creating internal bureaucratic rules, red tape, and procedural specifications in an effort to address the concerns of funders, regulatory agencies, or courts describes the influence of addressing external concerns. For example, it is common to hear service providers complain that a certain bureaucratic form is required by the federal government when in reality the form is not required but instead represents their organization's attempt to address a service quality requirement of the government. The leaders' decision to support a bureaucratic form in response to a service quality issue with minimal attention to the intended purpose of the form is usually an indication that the organization is rule driven rather than mission driven. Or, if the organization's deviation from its mission is recognized, the concern is placed well behind alternative priorities of addressing the concerns of funders and others. The rationale behind a rule-based organization is that prioritizing efforts toward meeting the demands of regulators and funders with additional paperwork and procedural specifications limits the organization's exposure to risk by providing documentation that certain behavior occurred.

Organizations that remain mission driven in practice have a distinctly different social context and response to external demands. Being mission driven requires a social context that goes beyond mission statements on the wall, marketing efforts to sell the organization's merits to external funders and stakeholders, and the use of bureaucratic paperwork and procedural specifications to document quality. In mission-driven organizations, leaders and staff consider the impact of all decisions or actions on improvements in client well-being. When external demands or internal limitations force leaders to consider priorities other than putting client well-being first, they work closely with managers and staff to clarify the conflicting priority and the underlying reasons. Leaders and staff use organizational tools such as team problem solving or continuous quality improvement (see Chapter 7) to limit the loss of focus on improving client well-being. Mission-driven organizations also invest in planning and initiate actions to minimize the impact of external or internal barriers that interfere with their mission, including coordinating with other service providers to address barriers and educating funders and regulators on the deleterious impact of new requirements.

Leaders of mission-driven organizations promote what we described as a proficient culture in Chapter 3, reflecting shared expectations about service providers' knowledge, skill, and practices that support high-quality service and a focus on positive client outcomes. We find in both our consultation and research that a strong sense of purpose for improving client well-being is shared among staff and leaders in mission-driven organizations and expressed in all facets of the organization's work. Normative patterns of behavior, the strategies that are employed by leadership and staff, staff attitudes about clients, as well as daily decisions and actions reflect attention to client well-being. Staff in these organizations are sensitive to events, cues, or signs of problems or barriers that interfere with improvements in client well-being, and they assume responsibility for addressing the problems. Inferences about clients' behavior result in manageable attributions for causes in the face of poor client outcomes. That is, the shared underlying assumptions of service providers in these organizations do not blame clients for service failures. Instead, failures lead to searches for client strengths and potential strategies for identifying and addressing service barriers to success. The underlying mental models and assumptions (as described in Chapter 8) that represent staff and leaders' understanding of their clients support improvement and change.

The mission-driven priority is expressed in a variety of organizational systems. For example, punitive discipline systems focused on rule infractions and procedural errors are replaced by purpose-centered, team-based monitoring and support that focus on efforts to improve client outcomes, often displacing the need for disciplinary practices with clear expectations that guide appropriate action. The social contexts of these teams are characterized by social expectations that organizational members will complete their work, support their colleagues' efforts, and focus on client well-being throughout their work. These efforts include feedback systems that provide client outcome data to staff as an essential tool for improving care. When less-than-desirable client outcomes occur, feedback motivates staff to find alternative approaches to improving services. Systems for staff orientation and on-the-job training are focused on developing skills and knowledge to achieve client well-being while minimizing an emphasis on bureaucratic paperwork and procedures. We have worked with a number of rule-driven organizations with staff orientation and training systems focused primarily on completing paperwork, along with staff evaluation systems that focus on process and timeliness instead of the intended purpose of using information to improve client well-being. Mission-driven organizations create engaged climates (Chapter 3) where staff report a personal sense of accomplishment in their work, shared responsibility for clients, and commitment to the success of their organization. An organization's clarity of mission provides a strong sense of common purpose, engenders team cohesiveness, and increases commitment among staff to reach meaningful client goals. As a result, the priority placed on mission reduces the need for procedural checklists and documentation of effort found in rule-driven organizations. Service decisions in mission-driven organizations are less dependent on policy manuals and more dependent on team-based monitoring, discussion, and participative decision making with client well-being in mind. Routinized behavior to meet perceived service requirements such as leaving rote phone messages to clients to document contact, a common practice in some organizations, is replaced with a greater emphasis on assuring meaningful client contact and individualized care that addresses the unique needs of each client. When errors or problems occur in mission-driven organizations, leaders are unlikely to overreact to errors or make incorrect attributions for staff failures. Staff members share the belief that their leadership is committed to high-quality service, and leaders' actions are perceived in this light. These expectations and perceptions are critical to the staff members' interpretations of documentation requests that are made by leaders. Focus on critical documentation requests embedded in a social context that supports the organization's mission to improve client well-being are more acceptable to staff who make positive attributions about their leaders' intentions.

A LEADERSHIP EXAMPLE

Leaders of mission-driven human service organizations are committed to improving the well-being of their clients and focused on delivering the most effective service possible. The mission to improve client well-being is explicit in their strategic planning, objectives, and organizational processes. Leaders place a priority on being mission driven with their decisions and the allocation of resources, and they recognize and reward staff decision making and behavior that reflect a commitment to the mission. A highly effective CEO with whom we worked to implement ARC provides an excellent example of such a leader.

An ARC front-line team, using the ARC component tools described in Chapter 7, identified the loss of a key team position as a service barrier to improving client well-being. Data gathered by the team to support their assessment provided evidence that indicated the loss of the position (a result of decreased funding) was linked to a decline in client outcomes as the position was incrementally eliminated. Although program directors initially used reserve resources to keep the position in place, the position was eventually lost, causing a noticeable negative impact on client outcomes. Solutions suggested by program members after the loss included other staff assuming the responsibilities and activities of the lost position. However, there was agreement that the solution could not be sustained long term and that the core activities of the position required reestablishing the position—a difficult solution because of the tight budget and little hope of increased funding during an economic downturn.

The OAT discussed with team representatives the proposal for position replacement and the associated costs. Limited expectations for success were shared by several program members who had witnessed their directors' failed efforts to keep the position funded. The CEO, who attended the OAT team meetings despite the many demands of his position, had read the proposal and was attentive to the ARC team's presentation. After listening to the discussion of the proposal by the OAT and being queried for his reaction by the staff, he said, "The data are clear and I know you have thought through the alternatives and costs. The question is not whether we'll replace the position. The question is how we're going to make this happen. We have to find a way to provide what we know works best for our clients." The OAT discussion resulted in a plan to connect the ARC team to the organization's development officer and for the CEO to approach new contacts for funding. As a result, the team garnered enough external funding from multiple parties, a mix of grants and endowments, to fund the position half time. The CEO leveraged their efforts to obtain the other half from a benefactor. Just as importantly, the CEO highlighted the ARC team's success in obtaining funding and months later celebrated data on client outcomes showing that improvements followed the reinstatement of the position. These data were shared with the board of directors, with staff in an internal newsletter, in presentations the leader made in the community, and with other funders.

The example is a simple one that describes a leader's response to an identified service barrier, but the importance of the CEO's response in the example cannot be overemphasized. We have witnessed scores of leadership responses to ARC team proposals and OAT discussions in many organizations over several years, more than a few of which provide examples of leaders who were unable to make the difficult decisions that demonstrated an organizational priority on mission. Our point here is that leaders' decisions are critical in creating and sustaining mission-driven organizations, especially when the decisions concern service barriers identified by those who are providing the service.

WHY AND HOW MISSION DRIVEN MATTERS

Mission-driven organizations are highlighted in the trade literature and often cited as essential to organization effectiveness, high-performance cultures, productivity, and ensuring success. Assessments of non-profit service organizations suggest that both economic success and positive service outcomes are more likely to be achieved when clarity of direction and meaningful purpose are ensured by a mission-driven focus on client well-being and improvement (Groscurth, 2014; McDonald, 2007). In other words, improved client outcomes and organizational economic health are not mutually exclusive when an organizational priority goes beyond espousing a mission to the enactment of a mission focused on client well-being. Based on data gathered via questionnaires, surveys, and structured interviews within organizations, the trade literature provides insight into both the positive outcomes associated with mission-driven organizations and the potential mechanisms that link a mission-driven priority to organizational success. A recent worldwide survey conducted by Gallup (Harter, Schmidt, Agrawal & Plowman, 2013) of 49,928 business units across 192 organizations in 49 different industries, found that maintaining a clear mission is linked to employee, customer, and organizational performance. Engagement and retention of employees are both supported by an organization's ability to emphasize their mission and provide staff opportunities to excel. That is, employees that have a meaningful purpose in their work and the opportunity to use their skills in achieving that purpose are predictive of low employee turnover and high performance.

The benefits of working within mission-driven, purpose-oriented organizations include increased job satisfaction, staff loyalty, less boredom, and happiness. These benefits are accompanied by higher staff engagement and retention (Larren, 2014; Ross, 2015). A Deloitte survey (2013) of more than 1,300 working adults found that employees experiencing a strong sense of purpose within mission-driven organizations were more than four times as likely (79% versus 19%) to indicate high employee satisfaction at their company. Within nonprofits, increased innovation, proactive problem solving, and perceiving opportunities where others see threats are all associated with being mission-driven (Davidoff, 2013). In challenging times, organizations that are not mission-driven rely on bureaucratic rules, red tape and the status quo, leading to poor performance, while mission-driven organizations approach challenges as opportunities to excel, allowing them to become stronger, more distinctive, and more successful.

Mission-driven organizations are associated with cohesive teams and coworkers who care about each other; leaders who are more invested in the well-being, growth, and development of staff; and increased trust, collaboration, and innovation among staff (Davidoff, 2013; Ross, 2015). Within mission-driven organizations, staff are more confident that their organizations will grow compared to staff in organizations without a strong sense of purpose and mission. Being mission driven is also identified as a key factor in the survival of organizations when facing financial or resource crises. Mission-driven nonprofit organizations are characterized as proactive and entrepreneurial with highly committed leaders, staff, and boards. Organizations that are not mission driven are described as low-energy groups with disengaged employees and boards who operate from a reactive stance. In other words, mission-driven organizations have proactive, committed organizational members who pursue success, eliminate barriers, innovate, and invest the effort necessary to succeed.

ARC strategies contribute to mission-driven priorities by creating social structures that encourage reflection among leaders and staff on whether their mission is being enacted. Efforts include specific mission-focused activities such as integrating mission into strategic plans, objectives, and goals. At the staff level, a mission-driven priority is reinforced as leaders are encouraged to teach managers how to align mission within daily activities and work completed by staff. ARC training materials emphasize leadership behaviors that place a high level of trust in staff to build teams, abilities, and processes necessary to address service barriers through collaboration and innovation. To sustain these efforts, mission-driven companies focus on mentoring and professional development as integral to employee selection and retention (Larren, 2014).

Underscoring leadership behaviors that promote a mission-driven priority are three themes that help explain the mission-driven influence on organizational success. First, maintaining a mission-driven organization ensures guidance and direction. That is, organizational members have a shared purpose that jointly guides decisions, judgments, plans, and actions. A strong mission allows leaders to establish and balance priorities, such as judgments regarding the allocation of resources, money, and time. A mission-driven priority emphasizes what is important for staff training, how systems need to operate (e.g., feedback data focused on improvements in client well-being versus controlling staff), how much focus is placed on staff development, and what daily activities are expected and reinforced. Organizations with a priority on being mission driven adopt innovations that help achieve their mission and moderate the amount of attention and energy given to externally driven demands that can push an organization in multiple, opposing directions. Being mission driven fosters shared goals across organizational members while aligning rewards and recognition in support of the mission (Wright, 2007). Being mission driven improves strategic alignment and eliminates silos in organizations via a shared common purpose that fosters joint action across departments, teams, organizational levels, and external stakeholders.

Second, a mission-driven work environment creates a sense of purpose and meaning within organizational members' work lives, which in turn enhances staff engagement, commitment, and tenacity in completing work. The mission provides the explanation and rationale for the work and an emotional connection to purpose that is shared with a community of service providers. Accompanied by leaders who foster staff input, innovation, and development and growth of staff, meaningful purpose allows organizational members to experience a strong sense of contribution to a worthwhile cause and a shared connection with colleagues in achieving that cause. The common purpose fosters trust across organizational members as they collaborate and support each other to achieve a common goal. Most importantly, perhaps, the mission promotes shared levels of energy, excitement, commitment, and persistence among leaders and staff.

Third, the trade and research literature documents the impact of being mission driven on innovation and change within organizations seeking to improve performance. Mission-driven organizations are associated with leaders who emphasize opportunities for growth and development among staff. These leaders focus on staff input and innovative ideas, and establish norms for both personal and organizational improvement. The three themes are interrelated. For example, higher levels of trust associated with mission-driven organizations allow members the autonomy and psychological safety to innovate and contribute (McDonald, 2007). Mission helps prioritize and focus attention on innovations that will contribute to the organization's effectiveness and creates a climate where change is supported. Clarity of mission, for example, weakens the presence of silos resistant to innovation and assures sustainability in the face of the inevitable barriers that occur during innovation efforts. It buffers innovation against undue criticism, political agendas, and embedded dysfunctionality among members that can sidetrack change efforts within organizations. In other words, being mission driven engenders the support, collaboration, motivation, and commitment of organizational members necessary for innovation and improvement. Furthermore, a priority on mission relies on expectations, norms, and beliefs that organizational change is possible and essential to improving client well-being.

EXEMPLARS OF MISSION DRIVEN

Systems and processes. The degree of mission clarity in an organization is expressed across all organizational systems and processes. Successful social enterprise startups such as Warby Parker, for example, cite their mission as integral to their 360-degree employee reviews, monthly feedback sessions, workshops, and outside speaker sessions (Stiverson, 2014). In a similar fashion, mission-driven human service organizations embed their mission throughout the practices, processes, and systems that compose the organization. For example, staff selection, promotion and dismissal processes in mission-driven organizations look beyond skill or knowledge qualifications. These processes include assessments of a candidate's fit with their organization's mission and culture. In human service organizations, this means recruiting and selecting candidates who share a personal commitment to providing services that improve client well-being and demonstrate the characteristics and abilities to develop relationships that support that effort.

In service organizations where a priority on improving client well-being has been lost, we see organizations make selection, retention, and promotion decisions that are not primarily influenced by the implications for quality care. A good example occurred early in our work within a state child welfare agency system. We had noted the skill of a case manager who was adept at connecting with children and their families. She effectively engaged clients under stressful conditions and was used as a resource by other front-line caseworkers with clients who were difficult to engage. When referred clients were angry, difficult, or had complex needs, caseworkers sought her help. Her paperwork, however, was inadequate. When we spoke to her supervisor about her ability to connect with clients he frowned and said, "Yeah, if she only knew how to do her paperwork, she'd be great." She admitted struggling with writing and documenting her work given her limited writing skills. She received poor job evaluations because a predominant focus of the evaluations was the timely and correct completion of paperwork. As a result of her poor evaluations, she was terminated for her failure to complete paperwork; the supervisor feared the lack of paperwork would leave the supervisor and agency vulnerable to negative reviews. When asked if anyone else could have helped with her paperwork, the supervisor replied, "This is one of the most important parts of the job. We need folks who can get their paperwork done." To his credit, when asked about her skills, the supervisor indicated, "She was fabulous at working with the clients. We just can't take the risk of having incomplete documentation." At the same time, he acknowledged that he had called on her to help other workers struggling with clients. He expressed no concerns, however, about retaining the caseworkers who lacked the skill to engage challenging clients and needed additional help.

In contrast to the work of the fired caseworker, we became familiar with the work of another caseworker who dutifully remained at her desk throughout the work day but ignored incoming client calls as messages accumulated on her answering machine. She occupied a significant part of her time playing a variety of digital games until late in the day, she then began returning phone calls to clients. She knew or should have known before calling that many of the clients would be unavailable at the time she returned the calls. We learned that she completed paperwork on time, sometimes by fabricating times and dates for documentation, and her paperwork was always complete. Her supervisor knew she was not always available and responsive to her clients, but she received satisfactory evaluations based on her paperwork and remained in her position throughout the several years we worked with the agency.

Beliefs, mindsets, and results. As the previous examples illustrate, being either mission driven or rule driven affects what is prioritized at work as well as the interpretation of events and decisions that are made. Consistent with ARC's mental model strategies that were discussed in Chapter 8, deeply held beliefs and assumptions underscore reasoning, decision making, and practices in work settings. In mission-driven organizations, leaders and members share a fundamental belief that remaining focused on improving client well-being drives success. When asked to explain why their commitment to client well-being is important, leaders in mission-driven organizations provided explicit examples of their beliefs and how their focus on client well-being leads to success. The leaders expressed how their focus on client well-being unites service providers in a shared purpose and how it directs work toward a common goal shared by all organizational members. That is, the leaders expressed a fundamental assumption that maintaining a clear focus on improving client well-being is the integrating force for motivating and driving coordinated action, decisions, and processes. More importantly, they weren't simply espousing this belief, they were living it.

The important point is that mission-driven beliefs affect the practices and approaches taken with clients in the care of human service organizations. Our work in pediatric emergency rooms, for example, illustrated striking differences in beliefs across ERs regarding family-centered care that affected health-care providers' interactions with children and their families (Hemmelgarn, Glisson, & Dukes, 2001). The behavioral differences were based partly on whether staff believed that family involvement is necessary to achieve the highest quality of pediatric health care. Associated beliefs included that a parent's input contributes to a provider's understanding of presenting medical problems and that parental support in treatment compliance is critical to long-term success. The idea that parents should be viewed as partners in their child's health care and that associated psychosocial support such as having a parent remain with a child during care are critical to medical success align with family-centered care. Research shows that family-centered pediatric care is essential to treatment compliance and therefore to the success of efforts to improve client outcomes. Yet, we found that the beliefs and willingness to engage in family-centered care varied significantly across different pediatric emergency-room settings and that these beliefs and behaviors were associated with the cultures and climates of the settings.

Our study found that ERs characterized by family-centered care established clear and ongoing communication with families beginning at intake, included family members in their child's care whenever possible, and provided emotional support to family members throughout care. When interviewed, these health-care providers reported that effective medical care went beyond medical procedures for children who faced serious illness or trauma. Behaviors with families included talking, hand holding, hugging, and comforting. These behaviors also occurred among staff where nurses and doctors would comfort each other after a child's death or during a particularly difficult case. As described by the social worker who worked closely with nursing staff and doctors during life-threat-ening pediatric emergencies in one ER, "We know very clearly that supporting each other and our families is critical to saving lives." Staff in settings not characterized by family-centered care resisted interacting with families, denied that staff were affected by a child's death or other poor outcomes, and had negative perceptions of parents who were seen as disrupting the providers' ability to complete their work. A staff pastor who worked in one of the ERs that devalued family-centered care described the medical staff as hard-ened and emotionally guarded. In those ERs, nurses avoided monitoring the reception desk to escape interacting with parents, provided little comfort to parents who lost their children, and limited the information and access they provided to parents from admission to discharge. Staff in these ERs established boundaries with parents at admission by not responding to parents' questions with such statements as, "We won't be able to answer any questions until all the procedures are completed, so please take a seat and wait." Interviews in one ER uncovered stories of a physician telling parents that their child had died without taking the time to sit down with the parents, to discuss any details, or to address questions.

In the ERs where health professionals were the most resistant to family-centered care, staff expressed negative attitudes toward parents. One nurse told us in an interview that "many of these parents are just too stupid to be helped," a belief that was expressed by several of her colleagues. On the other hand, in ERs that were focused on providing emo-tional support and family-centered care, staff maintained supportive attitudes toward family members even when families were upset or unable to understand. As one nurse indicated, "I feel so sorry for parents who can't understand the medical procedures we are trying to describe to them. They are so worried and feeling so out of control."

Our experience and research indicate that human service organizations vary widely in how their staff interacts with clients and families, which reflects their priority on mission versus rules. Our work shows that service quality and outcomes are best in social serv-ice and behavioral health organizations that are firmly driven by the mission to improve client well-being. Staff in mission-driven organizations are more likely to be available and responsive to clients and to establish continuity of care with clients' families and other service providers and stakeholders. These service characteristics are driven by beliefs about what it takes to be successful, including a consistent commitment to improving client well-being even when working on difficult cases. This commitment is represented by the words of a psychiatric therapist who conducted a home visit where the client became aggressive and punched her. "He didn't mean to hurt me," she told us, "he thought I was there to turn him over to the FBI—he was just not taking his medicine. Tomorrow he will hug me!" It is this positive attitude and commitment to improving their clients' well-being that is characteristic of service providers in mission-driven human service organizations. As shown in our pediatric emergency room study, staff working in settings supportive of family-centered care reported higher levels of engagement and purpose in their work that was associated with a shared mission of improving client well-being. The sense of purpose in these types of OSC encourages staff tenacity, persistence, and commitment in serving their clients.

The contrast is striking when working with an organization whose mission has been muddied by a priority on bureaucratic rules and documentation, misdirected by a focus on headcounts, or replaced by routinized client care that fails to recognize and address the unique needs of each client. When organizations are not driven by a service mission, staff members view families and clients as the architects of their own failures and cite poor results as a function of non-compliant clients. The shared belief within these settings is that some clients are broken beyond repair and that improvement is simply not possible, regardless of the service. Just as we found in the ER study, explanations of client behavior are reflected in explanations of staff behavior. Supervisor's perceptions of staff reflect similar attributions when staff problems occur. Supervisors attribute staff errors or failures to a lack of staff effort, motivation, or commitment to their work, which they assume are fixed predispositions. Conversely, staff members in these types of work environments believe it is unreasonable to hold them responsible for client success or failure. These front-line providers expect failure to occur and believe that too many factors contribute to client outcomes, which makes it impossible to reliably improve their clients' well-being. Empirically, we know from our research that a great deal of variation exists in the cultures, climates, and mission-driven focus of similar types of organizations that serve similar clients under similar constraints. We also know that the associated beliefs and assumptions held by organizational members vary by organization and, in turn, are associated with the variation in service quality and outcomes.

As we described in Chapter 8, OSCs are sustained by mental models and associated assumptions, inferences, and beliefs that are shared among leaders and staff members. Within mission-driven organizations, the belief that improving client well-being is possible and at the core of one's work is shared and unquestioned. Staff in these organizations believe that clients desire help in making improvements and that even incremental improvements in well-being are important. When poor service outcomes occur, staff members do not automatically assume it resulted from the client's ineptness. In a similar manner, if a staff member fails or makes a mistake, it isn't assumed that the staff member is characterized by lacking ability, motivation, or commitment.

When developing the capacity of staff members to promote client success, leaders and supervisors in mission-driven organizations share the assumption that the purpose of administering a successful human service organization is improving client well-being. They believe that the purpose and meaning of work is what creates the motivation among staff to succeed. These leaders view their job as developing organizational processes and systems that support staff efforts to remain focused on improving client well-being. For example, the performance data monitored in an organizational information system of a mission-driven organization include well attended indicators of client well-being and are not limited to indicators of client headcounts, billing amounts, or rule compliance. Training in mission-driven organizations strongly emphasizes improving service provider knowledge, skills, and use of best practices while emphasizing the completion of paperwork, rule compliance, and procedural requirements as necessary, yet secondary in importance. Underscoring these system approaches is the underlying mental model that staff are motivated to do a good job and want to succeed in improving client well-being. The assumption is that mistakes or poor outcomes are not intentional and provide opportunities for growth and learning. That is, the shared beliefs and mindset of leaders and supervisors support the notion that improving client well-being is paramount, that staff are trying to do the best work possible, and that success comes from supporting staff in conducting meaningful work aimed at improving client well-being.

Returning to the example of hospital pediatric emergency rooms, staff in the ERs that were not family-centered believed their responsibilities were restricted to medical procedures and did not include providing emotional support or engaging families of the children they treated. The staff in these ERs believed that tolerating the stress within the ER without expressing emotion or receiving emotional support from other staff demonstrated an individual's stability and professional competence. Similarly, staff believed that addressing the emotional needs of parents was neither their job nor important to medical care. In fact, they believed that engaging parents in care was potentially harmful because it deflected attention away from important medical issues. In other words, the shared beliefs among staff influenced their shared behaviors. At the same time, we found that the staff in the organizations that rejected family-centered care and the need for emotional support among staff reported the highest levels of stress. That is, the staff in those hospitals that rejected family-centered care and the role of emotional support in their work reported significantly higher levels of stress than staff in ERs providing family-centered care. Consistent with the application of mental models and social cognition research in our work to improve social contexts, the power of these types of beliefs and assumptions are that they guide the attention, interpretation, reasoning, and subsequent actions taken with clients, influencing client outcomes while also influencing staff well-being and functioning.

USING ARC TO CREATE A MISSION-DRIVEN ORGANIZATION

We worked with the executive leaders of a Midwest community-based mental health agency who expressed strong support for ARC principles during their initial meeting with the ARC specialist. The CEO noted in this meeting that the organization was beginning to move beyond financial difficulties after five years of budget deficits. In response to their financial problems, the board of directors had hired a financial director who was given the authority to establish program budgets, goals for each program, and to sanction or reward programs based on productivity. The financial director was also given the discretion to eliminate or add new programs as needed to create economic stability. The message to organizational members, including front-line staff, was that financial well-being was the top priority for the survival of the organization. Client well-being had taken a back seat.

We surveyed line-level service providers at the inception of ARC to assess program baseline OSC scores, which we provided to leaders. The service providers described rigid and resistant program cultures (see Chapter 3). The leadership team was anxious about the baseline OSC profiles but relieved to hear the explanation offered by the CEO. She explained that the director of the programs with the most rigid and resistant profiles was the problem and that she had considered firing him. That director, however, had built the programs from scratch and had the support of the financial director and some board members because of his productivity numbers. The CEO described the director as inflexible, highly controlling, and directly involved in front-line cases despite being two supervisory levels above frontline team leaders. We learned that the team leaders believed the program director contributed to high turnover among front-line staff, and there were examples of staff members being confronted in meetings with the program director. The impression provided to the ARC specialist was that front-line staff had very little discretion, faced unrealistic productivity goals, and were being led by an authoritarian, demanding, and punitive director who attempted to control decisions and actions all the way down to individual case details. During our initial ARC orientation meeting with front-line staff that included the director, they looked nervously at each other, asked no questions, and maintained a flat affect throughout the meeting. It was clear to us that frontline staff members had little sense of purpose in their work, were emotionally exhausted, and wary of their program director and organizational leaders.

Three initial steps were taken using ARC strategies: (1) The CEO and the ARC specialist identified an executive above the program director to serve as the ARC liaison (see Chapter 4). The liaison was selected because he was skilled at establishing relationships and trust at different levels within the organization, had been successful within the organization, and understood the importance of maintaining a focus on improving client well-being; (2) plans were developed to share the OSC data and previous research results with a broader executive group that included the financial director, with a focused discussion on how economic conditions had affected the organization's ability to be mission driven;

(3) planned ARC activities were begun with ARC team leaders and their front-line staff to engage staff in identifying and addressing barriers to service quality and outcomes.

The first step was designed to bridge the divide between front-line staff and leaders and regain some of the control that had been relinquished to the program director. The second step was to build support among leaders for the ARC process and its principles, particularly being mission driven. The third step employed ARC's sequence of activities with front-line ARC team leaders to increase the agency's focus on identifying and addressing service barriers, particularly at the front line. This step included developing team skills, establishing psychological safety (see Chapter 8) within the program teams, and teaching team supervisors to use the ARC tools and processes (see Chapter 7) with their teams to identify and address service barriers.

The first step resulted in the ARC liaison working closely with ARC team supervisors and staff to facilitate changes in control over decisions influencing their clients' care, such as transferring budget discretion for small resources provided to clients from the program director back to team supervisors. Additionally, the ARC liaison facilitated linkages between front-line teams, leaders, and departmental staff to address larger barriers, while discussing with the program director the reasoning behind his need to control program supervisors. The liaison's ongoing interaction with team leaders provided insight into the level of control maintained by the program director and the lack of discretion service team leaders had in making decisions that influenced the care provided by their teams.

The second step allowed the ARC specialist to review OSC culture and climate profiles with a broader group of leaders, including the financial director. Designed to create an understanding of the need for change, the review included empirical evidence of culture and climate's impact on client and staff outcomes, linking the ARC principles to effective OSCs, and discussing the importance of the ARC mission-driven principle for long-term economic health that included a reduction in turnover and an increase in program effectiveness. Participants, including the financial director, explored the impact of past financial difficulties on their mission focus, their beliefs, and assumptions that continued to guide their focus on productivity. This allowed the top leaders, including the financial director, to be recognized for their contribution to the economic improvements that were necessary for success. At the same time, it redirected the leaders' attention to a priority on improving client well-being as a first step in regaining this focus across the organization. This step also helped executive leaders develop a mental model of leadership that balanced productivity and improved client well-being. Specific targets for improvement included parallel feedback mechanisms for monitoring client well-being to balance the emphasis on productivity, formal and informal steps to recognize staff successes with clients, and additional work on creating psychological safety around the use of data and improvement. Leaders and mid-level managers agreed to consider practices that fostered psychological safety. The ARC liaison and others became increasingly aware of the fearful environment staff and program leaders were working in; it was an environment that was crippling staff motivation, inhibiting their ability to speak about problems and potential improvements, and exacerbating their loss of commitment to the organization.

As employed in all ARC projects, the third step guided front-line service teams through ARC activities designed to increase their focus on client well-being and the improvement of services. The five ARC principles (Chapters 9–13) are used to establish a framework that guides subsequent ARC work and activities. The third step included a detailed exploration of ARC's mission-driven principle, gaps in its application within their agency, and identification of potential barriers blocking its enactment within front-line ARC teams. Additionally, ARC activities allowed front-line teams and their supervisor to identify, analyze, and propose ways to address service barriers. Team leaders were trained in promoting teamwork and how to use meeting and team tools to support their work. The introduction of psychological safety in the teams and the corresponding enactment of behaviors to support psychological safety were critical requirements for this work. Initial team efforts led to additional psychological safety training as the ARC liaison helped coordinate training and activities among leaders and others to facilitate psychological safety throughout the entire organization.

As staff experienced improvements in group functioning, developed trust in the ARC liaison, and witnessed changes beyond their own program, they became more open about barriers that impeded their ability to serve clients. Using continuous improvement tools, they were asked to prioritize service barriers based on their impact on client well-being, further emphasizing a mission-driven focus on client well-being. Proposals for improving client care increased and were supported by the ARC liaison and OAT (Chapters 4–5). As progress occurred using these three steps, the program director began to recognize his own role in inhibiting psychological safety, the improvement of social context, and the enactment of a mission-driven principle. Sometime later, the program director asked to be moved to another position, which was more suited to his interests: that of providing consultation on difficult client cases and expertise on technical details to meet non-negotiable policies, regulations, and requirements for funding and reimbursement.

The successes that occurred in this organization were supported by developing an awareness among leaders (including the financial director) that although human services required the necessary financial resources to provide care, effective services required more than simply focusing on financial resources. Leaders successfully reoriented their organization to a more balanced blend of priorities on productivity for economic health and on improving client well-being to provide meaningful purpose and guidance to the organization's work. This was accompanied by a change in the leaders' shared mindset about front-line members' input and discretion into the decisions, processes, and approaches needed to achieve the organization's mission. The three steps described above allowed members to participate in identifying and addressing barriers to care using client outcome data and in a process of improvement that was supported by the principles, mental models, and specific organizational tools necessary for success.

10

RESULTS-ORIENTED VERSUS PROCESS-ORIENTED HUMAN SERVICE ORGANIZATIONS

The results-oriented principle requires that human service organizations evaluate performance based on how much clients' well-being improves and whether the assessment is at the individual-service-provider level, treatment-team level, program level, or organizational level (Glisson et al., 2016a). This principle addresses deficits in service caused by the conflicting priority of evaluating performance with process criteria such as the number of clients served, billable service hours, or the extent to which specified bureaucratic procedures such as completion of paperwork are followed.

Executives in Agency A from our example in Chapter 2 were committed to data-driven action and decision making. Leaders rewarded success in achieving established data-based goals both formally and informally. Promotions for team leaders and managers were influenced by meeting performance goals. Leaders, in turn, publicly acknowledged team and program supervisors' successes in reaching goals during staff meetings. Upper leadership frequently cited program and team accomplishments of achieving difficult performance goals as examples of excellence to board members and successful programs were specifically identified. Programs that achieved performance goals were also rewarded by a reduction in the monitoring of their program activities by middle managers and increased discretion in how they achieved their results. High-performing teams expressed a great deal of pride in their achievements. There was also positive, ongoing competition among team supervisors over who had the best results.

Agency A invested substantial resources in data information systems to assure that desired data-based outcomes were tracked and easily accessible. Training was available at all levels on how to access and use the data from the information system. The emphasis on performance data was reinforced in other organizational systems and processes. Individual performance appraisals at different levels, for example, included assessments on the individual's use of feedback for goal setting and action planning. The disciplinary procedures emphasized the use of data to support disciplinary actions and included information on failures in achieving specific performance goals. Ongoing data monitoring included the use of weekly reviews of program data with front-line supervisors and mid-level managers as well as monthly reviews of program outcomes by directors and upper leadership. Data trends were posted in meeting rooms for front-line staff to provide visual data for gauging movement toward achieving goals.

Although Agency A seemed to have a strong performance-based culture, there was a problem. Despite placing a priority on using data for decisions and actions within their organization, Agency A was not results-oriented. The data driving their organization focused on productivity: more specifically, the number of clients for which they received full reimbursement and the timely completion of documentation to assure reimbursement was not lost. Although client well-being data were monitored at the request of funders, data describing improvements in client well-being were reviewed only briefly in monthly leadership meetings to meet funder demands and were not incorporated into performance appraisals. Unlike productivity, there were no weekly goals for client well-being and no attention to trends in the improvement of client well-being across programs. Some program supervisors who were personally committed to tracking client well-being, spent time accessing, reviewing, and discussing wellbeing findings with their front-line staff; but this process was not highlighted or integral to ongoing performance monitoring.

This point is not that productivity and reimbursement data are unimportant. They play an undeniable role in program sustainability and in providing adequate resources for high-quality services. Agency A, in fact, had a stronger budget than many competing agencies; a budget that allowed for more training, sophisticated computer resources and other technologies such as iPads, cellular phones, and a shared internal communication and information network. Despite these resources, we found that Agency A was characterized by high levels of staff dissatisfaction and turnover, as well as low levels of engagement with clients compared to national norms. As described by the staff, they perceived their work as focused on making money for the organization and not on improving clients' lives. This money-focused perception was reinforced for program staff and supervisors who complained that their programs' discretionary funds failed to increase with the increased revenue captured by a program's high productivity. In other words, there was little monetary reward at the program level for meeting performance goals because funds were controlled centrally. Moreover, the agency's lack of maintaining an environment where poor performance was addressed in a safe manner with staff and supervisors was creating disengagement and turnover among staff.

As we learned in our work with Agency A, increased revenue was funding its geographic and programmatic expansion of services across the state. These expansion efforts were tied to productivity and reimbursement while the focus on improvements in client well-being was a secondary priority. Plans for organizational growth had shifted the leaders' priorities away from improving client well-being to headcounts and income. Ironically, the intention behind expanding facilities and services was to ensure more comprehensive care that provided for all the needs of clients and to ensure economic stability for all programs with the intended purpose of improving client care.

The agency's narrow focus on productivity and reimbursement, however, was only part of its problem. Managers responded to the emphasis on reimbursement by employing data with staff in an authoritarian, and at times, punitive and threatening manner. Leaders' and managers' approaches for correcting poor productivity were demanding, with simple messages such as "get it done" and "you'll be held responsible." Minimal discussion occurred between the supervisors and staff to examine service barriers or problems that staff felt were interfering with productivity goals. Not surprisingly, the authoritarian and sometimes threatening approaches exacerbated the impact of failures on staff morale. Staff expected that failures in reaching productivity goals would be attributed to their not trying hard enough or not taking personal responsibility for getting work accomplished. The problems behind low productivity were not openly discussed by staff given fear they would be blamed. Overall, responsibility for productivity failures cascaded down from leaders, flowing to each subsequent level of management until it landed on the laps of front-line staff. This created a work environment in which front-line staff members were monitored closely on their productivity while being unable to discuss organizational barriers that interfered with their productivity.

THE CHARACTERISTICS OF RESULTS-ORIENTED ORGANIZATIONS

Organizations that incorporate the results-oriented principle are noticeably different from organizations that are process oriented. One of the most important distinctions is a priority and focus on monitoring improvements in clients' well-being and using that information in decision making. In results-oriented organizations, leaders routinely discuss improvements in client well-being with a focus on reinforcing and motivating all organizational members to serve clients and to address service barriers. These interactions establish expectations in the organization for maximizing client improvement. Coupled with the mental models discussed in Chapter 8, program managers, and supervisors use results-oriented data in a psychologically safe manner. Psychological safety assures that barriers to improving client outcomes can be discussed and addressed openly without fear of reprisals or personal attacks. The focus on results is supported and sustained by leaders' receptivity to input on errors, barriers, and problems that interfere with client outcomes.

Furthermore, leaders support the results orientation by allocating time for reviewing, analyzing, and identifying targets for change. Leaders sustain this focus by providing simple, understandable, and usable client well-being feedback that supports action planning and change efforts among staff. Similarly, leaders provide support through processes and tools that are consistent with the design of organizational systems that attend to client results. Introduced in Chapter 7, for example, component tools of well-designed continuous improvement processes coupled with planning and goal setting are essential for service providers to identify, analyze, and eliminate barriers based on client well-being results. The success of these tools and processes, however, relies on leaders that maintain expectations of positive support for these tools and who establish formal and informal paths for collaboratively sharing ongoing client successes and improvements. These leaders' efforts are rewarded as their priority on being results oriented further ingrains a proficient culture where clinical skills and knowledge are expected and valued by staff.

The commitment to client improvement in results-oriented organizations is reflected in the leaders' recognition of excellence among staff members. Exceptional examples of improving client well-being are shared in results-oriented organizations. Program supervisors share success stories with managers and directors who, in turn, forward them to executive leaders. Executive leaders highlight stories of client success with board members, funders, and stakeholders who are vested in client improvement. Within results-oriented organizations, rewards, as well as recognition, are linked to success in improving client outcomes. More broadly, decisions and actions of leaders reinforce the organization's mission of improving client lives. Decisions made by leaders, whether about the distribution of resources, strategic goals, or the design of organizational systems and processes, are guided and assessed against their impact on improving client well-being.

A results orientation creates an organizational work environment where front-line providers have positive attitudes about using feedback on client outcomes and expectations that feedback will drive decision making at all levels. As described in Chapter 7, the use of feedback is one of the ARC component tools that support the organization's mission of improving client well-being. Coupled with psychological safety and participative decision making as described in Chapter 7, staff members are supported in reviewing feedback data to improve performance by identifying and addressing service barriers.

The expectations for improvement are met using results-oriented data that trigger constructive feedback from colleagues and leaders as they work to identify and eliminate service barriers. This process and support apply to productivity goals as well, but the focus on productivity does not replace the focus on client well-being. In the words of a staff member from a results-oriented organization we worked with: "I'll do whatever it takes in whatever form to make sure we help our clients, including worrying about productivity . . . but, I won't be a part of a program that isn't making a difference."

OTHER EFFORTS AT BUILDING RESULTS-ORIENTED ORGANIZATIONS

Osborne and Gaebler's (1992) *Reinventing Government* describes the weaknesses of process-oriented government organizations. Driven by funding based on process measures and a predisposition toward using standardized processes and regulations to guide behavior, client results or individual customer needs are lost. For example, paying higher rates to nursing homes for bedridden elders creates a built-in incentive for increasing the level of care while the goal of public funding is to prolong independence. Funding schools based on the number of students enrolled versus gains in academic performance leads to a focus on head counts, not quality education. Within mental health and social services, accreditation and certification requirements that are not results oriented often drive training. Attending training provides no assurances that training elements are implemented or that training improved client well-being. Within process-oriented contexts that have subjugated client well-being to headcounts and monitoring the completion of paperwork, the meaning of training shifts from skill development for improving client well-being to focusing on the minimum requirements for accreditation or licensing. As illustrated by Agency A in Chapter 2, the impact of a process-orientation (i.e., a focus on productivity operationalized as headcounts and reimbursements) decreased engagement with clients and reduced continuity in care as staff turnover increased. At the same time, headcounts and revenue increased. These gains were reduced, however, as turnover costs mounted. In the words of Osborne and Gaebler (1992): "What gets measured gets done ... if you can't reward success, you're probably rewarding failure."

Since the publication of *Reinventing Government*, there have been ongoing efforts to embed results-oriented approaches in for-profit businesses as well as non-profit human service organizations. The impact of a results orientation in these organizations has extended its reach all the way into the design of résumés and hiring practices. That is, the traditional focus on specific skills, competencies, and knowledge has been replaced on résumés to an emphasis on demonstrating one's ability to achieve results and get things done. Innovation based on results-oriented approaches has been reported in case studies from the private sector, such as Best Buy's Results Oriented Work Environment (ROWE) paradigm (Johnson, 2015; Stevenson, 2014). ROWE endorsed and increased discretion for corporate managers and teams for determining when and where they work. It was their choice as to whether or not they met with leadership on projects and they selected their own approaches to succeed in meeting results-oriented goals. The caveat, however, was that managers and teams were fully accountable and responsible for their results and could be fired for not reaching desired goals. Turnover was reduced up to 90% in some departments and productivity increased as much as 41% (Stevenson, 2014).

Lawmakers, funders, publicly funded assistance centers, private foundations, and other groups devoted to improving human service organizations have maintained efforts to create results-oriented organizations with the intent of reducing wasted resources and orienting organizations to client outcomes. Early efforts by lawmakers, such as the Government Performance and Results Act of 1993 stimulated ROMA, or Results Oriented Management and Accountability. This performance-based management system was designed to preserve the anti-poverty focus of community action groups and to promote greater effectiveness among the state and local agencies receiving Community Services Block Grants (CSBG). Over one thousand community-based agencies across the country have had access to support, training, and resources surrounding ROMA for improving results monitoring and accountability. In child welfare, the Child Welfare Information Gateway, funded by the Administration for Children and Families, provides links to multiple private, federal, and state supported interventions, training, and resources that help social service providers improve and use results-oriented measurement systems. Technical assistance centers funded by federal, state, and providers themselves help support training, education, technical assistance, and intervention to improve the use of results in assessing outcomes within human service providers. Federal funding agencies, such as the National Institutes for Health, have invested in staff development efforts to deploy results-oriented approaches in their own work and activities. These and other examples show that an array of organizations have recognized the value of employing a results orientation to improve services. The question is whether they can do it in ways that foster healthy cultures and climates in which these systems are embedded.

Applying feedback and goal setting evidence. At the core of these efforts to improve services via results-orientation is the belief that focusing on client results, such as improvements in client well-being rather than process (e.g., the number of clients served) can increase staff engagement and commitment as well as subsequent service quality and outcomes. According to Osborne and Gaebler (1992), "Organizations that measure the results of their work—even if they don't link funding or rewards to those results—find that the information transforms them." The implication for human services is that assessing improvements in client well-being encourages the leaders and staff to focus on client well-being and directs employee efforts toward improving results. However, researchers who study performance feedback and practitioners who use feedback data agree that the transformation to a results orientation requires considerably more work than the idea implies (see Kluger & DeNisi, 1996). At the same time, the research on the effects of measuring and employing outcome results in well-designed systems—systems that are supported by appropriate mental models, aligned organizational priorities, supporting organization processes, and positive social contexts—provides evidence that such systems can improve service quality and outcomes.

Three comprehensive reviews of empirical research provide support for developing a results orientation in human service organizations. These reviews include research on performance feedback (Kluger & DeNisi, 1996), self-regulation (Burnette et al., 2013), and goal setting (Locke & Latham, 2002, 2013). These comprehensive reviews and the conceptual frameworks they provide are based in multiple theoretical models backed by empirical research. Kluger and DeNisi's (1996) integrated model for performance feedback draws on other theoretical work from goal-setting theory (Locke & Latham, 2002), control theory (Carver & Scheier, 1981), action theory (Frese & Zapf, 1994), action identification theory (Vallacher &Wegner, 1987; and the theory of learned helplessness (Mikulincer, 1994). Taken together, this research confirms that providing feedback that drives focused effort and strategy development can achieve the outcomes desired in a variety of organizations. This research also identifies mechanisms and practical factors that must be addressed to ensure success.

Closely linked and often integrated into research, goal setting and performance feedback support common mechanisms of influence. Outlined in a comprehensive review of 35 years of research by two pioneers in goal-setting research, Locke and Latham (2002) concluded that goal setting, such as results feedback, impacts performance by (1) directing attention to what should and should not be addressed and (2) directing energy toward meeting desired results. Additionally, goal setting (3) bolsters persistence for achieving results and (4) stimulates arousal, discovery, or use of new knowledge and strategies that lead to goal success. Empirical evidence of Locke and Latham confirms that establishing high standards for desired results increases focused efforts toward achieving those results, particularly if there is specificity in what is to be achieved. The comprehensive reviews provided by Locke and Latham (2002) as well as Kluger and DeNisi (1996) reinforces that individuals search for alternative strategies when existing strategies prove unsuccessful in achieving results. Simply stated, if one wants to increase the amount of effort directed toward achieving results, set high standards for desired results, monitor them, and provide specific feedback. And if increased effort for reaching high standards for results doesn't lead to success, pay attention to assisting and supporting individuals in their search for strategies to achieve the desired results.

Although results-oriented goals and feedback direct energy toward the desired results, reviews of goals setting and performance feedback indicate that other factors moderate these effects. These moderating factors must be addressed to support the use of results feedback and goal setting in a service improvement effort. Research suggests that both the commitment to achieve difficult results (e.g., improving the mental health of clients) and the complexity of the work or tasks being accomplished can influence whether results feedback and goal setting will be successful in improving performance. Within the human services world of behavioral health, child welfare, and social services, complexity is an established characteristic. The more difficult and complex the task to be accomplished, the greater the need for commitment to achieving desired results. Ironically, we have long known that complexity can be addressed within human service work by creating bureaucratic work environments that simply ignore complexity and routinize (rather than individualize) services (Glisson, 1978). That is, the complexity of work can be reduced to completing paperwork to document specified steps in applying cookie-cutter approaches that require the same procedures for each client. We see this frequently in child welfare systems, for example, when guidelines require that each caseworker make a specific number of mandatory visits at set intervals—and regardless of whether the child is doing extremely well in an ideal setting or the child is doing poorly in a problematic setting. The point is that such specifications, while intending to establish a minimum standard of care, eliminate the discretion required for addressing complex cases. And when a service provider no longer feels they are providing individualized, high-quality care, their engagement suffers.

The importance of this research is that in addition to the presence of feedback, the level of commitment needed to address complex work demands requires attention. That is, human service providers must value the importance of the desired results and have conviction that their efforts can make a meaningful difference in achieving these results (i.e., self-efficacy). Multiple approaches have been proposed to enhance the importance of the desired results. These approaches include (1) developing public commitment to high standards for results, (2) leader communication and support of a vision for the importance of achieving the desired results, (3) establishing incentives, and (4) having service providers participate in establishing standards for goals with a clear sense of purpose and rationale. Using participative approaches to set the level of results that will be monitored and used to guide performance is found to be most successful when the rationale and purpose for preset goals are provided to staff appropriately. That is, simply allowing participation in setting standards for results without providing the purpose or rationale are less effective (Locke, Latham, & Erez, 1988). For example, the approach taken by Agency A in our example from Chapter 2 for achieving results is not well suited for complex tasks. That is, demanding difficult-to-achieve results for complex and demanding tasks by simply saying, as did the Agency A leaders, "get it done or else," does not work as well as it would for simple, straightforward tasks such as routine work on an assembly line where the purpose is clear.

Research suggests that leaders can address self-efficacy in complex tasks by (a) providing adequate training to ensure mastery, (b) establishing role models with whom the service provider can identify, and (c) using persuasive communication that expresses confidence that the service provider can attain the goal (Bandura, 1997; Locke & Latham, 2002; White & Locke, 2000). In other words, access to mentors who have shown that attaining results is possible, providing necessary skill development to achieve results, and building the providers' confidence in their ability to accomplish desired results through persuasive and motivational communication can alter efficacy. Just like effective coaching in a team sport, the ability to provide strong and passionate encouragement, connecting staff with successful others, and developing core skills can build the confidence and belief in one's ability required to succeed in complex work with high standards.

Central to these research findings is that complex tasks (e.g., achieving success in human services with complex client cases) and establishing demanding standards for these challenging tasks have the potential to lead to poor results. Poor results can occur when the energy aimed at achieving challenging results begins to narrow attention to limited cues and strategies that may be ineffective. This is particularly true if the uncertainty and unpredictability arouse high levels of anxiety and stress. In other words, under high anxiety or stress, our focus can narrow our attention to a singular strategy or a small number of specific strategies as we scramble to find an immediate solution. In these situations, attention to broader cues, alternative strategies, and systemic processing of information to achieve success becomes more difficult (Christiansen, 1992; Eysenck, 1992; Lewinsohn & Mano, 1993). Self-efficacy is the critical moderator. If one's self-efficacy is low, the perception of risk in challenging, complex work tasks is increased along with anxiety and stress. For those with high efficacy, they are more comfortable with high standards, show more commitment to difficult standards, and are better at handling negative results (Latham, Winters, & Locke, 1994; Wood & Bandura, 1989). In negative social contexts marked by punishment and minimal safety to discuss errors, anxiety can quickly dominate. In complex and demanding tasks such as those faced by human service providers, having challenging, results-oriented goals and monitoring client results to drive improvement requires the careful design of work settings. Organizational systems and processes must buffer potential risks to self-efficacy, help address the complexity of the work being done, and continually support the importance placed on achieving desired results. Leaders' and colleague's mentoring, encouragement, and active support in helping front-line service providers to solve complex cases and to maintain high perceptions of efficacy are essential. Opportunities for learning and processes that promote strategy development by front-line service providers must be in place. Effective teams that support effective problem-solving steps, continuous improvement processes, and activities such as brainstorming to identify alternative paths to success are essential in addressing the complexity. In addition, the training to build skills and a repertoire of strategies for responding to challenging cases must be available. This must be coupled with leaders' communication and encouragement for the importance of the work and the recognition and reinforcement for improving clients' lives. Although not exhaustive, these mechanisms increase the chances for success and for optimizing the impact that a results orientation has on the quality of care and outcomes. These mechanisms provide strategies and skills for complex work while lowering the risk of stress and building perceptions of self-efficacy. These mechanisms of support reinforce for all organizational members that the importance of improving client's lives is paramount to the organization's efforts. At the same time, these mechanisms do not guarantee success, which introduces the third area of research for creating a results-oriented approach, which is altering mindsets, mental models, and implicit assumptions.

Mental models and mindsets for a results-orientation. Mindsets, what we describe as the mental models and underlying implicit beliefs that support them, are critical to creating a results-oriented organization. Improving services require mindsets that guide a clear, undiluted focus on client results. The focus cannot lie solely on process results, such as headcounts or billable hours, or the amount of paperwork standards being accomplished. In the words of Jack Welch, the well-known CEO of General Electric: "Kick bureaucracy at every chance and poke fun at anyone who tries to install process for process's sake." Organizational members' mindsets must shift from relying on process outcomes to the broader and more challenging idea of achieving results. ARC strategies are designed to improve the social contexts of organizations and develop mental models and assumptions that complement the organizational priorities in each of the ARC principles, including a priority on client results. When staff and leaders are enmeshed in bureaucratic processes, red tape, and paperwork and unable to consider data on results as nothing more than bureaucratic minutiae, the challenge of improving services goes beyond simply introducing new data systems. It requires a change in the shared assumptions and conscious reasoning among members of the organization about data and its significance.

A results-oriented mindset is not associated with structured, rigid patterns of thinking that rely on routine processes. That is, results-oriented mindsets include essential beliefs that client outcome results are the primary concern and that positive results require multiple alternatives and innovative new approaches to achieve those results. In contrast, process-oriented mindsets focus on routinization and standardization while avoiding innovation and risk. We have worked with child welfare organizations that hold an inordinate amount of fear of being criticized for mistakes by the media, regulators, or funders. In some systems, leaders work with external stakeholders to manage these pressures. In others, leaders develop mindsets of protectionism where controlled approaches that accept minimal success are satisficing as long as work efforts are documented and no major incidents occur. In a results-oriented work environment, the shared mindset veers from a preoccupation with avoiding crisis to embracing the idea that innovation and flexibility are required for individualized care and optimal results. Mentioned earlier, ROWE (Results-Oriented Work Environments) requires shifts in mindsets that are difficult for more traditional leaders who rely on procedural rules, routine, and standardization. As described by one of its founders, process-oriented leaders with complex work challenges hold the following belief: "You're going to get the best out of people if you give them rules and make them stick to rules." The founder also describes the distinct nature of mindsets of employees in a results-oriented work environment. "Something happens to you when you feel like an adult again at work. It's the control, but it's also the clarity on top of it . . . I now need to know what my results are supposed to be so I can prove that I'm getting there" (Stevenson, 2014).

Results-oriented consultants urge leaders to promote the sharing of stories about their clients. They suggest one should take time to "walk in the shoes" of their clients, thinking about what they experience, what their needs are, and what priorities they may have (Mills-Scoefield, 2012). That is, instead of seeing work as a set of procedures or rigid steps that are followed and completed, a results-oriented mindset fosters envisioning the needs and experiences of clients and being responsive to them. The mindset of walking in the shoes of clients promotes both sensitivity and responsiveness to clients' needs. The latter has been identified as a marker for distinguishing human service cultures that succeed in using results feedback data to drive improvement versus those that are not as effective (Hodges & Hernandez, 1999). Cultures that expect the use of meaningful results are distinguishable by their appreciation for the importance of client results and its role in improving provider responsiveness. Members of these cultures view results-oriented feedback as invaluable for correcting and improving their services to clients. And not surprisingly, these perceptions are embedded in settings (cultures) that support a willingness to take risks to improve results.

Empirical research supports that participants' mindsets influence the impact that results-oriented feedback and goals have on their achieving results. Burnette and colleagues provide a comprehensive review of research that illustrates how implicit theories and corresponding mindsets influence self-regulatory processes, and in turn, determine reactions to feedback results and goals (Burnette et al., 2013). They describe how *incremental* and *entity* implicit theories drive self-regulatory processes when responding to results-oriented feedback and challenging goals (Dweck & Leggett, 1988; Molden & Dweck, 2006).

Implicit theories are assumptions or beliefs that without full awareness guide the meaning we experience from events. Incremental theorists hold an implicit belief that human attributes, such as intelligence or empathy, are malleable. In contrast, entity theorists hold an implicit belief that human attributes are stable and fixed, focusing more on trying to control or manage a fixed characteristic rather than attempting to alter it. Although implicit (i.e., operating without conscious awareness), these assumptions guide the conscious representations of events (mental models), reasoning about events, decisions, and actions. Applied to the challenge of expectations or standards for achieving client results, individuals holding entity assumptions approach the challenge with more trepidation, anxiety, and thoughts of failure that trigger strategies to protect themselves against failure. Incremental theorists, on the other hand, perceive challenging results-oriented goals as obstacles to conquer and opportunities to build capacity and skill.

In work environments characterized by high expectations, entity theorists are more likely to self-handicap or apply learned helplessness strategies than incremental theorists, even prior to reviewing their results-oriented feedback. Framing and mindsets determine how one experiences high standards for results as well as the reactions to those experiences. Those who hold implicit incremental theories are less likely to focus on whether poor results will show they are incompetent. Instead, they are more likely to focus their efforts on discovering strategies and increasing abilities to achieve difficult results. Those holding implicit entity theories are more likely to engage in self-handicapping approaches that can be used to explain their poor performance on factors they cannot control.

The important point is that implicit assumptions and corresponding mindsets determine whether results-oriented feedback and high standards contribute to improved outcomes. Success in improving human services is in part a function of whether the feedback and standards lead to self-handicapping or strategies to acquire the skills to achieve the desired results. What is critical, however, is that these deeply held assumptions are not necessarily fixed. That is, Burnette and colleagues cite evidence that these implicit assumptions are malleable and situation specific. This is critical to ARC's strategies for altering shared mental models and assumptions that influence organizational members' decisions and actions related to the results-oriented principle. The evidence suggests that these fundamental assumptions are influenced by the social context (e.g., culture and climate) and learning, as well as by the series of experiences and results that lead someone to hold a fixed or alterable theory.

We conclude that implicit assumptions related to improving human services can be altered through experience and socialization. ARC strategies that we have incorporated in working with organizations nationwide focus on creating organizational social contexts that support learning and development, even in the face of errors and mistakes, and shift shared assumptions of organizational members toward incremental mindsets. As organizational members recognize that problem solving and strategy development are supported—and that assistance to develop skills is available, experiences that could promote a sense of threat and risk are instead framed as changeable events that can be controlled and influenced.

We have observed service providers in poor social contexts who inundate new hires with messaging, examples, and attributions to unfixable entities for failure, socializing new staff in expectations that nothing can be done to improve the results of the services they provide. The initial enthusiasm and assumptions of improving client well-being held by newly hired staff in these settings are replaced by assumptions that both the organizations in which they work and the clients they serve are inherently fixed and unchangeable. The strength of these processes can be seen within individual organizations as individuals shift positions. We have watched clinicians driven by incremental theories in their work with clients begin to adopt an entity perspective as they take supervisory positions within rigid structures where leaders endorse fixed and negative assumptions about staff. The new supervisors are socialized into behaving as though staff is inherently lazy, chronically unmotivated, or innately inept when performance falls short. These examples of shared mindsets and assumptions within organizations are powerful forces in guiding members' reasoning, attributions, decisions, and actions, but they can be altered. ARC strategies are designed to alter them by introducing new principles, including a results orientation, and addressing the underlying assumptions that organizational members use to interpret and react to their work environment.

The impact of beliefs and assumptions on results-oriented services. The entity versus incremental mindset and corresponding shared assumptions can characterize the members of an entire agency or organization. We find, for example, that members of organizations with the poorest OSCs share implicit assumptions that organizational performance is fixed and cannot be altered to improve services. Organizational members, including leaders, believe that the organization is simply too ineffective or broken to improve and that efforts to fix it will fail. Individuals in these organizations can believe in their personal ability to do meaningful work with clients but also believe their successes occur despite their organization, not because of it. Strategies to build a results orientation must address these shared assumptions of organizational members. In ineffective organizations, staff is already predisposed to avoid what they view as futile engagement in efforts to deploy results-oriented feedback systems or to identify and address service barriers, particularly at an organizational level. These assumptions are prevalent in organizations with high staff turnover, burnout, emotional exhaustion, and disengagement with clients. In our work with organizations, we reference these indicators to trigger discussions of the shared assumptions preventing change and discussions of alternatives to not believing in or attempting change. These discussions provide the basis for directly addressing negative assumptions, which often leads to such statements as, "If you don't believe you can make a difference, how are you effective in this work," that are integral to creating support for a results orientation.

Service providers within organizations interact with each other in building mental models or representations that guide reasoning about clients or families and that can be harmful to improvement efforts when based on fixed theories. In our hospital study of emergency pediatric care, hospital personnel who worked in the ER with our "worst" culture profile promoted an internal, shared representation of not having parents involved in medical care. This shared internal representation (what we described as "mental models") depicted parents literally as too stupid to be involved in their child's care. It suggested that considering the needs of parents interfered with high-quality care and indicated that parents had to be separated from providers. Underscoring their representation of parents was an implicit assumption that parents impeded the care their child received. The nurses we interviewed provided examples that supported their beliefs, such as a mother who could not understand the medical information they provided about her dying child. When interviewed in groups, others shared stories that described parents who lacked the capacity to learn, were not emotionally stable, or were otherwise unable to contribute to quality care. Although each of these can occur, no examples of helpful parents were noted.

We concluded after watching these nurses function that they were unable to recognize parents with the capacity to support the care of their child or those with the knowledge and judgment to contribute critical information or ensure treatment compliance. We have also observed these assumptions in child welfare agencies where the staff shares beliefs that their clients cannot be helped. When these beliefs are implicit among staff and leaders, they are reluctant to monitor results based on improvement in their clients' well-being and are resistant to being held responsible for client outcomes. Staff in these work environment believes they should not be held responsible for failures and, in the worst cases, for the results of clients. When questioned about whether services should continue given no evidence of client results, service providers typically refer to process, affirming that they follow the legal mandates and do everything they are required to do. Used in this way, completing process requirements is used to justify service providers' beliefs that clients are to blame for failures and that clients cannot be helped.

Just as importantly, leaders' implicit assumptions about staff affect their framing, evaluation of events, and reactions to those events. When data reveal poor results, leaders who believe deficiencies are fixed within their staff, such as a lack of ability or motivation, tend to push staff members with threats or to simply replace them. These leaders fail to assess performance as a function of organizational characteristics, their own leadership, or the ineffectiveness of their training or mentoring systems. When holding an implicit assumption that fear and pressure are good motivational tactics, leaders use punitive and aggressive actions toward staff to achieve the outcomes they desire. The subsequent effect on staff is rejection of a results orientation, linking poor results and punishment (not learning), and the expectation that the leader will hold them responsible for results that are not under their control. The fixed versus changeable assumption is only one of many shared assumptions and beliefs that influence a successful results orientation. Others include shared beliefs that data cannot measure improvements in client well-being or that monitoring client well-being is dehumanizing and inappropriate. Another example is the belief that monitoring results impedes service improvement efforts by interfering with required processes such as paperwork requirements. These beliefs and their origins are at the core of being process oriented and demonstrate the impact of shared beliefs and assumptions on the reasoning and behaviors required for results-oriented services.

In process-oriented service organizations, shared assumptions and corresponding behaviors are not appropriately focused on improving client well-being as an organizational priority. Service and outcome data are collected mostly to meet the requirements of funders, regulatory agencies, or ensure reimbursement. In these work environments, staff members share mental models that suggest monitoring client outcomes is a required job task, rather than a meaningful activity that provides staff with information to guide decisions, actions, and paths to improved service. These mental models are reinforced among staff and leaders who are often inundated with data collection demands from multiple funders, regulators, and other stakeholders. These demands divert the organization's focus from using results to support service improvement to meeting funding or regulatory requirements. There are no inferences or connections between the data being collected and the potential for improving client well-being. Instead, organizational members frequently view data collection as meaningless bureaucratic nonsense that has to be completed, which increases the likelihood of their rejecting a results orientation. Beliefs shared among these members suggest that monitoring client well-being data actually degrades the quality of care. For example, staff conversations regarding data demands frequently center on how data collection reduces the time spent with clients and negatively affect alliances between service provider and client. In organizations that are results oriented, these conversations and conclusions are less likely to occur. If these concerns do arise in results-oriented organizations, the discussions are to examine how the data can be used or how the time required for collection can be minimized so that the other client data can be used to improve care.

USING ARC TO BECOME RESULTS-ORIENTED: A CASE EXAMPLE

As explained in Chapter 2, Agency A used data to attend closely to productivity rather than improvements in client well-being. Both leaders and staff held implicit assumptions that monitoring data alters behavior, not only from personal experience in their work setting but also in applications they had used with clients. Second, they understood the importance of processes and systems to support the use of feedback, including a user-friendly information system and clear goal-setting processes. Reward structures expressed as recognition, promotion, and advancement, as well as reinforcement by reducing management control over programs meeting productivity goals all reflected their clear understanding that data feedback is a powerful management tool.

Mid-level leaders, managers, and supervisors of Agency A viewed data feedback as a way of controlling and motivating front-line service providers to increase productivity. That is, they shared an implicit assumption and mindset reflecting McGregor's (1960) Theory X, versus Theory Y. That is, people are inherently lazy and have to be pushed to work (Theory X) versus people are attracted to meaningful work and motivated to accept responsibility completing their work successfully (Theory Y). Given the shared mindset in Agency A, little emphasis was placed on developmental or mastery-based approaches when reviewing data. Their Theory X approach was reinforced by the gains in productivity they produced and leaders' recognition that their approach did not require elaborate processes or sophisticated problem solving. Leaders identified simple strategies that improved productivity and instructed staff to follow them. Unfortunately, leaders and managers failed to recognize staff turnover, dissatisfaction, and disengagement was associated their approach to increasing productivity. Instead, attributions for turnover and disengagement were ascribed to unmotivated staff, reinforcing their Theory X mental model and escalating their commitment to their approach.

The ARC specialist who worked with Agency A faced the challenges of focusing leadership and staff on client well-being and helping leaders to understand that employing client feedback for improved outcomes would require a different approach. That is, monitoring client results and deploying feedback would not be effective by simply demanding that goals be met for improving client well-being. The greater complexity of achieving improved client results required additional mechanisms, including problem-solving techniques and continuous improvement processes at the program level to eliminate service barriers. Success also required a different leadership approach and mindset; one that supported learning, innovation, and mastery over control of staff, as well as greater psychological safety among staff in discussing errors, problems, and barriers.

The ARC intervention introduced leaders to the ARC principles, their impact on fostering highly effective social contexts, and their current deployment within the organization. During this work, executive leaders were frustrated that their front-line service teams were not accessing client outcome data via the information system they had installed. This frustration opened the door to a two-pronged approach using the ARC process that would embed a results-oriented priority. One approach assured a parallel emphasis and structure for client results that was on par with the agency's emphasis on productivity. The second approach was to create a social context where front-line staff could employ tools and processes to identify and address barriers to improving client results. This altered social context required a shift in managers' and supervisors' approaches to using feedback results and in their allowing increased levels of discretion and input for front-line teams in deciding how to improve their results.

The ARC strategies include organizational tools and processes to strengthen a results orientation. The biggest challenge for Agency A, however, was to shift the mental models and approaches that were being used leaders and supervisors. The ARC specialist began this process with executive leaders by examining the difference between the use of productivity data and the use of outcome data focused on client well-being. This process increased the awareness among leadership that a system for monitoring client results created an important gap in their data system. This discovery led leaders to examine their expansion efforts and increased focus on finances and productivity in light of the diminished focus on client results. Several of the leaders expressed their concern when realizing that they had extensive processes for monitoring and incorporating productivity data into program assessment and planning but had little capacity for monitoring and using data on client well-being. To ensure that the leaders' deployment of a new system for monitoring and using results data did not continue to follow the same approach they had used for productivity data, the ARC specialist and ARC liaison directly addressed the leaders' frustration that front-line staff were not using available data on client well-being. Specific activities for increasing the leaders' understanding of the need for a new approach to using results data included (1) sharing alternative models of feedback deployment and their implications for improving human services, (2) establishing the complexity of efforts to monitor and improve client well-being, and (3) providing information to leaders that described the status of their efforts to use results-oriented data. We explain these activities in more detail in the following paragraphs.

First, contrasting models of feedback based on control and monitoring versus development and mastery were examined. Designed for use in the ARC strategies, these models outline key elements that distinguish between the two approaches and have different implications for complex work tasks such as improving the well-being of social service and behavioral health clients. Among the key elements are implicit models that underscore the different approaches (e.g., Theory X versus Theory Y); the nature of contrasting supporting systems and their implications (e.g., using punitive disciplinary approaches that focus on failures versus developmental approaches that use errors to create new strategies); and leadership behaviors that foster or inhibit psychologically safe environments for staff to openly discuss problems and barriers. These models represent explicit attempts to alter or enhance mental models for effective feedback in complex task environments. Each of these elements was discussed with leaders in relationship to their frustration with the staff's minimal use of the available outcome data. That is, each of the elements were assessed to determine which would create an environment where front-line teams would be more likely to seek out and use results in their data systems to suggest improvements in client care.

Second, leaders were guided in exploring the nature of the work for achieving client results on improvements in well-being versus monitoring productivity. This process was conducted to build a clear distinction in the minds of leaders between work tasks with straightforward solutions and more complex, uncertain work tasks that require continual adaptation, adjustments, and problem solving. Many of the executives had been direct service providers earlier in their career, so they understood the link between the challenges of improving client care and the need for safe environments where staff could use tools and processes to discuss problems, barriers, and deficits impeding client success without fear of reprisal. Fortunately, this examination of the complexity of a results orientation focused on client well-being helped leaders reconnect with the mission of the agency and to the challenges that clients present to front-line staff. In the words of the CEO, "This takes me back to just how difficult it was to solve some of the client problems I faced when I was working the frontline."

Third, information was gathered about the agency's efforts to create change using results-oriented data. The ARC specialist learned from conversations with executive leaders and front-line staff that discrepancies existed in their respective perceptions of how managers and supervisors were using data. Feedback included revisiting OSC baseline results (see Chapter 3) to discuss how the organization's high rigidity scores were linked to productivity data and its use with staff. Direct feedback from staff was gathered anonymously regarding how results-oriented data created feelings of risk for staff and the need for transparent processes that allowed staff to address barriers, errors, and problems that led to poor results. Additionally, the ARC specialist shared observations with leaders throughout the ARC process that included examples of effective data usage that were driving learning and improvement in outcomes within front-line teams.

The information that supported a need for improvement in the organization's use of results-oriented data led to the ARC liaison and specialist collaborating with the managers and leaders to alter their use of feedback. A critical element of these activities was maintaining psychological safety for staff when reviewing results data (see Chapter 8). Simultaneously, the ARC process included work by ARC front-line teams in collaboration with OAT members to establish measures of client wellbeing that could be monitored and reported along with productivity data, with the agreement that problems would be addressed by collaborative efforts to identify service barriers with the support of leaders. Leaders agreed to allow time for the front-line to ascertain reasonable baselines for client outcomes and to set up data monitoring at regular intervals. And, front-line staff learned to use the ARC component tools (see Chapter 7) to identify and address barriers that were leading to poor results. Simultaneously, the

ARC liaison and specialist reinforced among leaders the benefit of a learning and mastery-based approach to using results-oriented data while maintaining expectations for improved results.

Some managers who were successful using authoritarian approaches with productivity outcomes found it challenging to alter their behavior. Leaders also struggled with the results-oriented findings that two of their highest productivity teams were moderately poor on measures of client success, an outcome of the teams' efforts to maximize billing without equal attention to the quality of care. However, there was recognition that punitive approaches did not support the optimal use of data for improving services whether assessing productivity or client well-being.

11

IMPROVEMENT-DIRECTED VERSUS STATUS QUO-DIRECTED HUMAN SERVICE ORGANIZATIONS

Leaders, middle management, and line-level service providers in improvement-directed organizations are never satisfied with the status quo and never stop looking for more effective ways to improve the well-being of the clients they serve (Glisson et al., 2016a). This principle addresses the conflicting priority represented by the tendency of individuals in formal organizations at all levels to resist change and cling to established protocols, regardless of whether the existing protocols promote improvements in the well-being of clients. Although the term "continuous improvement" is well known and popular in a variety of business and industrial sectors—and to a lesser extent, in human services—it is a challenge for organizations to continuously improve. Improvement-directed organizations continue to invest effort and resources in updating core technologies, modifying bureaucratic processes, and addressing service barriers to improve performance.

In our work with human service organizations over the last few decades, we have collaborated with many organizational leaders who focused to some extent on improvement and capacity building in their organizations; however, we met few leaders who had made it a priority before incorporating ARC strategies. Our experience is that even those organizations that report having adopted continuous improvement provide modest evidence of its implementation. The discrepancy between the ideal of continuous improvement and actually incorporating improvements into an organization's management in a way that improves services is a function of the expectations that are placed on organizational members. Improvement-directed work environments expect members to be invested in improvement, interested in alternative ideas, and eager to identify and address service barriers. This requires that members understand how decisions and actions, as well as processes and systems, fit together to improve client outcomes. The members must focus on the broader organization and how it can be improved to maximize effectiveness. This focus requires that members move beyond their immediate job tasks and personal experience to incorporate information from other members, levels, and divisions during their improvement efforts.

Organization members' pursuit of mastery, knowledge, and optimal strategies to improve their organization fosters interdependence and a sense of team within improvement-directed organizations. Leaders, managers, supervisors, and front-line providers share information, knowledge, and experience with each other to understand their organization as a complete system. In our work with ARC teams, the objective is to encourage the discussion of ideas, solutions, and strategies among line-level service providers to begin the process of identifying and addressing service barriers. Among leaders, program supervisors, and front-line providers who comprise the Organization Action Team (OAT), the objective is information exchange and discussion in a joint effort to solve problems and implement ideas generated by the ARC teams. These exchanges increase the organization's capacity to improve client outcomes. To do so, however, requires a commitment across organizational programs, levels, and departments to understand, coordinate, and facilitate functions so that the organization can deliver services effectively.

The ARC strategies for building improvement-directed organizations reflect a prerequisite that leaders elicit and attend to information and ideas from their front-line service providers. This attention to the contributions of front-line service providers encourages the identification of service barriers. It assures accurate feedback to determine what is and is not working, and it drives collaboration on incorporating suggestions from front-line staff that improves their organization's service capacity. Service improvement requires that front-line service providers receive information about proposed changes, agree with the reasoning behind the changes, and have opportunities for influencing decisions regarding improvement plans. The use of ARC and OAT teams introduced in Chapter 4 provides the organizational structure for leaders to collaborate with front-line staff on proposed changes and to address the capacity of the organization to eliminate service deficits.

Improvement-directed organizations employ mechanisms to provide feedback on client outcomes that support change. That is, feedback on client outcomes described in the previous chapter is used to identify problems, suggest innovations to address service barriers, and focus resources on the implementation of new practices. Within ARC, the ARC front-line teams and OAT teams use this feedback to initiate problem-solving steps and processes across organizational levels to eliminate barriers to high-quality care.

ARC provides the structure and process for generating improvement plans from the ARC teams, having the plans endorsed and improved by the OAT, and testing the plans within the organization. Improvement-directed organizations use these

ARC's structure and processes on an ongoing basis to ensure that their efforts to address service barriers continue. These organizations employ ARC generated improvement proposals, action planning, and assessments as needed for successful implementation efforts. Examples of efforts include the introduction of EBPs, changes in organizational rules such as referral criteria, or changes in procedures such as the intake process or case assignments. Improvement-directed organizations promote agreement among leaders and organizational members for change efforts by employing the ARC tools, mental models, and principles that support service improvement across organizational levels. The application of ARC principles, tools, and processes leads to consistency and agreement across all levels of the organization on what and how needs are addressed.

Within improvement-directed organizations, the sustainability of improvement efforts requires recognition and reward structures that share information regarding successes and increase members' awareness of improvement opportunities. Sustainment also requires that successful program directors and managers mentor others who attempt similar improvements. These protocols, efforts, and mechanisms are aimed at building the organization's capacity for improving services at multiple levels, whether at the front-line, managerial, systems, or organization-wide level.

NORMS AND EXPECTED BEHAVIOR WITHIN IMPROVEMENT-DIRECTED ORGANIZATIONS

Members of improvement-directed organizations share expectations for improving their individual skills and capacity for service, as well as those of their colleagues. In contrast, members of status quo–directed organizations expect that their skills and capacity for service will remain relatively unchanged and that improvement efforts will fail to alter practices already in place. These shared expectations for the status quo stimulate little investment in innovation and support passive and active resistance to change that is aimed at retaining familiar procedures and processes. For members of improvement-directed organizations, the expectation of positive change is associated with the expectation that client outcomes should drive problem solving and strategy development. Positive results gained from new approaches or change efforts are recognized, rewarded, and shared by leaders. These leaders work to identify and praise the staff members who contribute to improvements. Among front-line staff members, successful improvement is reinforced when team members celebrate their successes. We commonly witness a spirit de corps and camaraderie in these types of social contexts. These contexts generate norms and behaviors that include members actively seeking out other staff members and program leaders to learn from their experiences, knowledge, and expertise using new tools or approaches that contribute to successful improvements.

The expectation is that staff in improvement-directed organizations will routinely identify and examine areas of weakness and seek assistance in addressing those weaknesses by building skills and capacities. It is important to note that this same behavior can be interpreted as incompetence in status quo-directed organizations while it is valued and reinforced in improvement-directed work environments. As a result, leaders in improvement-directed organizations expect to provide ongoing mentoring and training for their staff and take steps to access requested resources needed to support those activities. Sharing knowledge, tactics, and strategies with other organizational members following training is the norm in pursuit of improving client outcomes. Unlike status quo-directed organizations that stick to well-worn paths, new approaches generate interest and commitment to testing rather than resistance. Expectations reinforce positive beliefs about improving services even when innovations or technologies are externally introduced. That is, norms focused on learning remain even when responding to the requirements of funders, accrediting agencies, and others. The important point is that the challenge of improvement and change does not create a fear of failure in improvement-directed organizations; it is viewed as an opportunity for additional potential success.

Discussion and analysis of alternative ideas for change are the norms in improvement-directed organizations. The need for resolving contrasting approaches and conflicting priorities is expected. These organizations' social contexts are flexible and open to change as opposed to rigid and resistant (see Chapter 3). Organizational members welcome opportunities for reviewing alternative views and encourage the assessment of current practices and policies. When poor outcomes occur, organizational members expect performance to be openly addressed and examined. Unlike status quo-directed organizations where members expect no change and explain failures on factors beyond their control, the staff in improvement-directed organizations engage in a normative pattern of searching for practices that can be changed to improve services. Members' attributions for poor performance in improvement-directed organizations focus on factors that can be altered, such as policies, procedural specifications, skills, or practices. In other words, while the members of many organizations identify reasons why improvement is unrealistic, members of improvement-directed organizations look for and expect to find solutions. Little effort is invested in attributing blame to an individual or focusing on causal factors that cannot be addressed. We have found that members of improvement-directed organizations rarely engage in disparaging messaging or rumination over what is uncontrollable. Instead, they challenge themselves and their colleagues to identify and address service barriers to improve client outcomes.

Leaders must actively develop the expectations and patterns of behavior in improvement-directed organizations. Leaders have to foster positive attitudes, mindsets, and beliefs (see Chapter 8) that promote improvement and ensure that mechanisms and processes are in place to support learning and problem solving. Just as importantly, the leaders celebrate successes, share stories of improvement, and reinforce excellence. Leaders promote service improvement as a core value of the organization and reward it in practice. When working with others, leaders model learning behavior and facilitate the behavior with explicit examples of their own learning and strategy development. This includes leaders seeking resources for training and workshops and fostering work environments where innovation and change are encouraged. Individuals who initiate new approaches or improvements are encouraged to share their successes with others in their organization, and they are provided the necessary support to help others adopt their innovations. In these ways, leaders champion new ideas for change in their organization, elevate the value of learning, and recognize and reinforce improvement efforts—all while diffusing successful innovations throughout their organization.

Leaders who promote learning must contribute to the shared beliefs that encourage organizational improvement and change. They recognize the need to alter behavior and reasoning away from simply reacting to crises to a proactive mindset that seeks opportunities for improving services. These leaders move members from a narrow focus on individuals and tasks in their immediate work environment to a longer and broader vision of the organization as a service system composed of multiple interrelated parts. In this way, leaders reinforce systems-level thinking where members examine improvement beyond their immediate department or program, and they foster relationships among organizational members to support integrated change.

Leaders of improvement-directed organizations understand the importance of their relationships with front-line and supervisory personnel in collaborative problem-solving and improvement efforts. The leaders of improvement-directed organizations ensure that supervisors' and managers' ideas and improvement efforts are recognized for their role in envisioning and creating change. These leaders recognize that the results of many individuals' efforts are not always clear to all members of the organization, such as a financial director's improved accounting system that facilitates staff reporting requirements or a receptionist's role in introducing the organization to new clients. They therefore explain and emphasize these links for organizational members by highlighting the work of all members in achieving client results. The leadership objective is to create a shared mindset among organizational members who focus on the organization as an integrated whole, where members understand their own roles in influencing and improving outcomes as part of a much larger system of efforts that include a variety of work behaviors that support improvement.

EVIDENCE ON BECOMING IMPROVEMENT DIRECTED

Strategies for creating improvement-directed organizations are used in multiple human service areas, including health care, social services, and mental health (Birleson, 1998; Lindberg & Merideth, 2012; Shortell, Bennette, & Byck, 1998). These efforts are aimed at developing flexible, innovative, and responsive organizations with the capacity to improve services while responding to continually changing political, economic, and knowledge environments, as well as supporting the complex work of serving clients. Employed across many hospital settings and applied in an increasing number of mental health and social service settings, continuous quality improvement (CQI) and similar strategies have become familiar and widespread to support innovation and flexibility.

Popularized by W. Edwards Deming in work that helped revolutionize Japanese manufacturing after World War II, CQI migrated from industry to other business organizations to human services, gaining considerable expansion into health care beginning in the 1990s. Early research on continuous improvement efforts within health-care providers yielded mixed results, yet leaders of health-care settings remained committed to CQI as a pathway to improving health care (Blumenthal & Kilo, 1998). Shortell, Bennette, & Byck (1998) reported promising results when looking specifically at CQI interventions aimed at clinical outcomes. More importantly, however, they provided additional insight into the mixed results and factors influencing CQI success. In their review of clinical studies, they described several factors that bolstered the impact of CQI including physician support and involvement, quality feedback to providers, and supportive organizational cultures. Using a framework introduced with additional colleagues (O'Brien et al., 1995), they concluded that improvement efforts address strategic, cultural, technical, and structural components surrounding CQI to ensure its success. For example, leaders using CQI and similar processes must use it in alignment with strategic goals (strategic); promote a work environment that supports discussing and openly addressing errors and problems (cultural); assure effective training on CQI and clinical practices (technical); and provide structural mechanisms for change such as improvement teams, improvement committees, steering teams, and redesigned communication and command structures. Our experience supports this framework that distinguishes successful versus unsuccessful efforts at fostering improvement within human services organizations (see also Solomons & Spross, 2011).

The research and trade literature identify key organizational characteristics that support the effective use of continuous improvement processes and efforts to build learning organizations (Birleson, 1998; Bersin, 2012; Garvin, Edmondson, Gino, 2008; Mancini & Miner, 2013). The key characteristics include: (1) systematic problem solving, (2) experimenting or testing new approaches, (3) gaining knowledge from their own experiences and history, (4) learning from others about the experiences and best practices that have been successful for them, and (5) transferring knowledge quickly and efficiently throughout their own organizations (Garvin, 1993). Consistent with ARC's three core strategies, the organizational characteristics necessary for continuous improvement are supported by the ARC principles, component tools, and mental models.

To illustrate, a CQI process provides the tools to identify and address service barriers in organizations that place a priority on learning and improvement. These processes increase knowledge of core causes to service barriers and foster potential solutions and strategies. Learning continues as the knowledge is put into practice in the planning, implementation, and evaluation processes that occur to achieve and assess success. Evidence suggests additional tools and processes are needed to support and sustain continuous improvement. For example, as indicated in our previous chapter, clear measurement processes and valid measures of service outcomes (Bickman & Noser, 1999) are essential to continuous quality improvement in social services and mental health. Organizations that are improvement directed rely heavily on teamwork and collaborative problem solving. Teamwork capitalizes on the input, ideas, and engagement of multiple organizational members to identify effective improvements and change, as well as implement efforts that reach across organizational levels, departments, and organizations (ARC's participatory-based and relationship-centered principles).

The practice and research literature agree that building improvement-directed organizations requires not only new tools and processes to create the capacity for improvement, it also requires supporting normative behaviors (cultures) and mindsets (mental models) that support learning and development (Mancini & Miner, 2013). Perhaps most importantly, as suggested by Garvin (1993), CQI requires a shared commitment to learning. Precision and practical specificity of CQI tools and mechanisms that put theory into practice are necessary but not sufficient without the norms that support their application and the mindsets that encourage learning and change. Several recent case studies of social services and mental health organizations illustrate how they have transformed into improvement-directed, learning organizations (Birleson, 1998; Lindberg & Meredith, 2012). In each example, leaders created mindsets and norms that supported improvement-directed behavior.

A leader's effort to encourage improvement-directed behavior begins with building an organizational context that supports innovations such as best practices (Solomon & Spross, 2011). Leader's collaborative efforts with staff help develop and maintain shared vision, enthusiasm, and strategic plans and objectives for being improvement directed. The leader's focus on learning and improvement is further supported by the allocation of resources and the commitment of time to improvement activities, problem solving, and strategic planning. This support is also expressed in the provision of concrete tools, processes, and mechanisms for organizational members to affect change. During efforts to embed improvement-directed thinking and processing among organizational members, leaders recognize and reinforce improvement efforts (see Bersin, 2012; Garvin, Edmondson, & Gino, 2008). Most importantly, leaders model and promote an array of behaviors that support learning within the organization. They actively question and listen to employees and prompt dialogue and debate, and they foster norms of inquiry and dialogue. When leaders allocate time for reflection and the application of knowledge for improving services, they establish norms for learning within the organization. The application of these norms depends on a systems approach: this approach is consistent with our research and experience and suggests that a combination of organizational tools, priorities, and mental models are needed for the development of improvement-directed organizations (Senge, 2006; Smith, 2001).

CASE STUDIES: THE IMPACT OF SYSTEMS, BEHAVIORAL NORMS, AND UNDERLYING ASSUMPTIONS

Below we provide case studies illustrating the importance of multiple organizational strategies to build effective services. These include improving systems and processes, establishing expectations that support a focus on improvement in client well-being, and addressing the beliefs, assumptions, and reasoning of organizational members that drive their actions and decisions.

Improving organization processes and systems. As we described in Chapter 2, the staff and leaders of Agency B believed that client well-being should be the primary consideration in all decisions and actions and were committed to altering clinical approaches to improve outcomes. The importance of focusing on clients and their improvement was expressed in their attention to clients' needs, such as responding promptly to client phone calls and concerns. The staff shared the expectation that they would be available and responsive to their clients. Additionally, compassion and concern were expressed in interactions with clients by clinicians, managers, receptionists, maintenance personnel, and executives. Nevertheless, staff and leaders believed they could be doing more to improve the services they were providing. They had failed in several improvement efforts, such as deploying a new measure of client well-being and implementing a new EBP that had been supported by a funder. Agency B's failures in the implementation of innovations to improve services did not result from members rejecting new ideas, resisting change, or the leaders' rejection of staff input. Their failures were due to weaknesses in their processes and systems for supporting, guiding, and sustaining the change they sought.

When the leaders were asked about the processes that supported their improvement efforts, they were confused and asked, "Do you mean for clients?" The ARC specialist explained that it included client-related processes but that it also included processes for eliminating organizational barriers to success, such as poor communication, the allocation of resources, or the service providers' need for support services. Leaders were open and enthusiastic in their response: "We would love to strengthen those processes!" They had a desire to learn, but the organization did not have the structures, processes, and systems in place to support learning and the identification of organizational barriers. They had no formal structure and process for continuous improvement. Leaders and staff simply addressed problems reactively as they arose, creating a crisis-driven work environment that put out one fire after another. Front-line teams openly shared ideas and information with each other to address client issues that arose, but the issues seldom focused on identifying the underlying long-term organizational factors that continued to influence service quality and outcomes. This reactive approach was reflected in their data monitoring. They collected standardized measures of client well-being for funders, but the programs were evaluated on recent anecdotal experiences with clients or incidents that occurred during the previous week. Understanding such incidents is necessary in identifying service deficits but not sufficient for improving service systems.

In response to questions about the need for training to address skill deficits, program staff said they discussed new approaches and training on a regular basis, but there was seldom follow-up action. The discussions occurred in regular front-line service provider meetings; however, as explained in Chapter 2, basic teamwork tools such as note taking were never used. On the positive side, meetings did include discussions of cases identified as having poor outcomes and the potential strategies to address these outcomes. When the need for additional training, a change in organizational policy, or program redesign would arise, no plans were presented to formulate the next steps to be taken. Follow through was limited. Unlike agencies that had lost their focus on improving client well-being or those that resisted change due to inertia and a reluctance to leave well-worn paths, Agency B leadership and staff were willing to learn and comfortable in discussing ideas for change but were unable to translate ideas into the actions required to address the identified issues.

Although improvement-directed organizations do not tend to be rigid and resistant, the example of Agency B illustrates that they do require the structures and processes necessary to support improvement efforts. The necessary structures and processes include procedures for assessing client outcomes at different levels, ranging from individual client results through agency-wide data on client outcomes. The assessments must allow improvements in client well-being to be examined at all levels: client, clinician, program, and organization. In addition, structures and processes are required for reviewing service outcome data to identify associated service barriers. Finally, organizational structures and processes are required to support the problem solving and action planning that addresses the identified service barriers within the organization.

ARC provides the necessary improvement-directed structure and processes with the ARC and OAT teams described in Chapters 4–6 using the three ARC strategies (i.e., principles, mental models, and component tools). To be improvement-directed, these teams use processes to identify and address service barriers at all levels, from altering an ineffective practice to changing an organizational-level policy. The training, mentoring, and coaching to develop the skills and efficacy required for success support these teams and processes. In other words, improvement-directed organizations are created and sustained by integrated systems that promote the staff collaboration, participation, and innovation necessary for problem solving, learning, and improvement.

Decisions, behaviors, and actions. A community-based, behavioral health agency located in the Northeast that we will call "Agency Learn," provides a clear demonstration of an improvement-directed organization. Its CEO, who had received an invitation to an introductory ARC meeting as part of a large funded study, e-mailed our office to request additional information about ARC before attending the meeting. The CEO also requested permission to bring additional members of the agency's leadership team, including the director of clinical services and the director of quality improvement and training. The

CEO and executives who attended the introductory meeting were attentive, articulate, and authentically interested in learning more about ARC and its implications for their organization. It was clear to us that they had read the material we provided and were intent on gathering as much information as possible about the project. They used the information we provided to expand their understanding of how their organization could be strengthened in serving clients. In our discussion following the meeting, we noted how different they behaved in comparison to two other leaders from another agency that attended the information meeting. These two leaders were affable and socially skilled, but their focus drifted in the meeting. They read and responded to their text messages and rejoined the discussion at intervals to support a point made by other leaders interested in ARC or to provide a witty comment to entertain the attendees. For the most part, they were not listening for content.

Towards the end of the meeting, we asked the group of leaders about their level of interest in ARC and whether they would like to consider participating in a project. The members of Agency Learn spent several minutes in focused discussion before the CEO replied, "We believe in what ARC is designed to do and I personally would like to see our organization participate." Before completing his comments, one of the other leaders who had drifted in and out of the group conversation, yet who listened closely to Agency Learn's CEO, quickly indicated that their organization would be conducting ARC as well. Agency Learn's CEO then continued by indicating that their final decision would be made after discussing ARC with their front-line program supervisors and others. One of the leaders who had asked few questions and seemed a bit disconnected with the discussion indicated that he knew his staff would be fine with their decision and gave his immediate commitment to the project. What was particularly striking about the commitment was that we knew he had paid limited attention to the details of the project and to the discussion that had occurred. Our view was confirmed later by another member of the organization who said that the leader returned to the agency after the meeting to report, "Everybody else was getting on board so I knew we needed to as well."

Agency Learn committed to participating in the project, and we worked with the agency for three years. The reflective, learning-oriented, and participative norms associated with Agency Learn in our initial meeting were not the only qualities that distinguished the organization. Not only were its leaders and members open to adapting their own thinking and approaches to the new ARC strategies, they thought about success in an integrated, systems manner. That is, they recognized that change and improvement influenced all their organizational members and that all organizational members had to be partners in creating effective change. There was recognition among members of the organization that improvement requires complementary changes in multiple systems of the organization and that improvements could not be restricted to a narrow CQI process or training program. In contrast, members of status quo–directed organizations frame the implementation of improvement processes as something that can address a poorly performing program or subdivision of the organization without requiring change throughout.

Members of status quo–directed organizations only marginally recognize that success is impeded by broader system failures in multiple areas such as hiring practices, training, and communication, and that service improvement requires more than isolated attention to parts of the organization.

Agency Learn members' understanding of this point was reflected in our subsequent work with the agency at all levels, including program supervisors. Beyond being reflective and open to new information while others in more status quo–directed organizations displayed skepticism and resistance during implementation, members of Agency learn recognized other facets within their organization to further support new approaches or tools acquired from the ARC strategies. For example, in the monthly ARC team leadership training on ARC component tools (Chapter 7), Agency Learn's supervisors and ARC liaison would report on what worked from the previous month's training as well as on additional efforts they had taken to develop their use of ARC processes and tools. Before we reached later stages of sustainability in the ARC process, they had integrated many tools into their organization's systems, including employee training to support the use of ARC tools. It was clear to us that they were pushing the ARC intervention along instead of being guided in enhancing their capacities and practices to support improvement. In some cases, they improved our processes and training tools to increase effectiveness.

Unlike ARC participants who need to be carefully guided and supported in addressing their fears, concerns, and small problems that arose, Agency Learn's members were predisposed to additional insights that could strengthen their implementation. They were supportive, open, and helpful to each other and to other organizational supervisors who tried to create improvement. In ARC's monthly training sessions that included program leaders from multiple agencies, Agency Learn's members openly shared their knowledge, additional tools, and even resources and connections to help other agency supervisors enhance their own effectiveness with clients. They invited other agency supervisors to attend trainings at their agency—trainings that were being conducted to respond to clinical weaknesses that they were experiencing in their own organization. And they helped make contacts for other agency supervisors in the broader community to help them strengthen critical links to additional services that could help improve services to clients. All of this was done with sensitivity to the other agencies' difficulties and a complete absence of arrogance. It was simply done because it helped support high-quality services, more effective capacities, and improved client care. We learned a great deal from working with Agency Learn, the most important of which is not all organizations begin at the same point in their improvement effort.

Beliefs and assumptions. The type of learning environment created by Agency Learn is difficult to achieve. As we have explained, resources and time are required for developing integrated systems, processes, and tools that support an improvement-directed organization. Our experience also suggests that becoming an improvement-directed organization requires more than just supporting tools, systems, and processes. It requires shared mindsets and underlying assumptions that drive improvement and learning. Our mental models chapter highlighted the importance of holding an implicit theory that abilities and other characteristics are changeable (incremental) rather than fixed (entity). The implicit theory influences how we frame our work as well as guides strategies for success. As we have explained, these implicit assumptions can be learned. An example is that of OSCs where new staff members come to believe via their emotionally exhausted and burned-out colleagues that nothing can be changed or improved. This assumption is at the heart of one of the most prominent barriers facing external consultants and internal change agents who often give up after being frustrated and derailed from their efforts to improve human service organizations that continue to fail.

Within improvement-directed organizations characterized by the capacity to learn, there is a shared belief among members that things are not in fact fixed or unalterable. There is an even more fundamental belief that continuous improvement, learning, and capacity building are critical paths to achieving success. While members of status quo–directed organizations believe that continuous change and improvement put their agencies at risk, members of improvement-directed organizations believe that not changing and making improvements guarantees failure. Members of status quo agencies fear that adaptations to processes, structures, and approaches create instability and fragility by eroding what is familiar to them while those in improvement- directed organizations focus on enhancing processes, structures, and approaches in a way that meets their shared goals. Members who fear change envision negative outcomes resulting from altering processes, expecting chaos if front-line staff members are given the discretion to help make changes. They envision disparate improvement ideas pulling the organization in different directions. They are unable to envision how altered structures, processes, and approaches can be cohesively integrated across multiple organizational systems within effective improvement-directed organizations. The reason for this difficulty in envisioning the positive potential in change is they do not hold implicit assumptions associated with successful, improvement-oriented organizations.

For those who work in improvement-directed organizations, there is an implicit assumption that improvement processes and change cannot be successful without considering the multiple parts of the system and how each of the parts influence the whole. Our example of Agency Learn pointed out how front-line supervisors worked on additional changes in other processes and systems to ensure that changes would be sustained. That is, they held the implicit, underlying assumption that change must be embedded in a social context where all parties, systems, and processes are aligned with the same priorities. Building improvement-directed organizations depends on systems thinking: that is, searching for and understanding linkages and relationships between processes and approaches to create an integrated whole (see Senge, 2006).

Members of improvement-directed organizations assume that addressing daily crises and events does not replace investing effort in long-term plans for improvement. That is, there is a shared assumption that a crisis-driven work environment diverts energy and attention away from long-term problem solving. This assumption is reflected in leaders' recognition and support for reflection and planning within their organizations and active efforts to put processes in place that proactively address upcoming crises and problems. What we know from experience is that the most effective organizations allocate time for long-term planning and strategy development for broader improvement. In practical terms, these organizations ensure that reflection and planning take place at all levels to address the factors contributing to daily crises persisting as a function of service barriers.

More specific to the ongoing activities required for improving services, individuals in improvement-directed organizations share underlying assumptions and beliefs that bolster individual learning and capacity building. These beliefs and assumptions distinguish successful from unsuccessful learning organizations. In improvement-directed organizations leaders, managers, and staff believe that unintentional errors and problems are opportunities for improved learning, skill development, and capacity building for staff and teams. Members of organizations that demonstrate little or no learning or capacity for improvement react differently to errors. These ineffective behaviors include simply not doing anything, overreacting using punitive approaches, or hiding errors and problems. Punitive reactions are backed by assumptions that explain poor performance as laziness or lack of motivation and an assumption that the use of intimidation is a useful motivational tool.

Implicit assumption that errors can be used to create learning and improvement are encapsulated in various beliefs that individuals hold about their own learning. Both front-line providers and leaders have talked to us about the beliefs they sustain to strengthen learning. For example, a leader described how he trained himself to stop his emotional escalation and assignment of negative attributes to others when hearing views or perspectives that conflicted with his own. He consciously used a mental model that explained conflict or disagreement as a function of missing information that might enhance his understanding and capacity to resolve the problem. His mental model included his inability to listen and learn when he experienced negative emotions while hearing conflicting views. His new model included the assumption that one cannot know everything and that others hold conflicting opinions out of their own knowledge and experience. His model also contained the expectation that if he listened closely and tried to understand other perspectives, he gained knowledge that increased his own ability to influence change. The implicit assumption of his new mental representation (mental model) of conflicting views is that disagreement can lead to additional information that is missing or needs to be uncovered. As highlighted in Chapter 8, these types of thinking patterns can be taught and reinforced to develop mental models for learning.

ARC is designed to promote the development of assumptions and beliefs that support an organization's capacity for improvement. As shown in the example below, we guide activities at all levels to target specific assumptions directly related to altering mental models to enhance this learning and capacity building.

BECOMING AN IMPROVEMENT-DIRECTED ORGANIZATION

Agency B, introduced in Chapter 2, was characterized by the desire, willingness, and psychological safety necessary to support learning and improvement. However, the organization did not have the necessary tools and processes to support learning and an improvement-directed work environment. We explain below how ARC strategies were used in Agency B to develop the tools and processes to support learning and improvement. As we discuss later in our description of Agency B, these efforts also addressed fundamental assumptions that were hindering their efforts to be a highly successful, improvement-directed organization.

ARC provides an ordered approach for organizations to implement innovations that address service barriers. Our initial work with leaders in Agency B focused on preliminary steps to build a foundation for introducing improvements. These preliminary steps included identifying strategic measures or outcomes to monitor the improvement process, establishing the leaders' commitment to their responsibilities for supporting change, and clarifying the leaders' reasoning and objectives for engaging ARC strategies.

Given the work environment in Agency B that we described in Chapter 2, supervisors of front-line teams engaging in ARC, the OAT team, and upper leadership all benefited from initial training in the use of basic meeting tools that supported planning and follow-through with action items. The training included the use of note taking, establishing and following team meeting rules, stating clear objectives for meetings, and the use of pre-meeting and post-meeting reviews. These initial steps prepared Agency B program teams and leaders for the planning and implementation of service improvements. Basic team tools such as using inquiry and dialogue skills, team problem-solving steps, action planning, and brainstorming helped staff and leaders create continuity in their efforts to improve. The biggest changes, however, occurred with enhancements in their data monitoring and feedback system and the introduction of an improvement process to analyze and address service barriers interfering with the quality of care and outcomes.

The ARC teams in Agency B learned to apply continuous improvement steps to scan data, identify barriers, analyze causes, propose solutions, and enact plans to address the barriers. To reinforce these efforts, feedback processes were created to ensure ongoing monitoring of key indicators of improvements in client well-being at both the program and organizational levels. Consistent with ARC processes described in Chapters 4–6, these efforts were driven by the front-line service providers comprising the ARC teams. These providers worked with leaders and OAT members to establish easy-to-understand graphs of client progress on meaningful client outcomes for monitoring client and program success. Although progress was made in using data, meeting protocols, team tools, and problem-solving steps to identify and address service barriers, progress truly began when front-line program staff experienced the responses and reactions of leaders to their proposed change. The first barrier the program staff proposed to address was one that had been identified by staff members previously, prior to their engaging in the ARC process—one that had hit a dead end with no explanation. ARC's improvement process and mechanisms for change, including the initial proposal created by the ARC team and the OAT team's support for enacting the proposal, contributed to a level of improvement that was unexpected by staff. The elimination of the barrier, therefore, created an increased level of engagement by both staff and leaders. The commitment and involvement of staff, as well as the support of leadership, triggered many more proposals and a series of successful collaborations with receptive leaders to continue the improvement effort.

The success of the initial efforts required more than the ARC tools and processes. In the beginning, the CEO struggled with a concern that the increased attention being paid to processes and tools might diminish the staff's intrinsic passion for their work and their focus on improving clients' well-being. That is—and this is a key point in understanding the agency's social context—she held an implicit assumption that too much structure and process could misdirect the agency's core mission of serving clients. This assumption troubled her as the ARC process began to produce client measures and feedback that staff would monitor on a regular basis. Her experience some years earlier in a centralized, process-driven organization was that client feedback results led to the punitive use of data that demoralized staff and increased turnover.

The ARC specialist and ARC liaison worked with the CEO to alter her underlying beliefs to include the idea that structure, process, and monitoring client outcomes did not preclude a focus on improving client well-being, nor did it prevent staff from retaining their passion and desire to serve. Her stated concerns actually made a positive contribution to the organization's improvement effort by leading to discussions that reinforced with staff a clear focus on remaining mission driven throughout the ARC intervention and on sustaining the passion and intrinsic motivation to resolve the complex problems staff faced in serving clients. Her experience with the changes that resulted from the ARC process altered her views of structure and processes as she saw program staff engaged in follow-through behavior beyond talking about improvement to focused work within their programs to implement improvements.

While we were preparing for ARC, Agency A lost one clinical treatment program because of low productivity yet gained the capacity for improving client care and met productivity goals in other programs as the ARC process continued. Increases in psychological safety encouraged staff to discuss issues, errors, and problems that supported personal improvement and learning. Combined with the CEOs insistence that anecdotal stories of qualitative improvements in client well-being be recognized as well, the feedback on measures of client well-being sustained a focus on client improvement. Perhaps most importantly, the CEO altered her mental model and assumptions regarding the structure and process necessary for innovation, learning, and service improvement. She stated later that the experience helped her recognize that her effectiveness as a leader depended on a balance between maintaining staff passion and intrinsic interest in their work with maintaining the structures and process to ensure that ideas and plans for improvement were followed by action. Fortunately, the CEO also gained an understanding that she had to trust and support, without directly intervening in, her staff's efforts to address service barriers while avoiding becoming sidetracked with daily crises. This proved important for the organization as it allowed her to promote training and other support mechanisms that were necessary for long-term, sustained change.

Before concluding the ARC process, two additional changes occurred in the organization. First, staff members and leaders adopted another assumption in their work. From the beginning of their participation, both staff and leaders routinely spent time addressing crises on a day-to-day basis. They had difficulty relinquishing this approach and tended to use the new ARC processes and tools to focus on immediate critical incidents. The ARC strategies and support of the ARC liaison helped staff and leaders recognize that although critical incidents influenced service improvement, a long-term vision of improvement was needed or the organization would forever be stuck in addressing only the immediate needs that resulted from the sequence of crises. That is, an underlying shared assumption of the members of improvement-directed organizations is that long-term success requires looking beyond the immediate crisis. Both the ARC specialist and liaison worked with leaders and staff to explore the implications of addressing primarily immediate crises versus looking at long-term improvement efforts. This comparison resulted in organizational members using periodic analyses of service barriers to find core causes that required extended efforts and action plans to resolve. In response, leaders and staff planned semi-annual retreats, free of their crisis-oriented work environment. In these retreats, broader, long-term issues could be explored, analyzed, and prioritized to identify barriers, establish action plans, and create objectives to meet over six months.

Finally, given the level of enthusiasm and desire to learn among members of the organization, the ARC specialist and liaison, along with the CEO, worked with supervisors of several ARC program teams to identify collectively the shared mental models they used as a way of learning for colleagues in other programs. This led to identifying and distributing literature on models of learning that could be associated with addressing service barriers. That is, models of learning that dealt with underlying assumptions that inhibited learning and improvement-directed behavior in the organization could be explored. Through social diffusion, other teams started to use these new ways of thinking to improve their team's functioning and success.

12

PARTICIPATORY-BASED VERSUS AUTHORITY-BASED HUMAN SERVICE ORGANIZATIONS

In participatory-based organizations, front-line service providers collaborate with middle managers and leaders to identify service barriers, prioritize needs, and contribute to solutions that address both practice and policy issues (Glisson et al., 2016a). The participatory-based principle describes the active, open participation of front-line staff, middle managers, and top administrators in decisions about practices and policies that affect the well-being of clients. Placing a priority on participation improves the organization's capacity for building knowledge, its openness to change, and the sustainment of improvements. A participatory-based priority counters the conflicting priority of administrators prescribing innovations to improve services in a top-down manner without the benefit of the experience, knowledge, and input of managers, supervisors, and frontline service providers.

THE POWER OF PARTICIPATION

Front-line service providers in participatory-based organizations are included in the key decisions that affect their work and the services they provide. These service providers recognize the value that managers and leaders place on their input and collaborate with leaders and other organizational members to share ideas, information, and knowledge. Their engagement and sense of responsibility and commitment to change is expressed in their interactions with colleagues as they obtain and provide ideas and solutions for achieving shared objectives and goals.

Participatory-based organizations are characterized by a mutual respect for the opinions of coworkers—respect that extends across positions, titles, and the formal hierarchy. When an ARC front-line service team proposes a successful innovation to address an identified service barrier, leaders respect and defer to the team's practice experience and expertise. Middle managers seek opinions and support from front-line service providers in their own efforts to address service barriers. Participatory-based organizations are not characterized by rigid hierarchies of authority and centralized decision making. Subordinates are not supervised exclusively by dictates from above, and there is the shared expectation that barriers to effective services and quality of care are best addressed in a collaborative fashion. Leaders and managers expect that their input will be valued and sought by staff because of expertise and respect, not because of title or position. Also, in times of crisis, the staff will follow the lead of the leaders and managers. However, the leaders, managers, and front-line staff in participatory-based organizations understand that no one individual or group of individuals has sufficient expertise to address all service barriers, but that the members of the organization collectively have the knowledge and expertise to achieve desired improvements and outcomes.

Leaders in participatory-based organizations recognize their limitations in understanding the practical barriers and problems their front-line staff experience when providing service to clients. Unlike authority-based organizations that seek control through centralized hierarchies and decision making, leaders in participatory-based organizations recognize that centralized decision making limits the contributions of experience and knowledge from the individuals who make the decisions that affect client care. Leaders in participatory-based organizations, therefore, depend on the input of front-line staff that know the idiosyncrasies of their work impeding implementation or improvement efforts. The leaders build an environment that encourages and supports the open and honest input from front-line staff. The value that leaders place on staff input enhances and sustains staff commitment to change by improving their sense of autonomy and control over a shared mission and purpose.

Participatory-based organizations improve by drawing upon the talents, skills, and perspectives of those providing the services. Instead of viewing direct service providers as automatons on an assembly line, leaders recognize the differences and strengths among the individuals who provide their organization's services. Leaders understand that their role is to help staff coordinate their varied skills to maximize their collective contribution to organizational performance. Improvement efforts often include working with staff to redefine individual work roles and responsibilities. In this way, the diversity of ideas, skills, and expertise among staff contribute to effective approaches that evolve from a community of providers who share responsibility for improving services.

The emphasis on integrating the knowledge and skills of staff at multiple levels of the organization enhances learning in participatory-based organizations, both individually and collectively. This emphasis also promotes development and growth that is sustainable. Sustainability is a function of more informed decisions and approaches that are reinforced by success and increased commitment to decisions and approaches made in a participatory manner. The contributions of members at different levels ensure that the organizational improvement processes and procedures have been collaboratively implemented by organizational members. For example, direct service provider input in identifying barriers and logistic problems while planning for a best practice implementation improves staff commitment and the feasibility of plans by allowing for preliminary critiques and adjustments prior to implementation. Unlike authority-based organizations that do not value input from front-line providers before implementation, participatory organizations are less hampered by negative staff perceptions and attitudes that interfere with success. Instead, both line-level staff and leaders perceive problems during implementation as issues that both staff and leaders share responsibility for identifying and addressing.

In participatory-based organizations the identification of service problems flow in both directions, up and down the organizational chart, as does the shared commitment to support efforts across organizational levels. Participation across levels increases access to essential information for both leaders and front-line service providers. Conversely, authority-based organizations restrict access to information to maintain power and control, often granting access as a privilege to reward selected individuals. In participatory-based organizations, power is exercised by sharing information to build expertise through collaboration. This requires that staff members have full access to information that will contribute to the organization's success.

In our experience, participatory-based organizations do not gain buy-in from subordinates on ideas that are generated solely by the leaders. In organizations that are authority based, however, it is common for participation to be touted by leadership to convince staff they have input into decisions that have often already been made. The intention is to increase commitment to centralized decisions by creating the impression of participation. When staff input is consistent with the centralized decisions, follow-up messages emphasize that staff input was heard and used. When staff input is inconsistent with the centralized decisions, attributions to factors beyond the leaders' control are cited, apologies are made for having one's hands tied, or more simply, no feedback is provided at all. The shared belief among leaders in authority-based organizations is that they are increasing staff commitment by allowing staff to express their opinions without appreciating the value of the staff contributions.

Leaders of participatory-based organizations actually value and listen closely to staff input whether from frontline providers, middle managers, or other leaders. Our experience is that the openness to ideas from all levels in participatory-based organizations occurs in individual interactions and group-level interactions. We see this in both our ARC teams and OAT teams when they operate successfully (see Chapters 5–7). Leaders model information seeking and promote discussion among organizational members at all levels. Front-line service providers expect colleagues as well as leaders to seek information from each other and to closely attend to the information that is offered. It is assumed in participatory-based organizations that members will seek clarification and respectfully present counter arguments. The aim is to obtain additional information, whether one is speaking to a colleague or supervisor. Leaders model sensitivity to identifying and addressing unproductive disagreement or conflict. They foster expectations for this sensitivity among staff as they mediate conflict to deepen understanding and learning in the face of discrepant views. When differences in perspectives are evident, leaders model rational and neutral processing of these differences, exploring the conflicting ideas to promote learning versus unproductive conflict. Front-line team members follow these patterns. They learn to address conflicting views and to direct colleagues toward controlled inquiry and dialogue with the explicit purpose of learning more from their discrepant or conflicting views.

Organizational members in participatory-based organizations feel a strong expectation to follow strategic objectives that focus on mission and ensure that approaches lead to desired goals. That is, consistency and control are promoted through shared purpose, objective, and mission; it is expected that members will maintain this focus in all decision making, planning, and behavior. Within work teams, members of participatory-based organizations contribute what they know and work toward the shared objective of improving client well-being. Each member is expected to have a voice within the team, seek information from other members, consider conflicting ideas, and avoid behavior that limits input from others. When discussions, planning or meetings lose focus, team members redirect others to their shared mission or objective to return to the task at hand. In a crisis, members of participatory-based organizations accept more directive approaches and are committed to following directives if needed. To quote a leader with whom we worked in one effective participatory-based organization, "My folks don't waste time on extensive discussions when a crisis occurs and debate isn't possible. They follow my lead or someone else who holds the expertise. We discuss later whether we could have avoided the crisis or have taken a better approach." That is, participatory practices recognize the need for directives because staff members attribute leaders' directive behavior as necessary for solving an immediate problem, not as an ongoing approach that dismisses their valued contributions.

THE EVIDENCE BEHIND PARTICIPATORY-BASED APPROACHES

The value of participatory-based work organizations has been acknowledged in practice since the mid-20th century. Deming's *Total Quality Management* (1986) incorporated participatory approaches as a central requirement for improving the quality of manufactured products in Japan following World War II. Osbourne and Gaebler (1992) used case studies to describe a participatory-based approach in public service organizations. These case studies outlined several benefits of participation that included: (1) organizational flexibility, (2) innovation, (3) organizational effectiveness, and (4) improved employee productivity, morale, and commitment. Flexibility is improved by replacing centralized decision making with increased staff discretion to identify and address service barriers without burdensome approval processes. Second, as increased discretion and control are placed in the hands of those with firsthand knowledge of how to get their work done, effectiveness and efficiency increases. Decisions are based on detailed knowledge from front-line staff regarding constraints, as well as shared histories of failures and successes from previous improvement efforts. This knowledge includes extensive detail on practical limitations and strengths. Not only is front-line decision-making quicker as bureaucratic approval is diminished, the quality of decisions is improved by the knowledge and experience of those providing the service. Third, innovation is increased by freeing front-line staff from rigid procedures and structured guidelines to propose adjustments, test new approaches, and search for solutions to service barriers. Furthermore, the increased motivation and commitment to engage in these activities is linked to core motives such as understanding, control, and purpose. Satisficing these motives is central to improved outcomes as participatory practices support these motives and associated cognitive mechanisms such as creativity, collaboration, and feelings of satisfaction.

The positive effects of participatory-based approaches are attributed to commitment and satisfaction of staff, which result from their increased sense of responsibility, ownership, and pride in their work. Individuals are motivated to work harder and are more creative in solving problems when they share ownership and control of their personal work environment. As organizational members enjoy an increased level of participation in decision making and access to leaders, they experience greater integration with other members of their work team and a stronger sense of mission. Participatory approaches require greater collaboration and communication within and between teams, providing both positive social interactions characterized by trust and less reliance on hierarchical authority, centralized decisions, procedural specifications, and bureaucratic red tape that undermine one's sense of autonomy and control.

These positive outcomes of participation are a function of basic human motives. Social cognition research, neuroscience, and the trade literature have identified core motives that explain the effects of participatory-based approaches on human emotion and behavior. Daniel Pink's (2011) bestseller, *Drive*, provides a comprehensive review of motivation research that describes the innate need for a sense of purpose, mastery, and autonomy. Fiske and Taylor's (2013) *Social Cognition* provides a comprehensive review that explains social motives underlying the needs of belonging, control, enhancing self, and trust in social contexts. Recent neuroscience based models, such as SCARF (Rock, 2008), document human motives within our neurological systems that include status, certainty, autonomy, relatedness, and fairness.

This literature also explains the mechanisms through which the effects of human motives operate. From neuroscience, we learn that motives are basic in their functioning and guided by an overall approach-avoidance theme inherent in our neurological systems.

If motives are met, reward and pleasure systems within our brains are triggered; but if they are not met (for example, if we are socially isolated) we experience physiological reactions of physical pain, stress, or flight responses. When motives are satisfied, the stimulation of brain centers associated with reward and pleasure are accompanied by positive behaviors and cognition that parallel those achieved by using participatory approaches. That is, satisfying these motives triggers brain activation that supports increased perceptions of satisfaction, enhanced problem-solving, better decision making, creativity, increased innovation, as well as cooperation and collaboration (see Rock, 2008). Blocking or impeding these motives narrows attention, reduces problem solving, and increases discomfort.

As described in Chapter 8, social cognition theory suggests that threats to core motives, such as our need for certainty or understanding, stimulates conscious cognitive processing and reasoning to retain or regain a sense of understanding, control, and predictability (Fiske & Taylor, 2013, pp. 48–51). Despite the narrowing of cognitive functioning in reaction to threats, we more actively process our experiences to envision different ways of acting or thinking to increase our sense of control and understanding. These processes establish implicit monitoring mechanisms that are sensitive to potential risks or threats that may be repeated in the future. In other words, our brains actively respond to perceived threats and avoid the same negative event in the future by thinking through different alternatives or actions. We collect information from others and adjust beliefs and assumptions to form new inferences and strategies that prevent a future loss of control or understanding. If we are unsuccessful in this effort, options include attributing failures to circumstances beyond our control. Or, organizational members simply give up—a pattern we have seen frequently among overwhelmed service providers embedded in dysfunctional OSCs.

Although differences in nomenclature exist across these different lines of research, the core themes among motives include understanding and certainty, control and autonomy, status, relatedness, and a sense of purpose. Increased understanding and certainty are gained as participatory approaches provide access to information, explanations of the reasoning behind leaders' plans, and the opportunity to learn from other organizational members. Control and autonomy are increased as organizational members provide input into decisions and plans, experience greater flexibility in how they work, and are provided the opportunity to explore and implement alternative solutions to problems they encounter. Status for organizational members is improved as organizational members gain access to leaders and have the opportunity to influence organizational plans. When members are recognized for their input, treated as equals in multilevel teams, and rewarded for mastery and sharing of their expertise with others, then status motives are enhanced. When placed in the position to guide others and share their expertise based on personal success within the organization, their status increases. Finally, participatory-based strategies, such as reliance on teamwork and social interaction to identify and address service barriers, promote interrelatedness. Associated with a meaningful purpose and focus on improving client well-being, a sense of shared purpose among organization members stimulates a sense of relatedness and meaning. Satisfying these motives in our work produces physiological changes in our neurological functions that support complex problem solving, innovation, creativity, collaboration, and positive attitudes about the work.

Empirical support of participatory-based approaches. Meta-analytic studies describe variation across studies in the effectiveness of participatory-based change efforts, but participatory approaches influence performance outcomes such as productivity and various satisfaction indicators (Cotton, 1995; Cotton, Vollrath, Froggatt, Lengnick-Hall, & Jennings, 1988; Doucouliagos, 1995; Pollock & Colwill, 1987; Wagner, 1994). Wagner's (1994) meta-analyses of participatory studies suggest that participation's influence on outcomes may be modest, while several other reviews find that on average, participation has positive effects. What is apparent in these reviews, along with some mixed results, is the differences between the precise efforts of science in isolating mechanisms of action and the practical efforts to change organizations. That is, research reports better outcomes from more extensive, multidimensional, direct, and long-term organizational interventions, while the outcomes of more defined, limited, and precisely targeted participatory-based interventions that are not carefully supported by other strategies and tools demonstrate weaker results (Cotton, 1995). Broader more intensive efforts that include multiple strategies create alternative paths for explaining participatory effects when viewed from a science methodology lens.

Correlational studies conducted with existing organizations employing survey techniques are criticized for inflating effect sizes with common method error variance (i.e., self-reports on both participatory practices and the outcomes). These correlational studies suggest moderate relationships between participation and outcomes, including job satisfaction, organizational commitment, customer service, errors, burnout, and turnover intentions (Hulpia, Devos, & Rosseel, 2009; Angermeirer, Dunford, Boss, & Boss, 2009). Given their correlational nature, these studies provide no basis for inferring causation. Nonetheless, both studies of practical interventions that employ multiple strategies and correlational studies of existing organizational social contexts support the benefits of participatory practices.

Participatory approaches in organizations continue to be used in practical efforts to improve organizational performance, with some strategies expanded to include more comprehensive organizational improvement efforts such as empowerment initiatives (for reviews, see Spreitzer, 2008; Spreitzer & Doneson, 2005). These improvement efforts introduce additional participatory components beyond participatory decision making or participatory leadership practices to assure effectiveness. Outlined in several reviews, empowerment initiatives are empirically linked to indicators of satisfaction (with pay, promotion, and work), less turnover, and decreased job strain (Spreitzer, 2008; Spreitzer & Doneson, 2005). Beyond the effects on attitudes, additional performance outcomes include increased managerial effectiveness and innovativeness, employee effectiveness, employee productivity, and work unit performance.

In practical terms, studies of participatory-based approaches have moved beyond the question of their impact on organizational performance. The question now focuses on the mechanisms, paths, and variables that explain participatory effects and how the impact of participation is assured by attending to the mediators and moderators of participatory effects. Psychological empowerment, for example, has been identified as a moderator of transactional and transformational leadership's impact on innovative behavior. That is, transformational leaders' influence on innovative staff behavior is contingent on whether empowerment is high for staff, including staff discretion in initiating and controlling actions within their organization (Ismail, Zainuddin & Ibrahim, 2010; Pieterse, Van Knippenberg, Schippers, & Stam, 2010). Participative and consultative leadership styles are linked to organizational commitment as an antecedent of job satisfaction (Ismail, Zainuddin, & Ibrahim, 2010). Leadership trust has a stronger impact on employees' perceptions of having a strong voice in one's work when leaders practice and employ empowering behaviors (Gao, Janssen, & Shi, 2011). In education settings, teachers' public service motivation and its influence on educational outcomes is moderated by the extent to which teachers perceive work autonomy and discretion to affect their organization's service provision (Lynggaard, Pedersen, & Andersen, 2016). In an example from child welfare, the staff who feel included in decision making are more likely to voice concerns and less likely to disengage from their work (Travis & Mor Barak, 2010). And feedback seeking from leaders is influenced by participatory decision making through the mediating variable of job-based psychological ownership (Li & Qian, 2016). That is, participatory decision making in settings where staff experience psychological ownership leads service providers to seek feedback, helping to drive improved outcomes. In summary, these researchers and others are focused on understanding the mechanisms and paths by which participatory-based organizational strategies influence critical outcomes.

In other studies, researchers assess how organizational social contexts that are participatory in nature support effective practices. Consistent with the ARC model, researchers recognize the broader effects of participatory social contexts on a variety of organizational systems, outcomes, and processes. For example, in a study of over 2,522 health-care providers across 312 departments within a large U.S. health-care provider, participative versus authoritarian-based climates were linked to positive outcomes (Angermeir, Dunford, Boss, & Boss, 2009). Highly participative climates provided improved customer service, fewer clinical errors, less burnout, and lower intentions to leave the organization. Efforts to transform large, bureaucratic agencies suggest that failures are due to the influence of non-participatory cultures that constrain employee empowerment and overwhelm efforts to alter established cultures (Foster-Fishman & Keys, 1997).

Branch's (2002) chapter, "Participative Management and Employee and Stakeholder Involvement," describes the breadth of work in changing mindsets and multiple systems, processes, and organizational levers required to achieve success with participatory-based organizations. As we have explained throughout this book, our experience is that successful improvement efforts require change in more than just one isolated process or system within an organization. Consistent with Parnell & Crandall (2003), we find that changes in culture, ideologies, mindsets, and associated organizational processes and systems are necessary to ensure the positive effects of participatory-based strategies.

PARTICIPATORY-BASED APPROACHES AND ASSOCIATED BELIEFS AND ASSUMPTIONS

A premise of the ARC model is that beliefs, reasoning, and assumptions must be aligned with the desired behavior to enact the priorities of effective human service organizations. Participatory-based organizations require organizational social contexts and associated assumptions, mindsets, and beliefs that support participation. Participatory-based human services are linked to broader philosophies of care that are rooted in a belief that participation is an intrinsic value. This includes its embodiment within both service organizations as well as the broader community of service. Human service examples include encouraging and supporting clients' efforts to become more active in their own care decisions within a human service agency, or recruiting members of the community that is served by the organization to participate in policy and practice decisions through membership on organizational boards and committees. The idea is that the participation of clients is necessary for change efforts to assure effective and sustainable improvement in outcomes (Bess, Prilleltensky, Perkins, & Collins, 2009).

At the organizational level, ARC provides the structure and process for staff input into decisions, plans, and strategies. The success of this strategy requires a parallel mindset and reasoning that include core beliefs engendering participation. Parnell and Bell (1994) and Parnell and Crandall (2003) identified key beliefs surrounding the effective deployment of a participatory approach and its influence on empowerment. To be effective, those applying participatory approaches must believe the approaches will lead to increased effectiveness and that problem solving and solutions can be enhanced and improved by participation. This includes the belief that participatory efforts lead to outcomes such as improved client outcomes or productivity as well as the belief that staff motivation and commitment will be increased by participation. Success also requires that leaders believe participation does not mean a loss of control and power, or that power is not a zero sum game where increasing staff discretion and control reduces leaders' power.

An example of a participatory-based organization. We worked with a mental health agency that we label Agency Participation. The organization was characterized by openness among staff, a shared emphasis on collaboration and growth, and a history of using outside experts to support their improvement efforts. These characteristics encouraged members to share their experiences relevant to ARC's participatory principle. They described numerous efforts and processes they had already put in place to promote participation and active involvement of staff in decision making. They described self-selected approaches to client care and tailoring their program's design by front-line service providers. When questioned about why they engaged in these participatory efforts, they expressed multiple beliefs and rationales. First, a leader indicated that participation assured all staff was integral to their organization, that participation guides what they do, and that all shared the same purpose. Other leaders outlined beliefs they held, such as the belief that allowing staff more discretion and control increased staff commitment and performance. Another indicated that she had found over the years that inviting everyone into decision making and planning created better plans and solutions as well as increased commitment to solutions. When specifically asked for additional beliefs about participation, others stated a belief that success with clients and improvements had a lot to do with staff being more involved in decisions. The human resource director said he believed letting the staff make decisions, not only about clients but about how the program operates, reduced turnover and absenteeism. The CEO indicated that his belief in a more participatory approach developed over many years as he felt more comfortable allowing staff increased discretion and control. "What I discovered," he said, "was the more I was able to let go, the more my staff amazed me by what they could do. I had to trust them and if I did, they did extraordinary things." When asked if he felt like he lost power or control, he indicated that he always feared losing control but realized he gained much more power to achieve the organization's mission by trusting his staff.

When we talked to ARC participants at the front-line level, they expressed their satisfaction with having discretion and control of their work including, "I love this place because we get to think on our own and try things that make us more successful" and "We feel like adults who get to control our own work lives." They shared the belief that their leaders supported them and provided the resources they needed to get their jobs done. They also believed that their effectiveness with clients was dependent on engaging clients and families in the same manner. They agreed that successful client outcomes were due to client and family input into their treatment plans and decisions. The members of the agency shared a philosophy of participation that went well beyond the staff. Clients sat on advisory boards, were involved in part-time work within the organization, and served as volunteers. Others in the community, including providers from other agencies, were invited into the organization for training events and to discuss successful programs and practices.

When considering the opportunity to participate in ARC, the CEO made it clear that the decision to participate would depend on whether front-line programs agreed to the process. The CEO requested that the ARC specialist meet program staff to answer questions and concerns of front-line providers, program heads, and middle managers that would be participating in ARC. At the meetings, front-line staff asked thoughtful questions to evaluate whether a commitment to the ARC intervention and its associated workload would be balanced against gains in learning and service improvement.

The staff agreed to participate, and we quickly learned the depth of their emphasis on participation. We discovered that the staff worked effectively as members of program teams by promoting dialogue and inquiry to draw out ideas and contrasting opinions on best practices and approaches to employ with client cases. The program teams were involved in the selection of new staff, interviewing as a group each of the final list of candidates selected by human resources, and then working with human resources collaboratively to make a final decision. Individual service providers actively participated in their own performance appraisals via a 360 feedback system that allowed self-ratings as well as ratings from colleagues and supervisors. The supervisors and front-line staff members discussed progress on improvement in the areas they had jointly identified for capacity building. The assistance of other program members was sought and provided by staff members and supervisors to support capacity building. The feedback system provided substantial access to front-line staff for viewing their own individual results, their program results, other programs' results, and any reports created for leaders to evaluate programs and the agency. Staff members worked with program supervisors to set realistic goals based on feedback data, including input from leaders on trends in service outcomes.

Front-line teams also had access to budget information for their programs. Individual program staff members were provided discretionary funds for training; the teams could collaboratively allocate funds to support clients, families, or their own team resources. Although training was required to address regulatory concerns, most of the training decisions were driven by the front line. Staff described their key training needs while managers and human resource representatives worked closely with front-line staff to identify training options. When viable training options were identified, staff discussed with leaders the option they expected to provide the most benefit. After training, staff developed action plans based on what they had learned to test changes. They also reported their experiences to program leaders, often sharing useful skills or knowledge with other programs. Leaders also discussed plans with program leaders and staff to assist in disseminating new practices in multiple programs. This process encouraged other program leaders' involvement and subsequent discussion with their staff. Although all of this would seem overwhelming, it occurred quickly as all levels of the organization interacted in a focused manner to communicate and share information.

A decentralized, participatory process was also incorporated into the agency's discipline system. Ongoing performance appraisal processes by front-line supervisors addressed most deficits or problems before the discipline system was necessary. When disciplinary practices were needed, leaders approached staff members to discuss why certain inappropriate behaviors or actions had occurred. Leaders focused on whether organizational barriers had led to the problems that occurred or if the behaviors were associated with a poor fit between the staff member and the work assignment. If the behavior was due to inappropriate behavior, a staff member was asked to take a paid day off to reflect on what occurred and to return with a decision plan for going forward. The result of their process was that in a few cases, organizational members chose to leave the organization due to a poor fit with the work. As described by the human resource director, all but one of the cases resulted in the staff member apologizing to their team and leaders for their behavior and acknowledged it was their issue, not the organization's that led to their decision to leave.

The importance of norms, expectations, and behavior patterns. We worked with another organization that was the antithesis of Agency Participation, that we will label Agency Isolation. Staff at all levels of the organization reported low morale on the OSC (see Chapter 3), turnover was high, and our efforts to engage organizational members in the ARC process were tremendously difficult. We discovered early in the process that the director and organizational culture was authoritarian, resistant to change, and rigid. Upper leadership two levels above the program supervisors of six different programs were involved in minute decisions for front-line staff. For example, approval for spending $3 for a bus pass had to be formally approved by the director in each case. As a result, requests faced weeks of backlog. The director also reviewed difficult cases with front-line staff members, often with no input from the program supervisor, to determine what to do. During an orientation meeting with over 45 staff members conducted by the ARC specialist, not one individual in the room offered any questions or comments regarding the work and activities that would compose the ARC strategies until the leaders departed. Front-line staff had not been consulted on the decision for the organization to participate in ARC and none appeared to have an interest in the process.

The norms and behavioral expectations within Agency Isolation dictated that staff input on decisions would occur only when specifically requested by leaders. Without a direct invitation, few would speak, and even with an invitation, comments were generic and vaguely positive. This pattern of behavior characterized each level of the organizational hierarchy, with a clear norm that any staff member accompanied by their boss in a meeting would follow the boss's lead. A few staff members who had been with the agency for an extended time (10 years or more) spoke in meetings without an invitation from a leader. It was clear that the expectation among organizational members was that supervisors would tightly control staff behavior. Members at all levels did little beyond what their supervisors told them to do. The staff we interviewed feared taking actions outside of what they were told to do and admitted that they were not motivated to help bosses who had little respect for their opinions.

We also found that informal strategies had developed in the organization to adjust to the resistance and rigidity. For example, program supervisors routinely buffered their staff from unreasonable requests from leaders. They cautioned staff on what issues or problems they should pay close attention to as well as issues or problems they should carefully avoid. In terms of input to leaders for program improvement, ideas were filtered through each subsequent level of leaders to ensure the messages were safe and appropriate. Problems and errors could be addressed with some immediate supervisors, but deference to upper leaders' opinions and decisions was taken for granted. There simply was no open and honest feedback about serious problems existing within the organization, and almost no negative feedback made its way up the hierarchy, which allowed problems and failures to persist.

From a participatory perspective, little opportunity existed in the organization to share opinions or ideas about new ways of doing things. What occurred instead were routine complaint sessions among cohorts within the organization about their bosses and the dysfunctional nature of their organization. A great deal of staff time beyond the eyes and ears of supervisors was spent commiserating with small groups of colleagues. At the same time, the norm in these informal sessions was not to question a colleague about their efforts to solve problems or to challenge someone about not doing much to accomplish meaningful work with clients. Immediate supervisors ignored these conversations (if they were aware of them), doing little to prevent them or to reorient staff to more productive conversations. Unlike participatory-based organizations where staff members push each other to perform well or expect to share information with each other, each person in this organization worked as an isolated individual, receiving support mostly for derogating the organization's leaders but not for solving problems. Instead, staff waited until problems occurred and then asked what the leaders wanted them to do to address them.

The director expected his program leaders to control staff. Reflective of his beliefs, the director stated, "I would be shirking my job if I didn't carefully shepherd my flock." Supervisors who did not follow these control norms were at risk of being criticized for assuming greater discretion or encouraging staff to discuss problems or innovative solutions. In our experience of assisting organizations to implement the ARC model, Agency Isolation exhibited some of the least participatory-based behavior we have seen. Yet, it was also clear that the leaders embraced their approach as effective, despite high levels of turnover, reoccurring service problems, and difficulties in recruiting for vacant positions. The organization was trapped in normative patterns of behaviors and expectations that contributed to poor quality of care, high turnover among front-line staff, and poor organizational functioning.

AN EXAMPLE OF IMPROVING PARTICIPATORY-BASED FUNCTIONING WITH ARC

Agency Youth provided multiple programs for delinquent and runaway youth including a children's homeless shelter, a transitional living program, an emergency crisis center, and several outpatient programs for younger children and adolescents. Our initial work with leaders and subsequent work with front-line supervisors revealed a modest level of support in the agency for participatory practices. Although leaders were open to staff participation, they believed the staff lacked an interest in extensive participation because they were too invested in their day-to-day work with youth. When we spoke with front-line supervisors, the ARC liaison, and several team members while attending a meeting of one of the ARC program teams, a slightly different picture emerged. A supervisor stated that the CEO, who had begun approximately a year earlier, had assembled staff previously to identify and eliminate problems or barriers to services. She indicated that they had presented several ideas, one of which she suggested was still a serious problem for the shelters. The program supervisor and direct service staff reported that their input was solicited, but no follow-up action was taken. The staff members were demoralized by the inaction and felt their input was not valued. As a result, the supervisor said their experience had negatively influenced her staff's motivation and commitment.

In the early stage of the ARC process, the ARC specialist was working with the ARC liaison and several of the top leaders to explore the ARC principles. A self-report measure of how participatory the organization was in terms of leadership practices was completed, accompanied by exercises to explore the leaders' beliefs and assumptions that supported or inhibited a participatory-based approach. The reports revealed modest scale scores on being participatory in their leadership approach and identified several beliefs that explained their moderate scores. These beliefs included leaders' views that the staff was unable to recognize the real issues that needed to be addressed to increase effectiveness and that staff were not adequately trained. They believe the staff was unprepared to be involved in problem-solving and had minimal interest in doing so. During this same period in the ARC process, we also obtained the perceptions of staff regarding their leaders' commitment to participatory decision making, which was used later in the ARC process.

ARC activities were progressing in ARC teams where improvements were made in team functioning, cohesiveness, psychological safety, and meeting effectiveness. Additionally, teams were learning to employ problem-solving steps and processes to identify barriers, write proposals for change, and to forward them to the OAT team for review and potential support for implementation. The external ARC specialist and the internal ARC liaison worked closely with the team to make sure that the members thoroughly analyzed the identified barrier, established its impact on care, and clearly addressed potential solutions and difficulties in implementation. The identified problem was on the surface a simple, but unusual one. A single water heater was being used to heat water for dishes, showers, and all other hot water uses for the residential programs. The problem was that dinner occurred in early evening; by regulation, this required washing dishes with at least 110-degree water for sanitary purposes. This meant that all of the available hot water had been used as the showering schedule began. The various age groupings of children and the range in aggressiveness and size of the children varied greatly, as did their presenting problems. The first few showers were the only hot showers given the facility's geographical location with many days of subzero temperatures during the winter. The bigger, more aggressive youth were traumatizing the younger, smaller, less aggressive youth for access to hot water. Although staff had tried to manage the shower use issue, the problems created conflict between staff and the more aggressive youth, as well as between the youth who got hot showers and those who did not. The conflict spilled over into all activities that involved the children as a group, as well as confrontations away from the shelter staff.

When presented with the proposal, the team provided several pages of supporting documentation. This documentation included multiple incidents and problems occurring between clients resulting from the hot water shortage, a thorough explanation of how the shower crisis was leading to harmful dynamics within the program, and several estimates of getting the work done to install separate and sufficient water heaters to solve the problem. The latter included additional ideas and concessions that could be made to reduce the overall cost. As the leaders began to recognize the level of work the team had put into the proposal and the ideas provided, they began to be more receptive to what was occurring. They also apologized for having earlier dismissed the issue, not realizing the actual impact the problem was having on the program's functioning. Most importantly, they learned the importance of information provided by front-line staff and recognized the staff's ability to understand the dynamics of what appeared as a simple problem that was causing complex results. After this first barrier was addressed, the participation and commitment of all parties began to change. The leader of the team became much more trusting of his staff's desire to help improve the program. The team and its leader began to more fully trust leadership. Front-line members' engagement increased significantly. We presented the leaders with their previous assessment of participation and allowed them to reevaluate participation behavior and beliefs. We also provided feedback on the increases in participation reported by front-line staff. The message was clear that change was needed, that it was occurring, and that it needed to continue.

The dynamics were altered within the team and between the team and leaders. Conversations with the ARC team supervisor indicated that staff perceptions regarding leaders had changed and the team developed a new sense of efficacy. The supervisor suggested that many of the processes introduced in the ARC process helped her become more effective in her own management of tasks and those of staff. She explained that success required more than a process for staff to offer ideas to leaders. Success was also a function of the team building its teamwork skills and creating a context of psychological safety in working with each other on identifying and addressing service barriers. Success also required more than leaders exploring their beliefs and assumptions regarding being participatory. It was important that leaders saw the evidence, as did the team, that change could occur and that the leaders' assumptions about the staff's limited capacity and motivation for improvement had to be questioned. As explained earlier in the chapter, narrowly defined participatory interventions are unlikely to succeed and additional processes such as recognition and reward or the use of feedback and data are all part of ensuring success. For this reason, the ARC model includes five principles of effective service organizations and creates organizational change with comprehensive approaches that include multiple tools, systems, and shared mental models that complement change efforts associated with each principle.

13

RELATIONSHIP-CENTERED VERSUS INDIVIDUAL-CENTERED HUMAN SERVICE ORGANIZATIONS

Relationship-centered organizations attribute positive service outcomes to the characteristics of the social networks within which the services are provided and within which clients live and function (Glisson et al., 2016a). Following this principle, successful human services place a priority on developing and sustaining a network of inter-organizational and intra-organizational relationships to serve their clients in the context of their family, school, work, and community. This principle addresses the conflicting priority of attributing service outcomes to the characteristics of specific individuals, such as an individual service provider, rather than to the system of relationships that support the client. To improve the well-being of clients, relationship- versus individual-centered organizations focus on the network of relationships that compose the social contexts for both service providers and clients.

Members of relationship-centered organizations cultivate positive relationships by being available and responsive to coworkers and by sustaining continuity in their efforts with others to ensure success for their clients. The ARC strategies are designed to promote these characteristics. The focus on building and maintaining quality relationships is reflected in shared organizational norms, expectations, and beliefs that characterize an organization's social context and the social networks that compose it. These networks support integrated efforts among providers and stakeholders both within and outside the organization. This principle is based on the idea that successful service providers do not work to improve client well-being in isolation or without including key stakeholders.

Instead, successful providers view client outcomes as a function of the social networks within which they work and within which their clients live.

In relationship-centered organizations, service providers in front-line teams communicate openly and collaborate to share resources, knowledge, and ideas that identify and address barriers to their clients' success. These interactions and the sharing of resources and knowledge extend beyond the teams as well. Program supervisors and staff interact with personnel from other programs within their organization, sharing information and resources. Program teams and their members interact with administrative personnel in human resources, training, and finance to ensure appropriate resources and an effective system of care. In system terms, the departments and programs that compose a service organization understand their interdependence and work to support each other to be successful. Individual-centered organizations provide a contrast where silos, guarded boundaries, and protective self-interests leave departments and programs working in isolation and competition with each other. Valuable information and resources are inadvertently or purposely withheld that could benefit others in the organization. The isolation, insularity, and focus of individual-centered organizations are replaced in relationship-centered organizations with an understanding that the success of one's program, department, and individual efforts is a function of effective relationships and mutual support. To build these relationships, ARC strategies depend on integrated, collaborative processes and behaviors that encourage the development of social networks, particularly those that support collaboration focused on service improvement.

The networks of essential work relationships extend beyond the provider's agency. Front-line staff, managers, and leaders must interact with other external service providers and stakeholders to achieve success. This includes relationships with key members of client social networks (e.g., family, community members). For example, effective services for children's mental health can require relationships that extend to schools, social services, churches, and extended families that are invested in the children.

Organizational supervisors and leaders promote these relationships among stakeholders and organizational members and build their own internal and external networks to foster success. Beyond client networks, these relationships include funders, regulators, politicians, business leaders, philanthropists, community groups, additional service providers, advocacy groups, and others who influence the effectiveness of organizations and their direct service providers. In essence, effective services and the success of improvement efforts are a function of the organizational members' capacity to identify and address deficits in these networks of relationships.

Our experience with relationship-centered organizations provides examples of organizational members who depend on collaboration and interdependence with colleagues for essential resources and expertise. Leaders of relationship-centered organizations are explicit that organizational members rely on each other to provide high quality services and to produce the best outcomes. Members at all levels support collaborative problem solving and the integration of members' skills and knowledge to solve complex tasks and problems. This support is guided by leaders' recognition that the social contexts of staff and of clients heavily influence behavior, motivation, and intentions. Likewise, leaders and front-line service providers in relationship-centered organizations understand that these relationships provide the basis for information sharing, resources deployment, and collaborative efforts that lead to success. Furthermore, leaders recognize that relationships influence stakeholders such as funders, policy makers, regulators, or other officials (e.g., judges, commissioners) who impact client outcomes through the allocations of resources, development of policies, or exercise of authority.

The mental models and implicit beliefs (see Chapter 8) shared within relationship-centered organizations support the quality of network relationships. Among these is the fundamental, implicit belief that creating positive, integrated social contexts within which organizational members, stakeholders, and clients function, is essential to success. Conversely, remaining isolated and independent from key stakeholders creates silos and barriers that impede high-quality care. Direct service providers in relationship-centered organizations cannot envision achieving success without their network of colleagues and without developing and working with the networks that make up their client's social system. Much like the characteristics of successful sports teams, individual skills and talents are valued and recognized, but success depends on integrating those skills, resources, and influence on behalf of the whole. Members of relationship-centered organizations focus on the importance of integrating the skills, talents, shared knowledge, and resources of various colleagues and programs in serving difficult and complex cases. This inclusiveness and participation engenders shared purpose, commitment, and motivation for shared action. Similarly, it provides, the emotional and practical support that is needed as front-line service providers address difficult and complex client problems.

Our experience confirms that relationship-centered organizations promote member norms (culture) and perceptions (climate) that sustain positive and productive working relationships. Staff interacts in an open and respectful manner with individuals at all levels of the organization. They work collaboratively to support participative decision making and to achieve mutually desired outcomes. The expectation among members of these organizations is that they cooperate across programs to ensure continuity of care and information sharing. Program supervisors share training materials and access to resources in support of other programs and establish links to others with similar clients and needs. Leaders foster connections between organizational members and encourage the distribution of information and resources that benefit other programs. A priority of leaders in relationship-centered organizations is facilitating relationships between members within their organizations and recognizing organizational members' efforts to assist colleagues.

The perceptions, attitudes, and beliefs among members of relationship-centered organizations are aligned to encourage and support collaboration with others in the organization. This is reflected in ARC processes, where component tools (see Chapters 5–7) are used to identify and address isolation among organizational members or programs by connecting isolated members and programs into the broader efforts of the organization. Creating relationship-centered organizations requires that integra-tive networking efforts extend beyond clinical programs. Support departments such as human resources are recognized in relationship-centered organizations as essential to effective services. Leaders build relationships among these support departments and direct service programs to promote collaborative work around planning, allocation of resources, and staff development.

Shared perceptions, attitudes, and behavioral norms contribute to collaborative efforts with external parties as well. Relationship-centered organizations expect staff to seek and engage new external partners. Norms for developing relationships with courts, schools, police departments, social service providers, health-care professionals, and other stakeholders are firmly in place. These efforts are expected to reinforce the success of service providers in achieving client improvement, increased credibility and status with stakeholders, and increased social influence on external factors that are controlled by external stakeholders and impact clients' outcomes. Leaders recognize and cele-brate successes in developing collaborative efforts with external stakeholders and rou-tinely spend time to strengthen partnerships and build networks within the community they serve.

In summary, relationship-centered organizations recognize the quality of internal and external relationships that exist at varying levels as essential to effectiveness. These organ-izations reward behavior that fosters effective relationships characterized by availability, responsiveness, and continuity. Organizational members believe that these characteristics are as important to improving services as are the characteristics of the individuals that compose the networks. That is, they understand that the nature of the relationships in which they and their clients are embedded is a core determinant of personal and client success.

EVIDENCE AND SUPPORT FOR RELATIONSHIP-CENTERED ORGANIZATIONS

Pfeffer and Sutton (2006) concluded that the power and influence of individual organ-izational members were less than that of the social context in which they work. That is, the social patterns existing with a network of work relationships affect performance more than the characteristics of individuals within the systems. Organizations are largely guided by the nature of social networks that define member interrelationships, guide member interactions, and affect the integration and coordination of activities necessary for success. The best-known example is the 1986 Space Shuttle Challenger explosion. This explosion was attributed to failures in socially constructed patterns of decision making and communication engrained within the social context of NASA. Despite cadres of in-telligent, skilled, and highly motivated scientists and engineers, relationship flaws within NASA created barriers to addressing design and production problems that were identified by line-level engineers. The difficulty in addressing those flaws within NASA's social context was tragically illustrated 17 years later when the Columbia disintegrated upon reentry. What was discovered, for the second time, were errors resulting from a dysfunctional bureaucratic culture that impeded a functional network of relationships among engineers and management. Hierarchical and centralized social structures placed control of production decisions in the hands of administrators who were isolated from the engineers closest to the production process and best able to identify problems. Socially embedded norms narrowed the engineers' control of the production process, preventing those with less formal power in the organization (but more engineering knowledge of the shuttles) from participating in key decisions regarding production and launch schedules. Pfeffer and Sutton (2006) used these and other examples to illustrate how the network of social relationships and behavioral norms within an organization affect the capacity of individuals within the organization to identify and address problems that undermine organizational performance.

Internal social networks in human services. The performance of human service organizations is also dependent on social networks and norms, as we describe in our research and throughout this book (Glisson, 1978, 2007, 2009, 2010; Glisson & Green, 2006, 2011; Glisson & Hemmelgarn, 1998; Glisson & James, 2002; Glisson & Williams, 2015; Glisson, Schoenwald, et al., 2008; Glisson et al., 2016a, 2016b; Hemmelgarn, Glisson, & James, 2006; Schneider, Brief, & Guzzo, 1996; Williams & Glisson, 2013, 2014b; Williams et al., 2016). Human services such as behavioral health and social services involve complex client problems that are embedded in multiple and complex social relationships. Attention to both the nature of relationships in which the client is embedded and the network of relationships that provide the service is critical to positive outcomes. This is reinforced by the fact that the technologies employed within social services and behavioral health are softer technologies—as compared to engineering or manufacturing that are even more vulnerable and dependent on social processes (Glisson, 1978, 1992; Glisson & Green, 2006). In other words, human interaction and relationships define the core technologies of social service organizations as well as the social context in which those technologies are implemented (Denison, 1996). Our research confirms that shared social norms (cultures) and shared perceptions (climate) that define a service organization's social context determine the nature and tone of interactions that influence service outcomes. These norms define the patterns and nature of interactions among organizational members that affect how staff members serve clients. In organizational cultures that emphasize top-down, centralized decision making and formalized rules and regulations, individualized client care is replaced by routinized, standardized care that ignores the individual needs of clients (Glisson, 1978; Glisson & Green, 2006; Martin, Peters, & Glisson, 1998). When work environments are characterized by emotional exhaustion, role overload, and depersonalization, the responsiveness to the unique needs of individual clients is compromised (Glisson & James, 2002; Nugent & Glisson, 1999). As illustrated with the NASA failures, social structures and norms guide the social interactions and patterns of decision making within an organization that, in turn, influence the quality and outcomes of problem solving. And like NASA, an organization's norms, expectations, and social relationships can put the well-being of individuals—or clients who receive services—at risk. This occurs despite well-intentioned, competent individuals who are willing to work hard yet are embedded in organizational social contexts that create barriers to their capacity for problem solving.

Our study of pediatric emergency rooms reinforces these points (Hemmelgarn, Glisson, & Dukes, 2001). The nature and quality of relationships among staff members and between staff and their patients and families were defined by socially shared beliefs, attitudes, and behavioral norms within the different emergency room settings we studied. Distinct differences distinguished hospital emergency rooms in terms of staff interactions among themselves and with patients and their families.

In some emergency rooms, interactions were warm, supportive, and inclusive while in others they were cold, distant, and exclusive. In the latter, client families were excluded from participating in the care of their children and provided limited information regarding their children's treatment. Staff attitudes toward parents were negative, and collaborative interaction with parents was minimal or nonexistent. Staff operated mechanistically rather than as emotionally connected humans, with effects on both staff and patients' families. Families were agitated during their child's care as little information was being provided and as medical staff actively avoided their requests for information. Staff in these environments reported that they experienced low levels of emotional support from their colleagues in their work environments and described feelings of being emotionally drained and minimally engaged. The characteristics of their interrelationships ensured that staff turned off their emotional connections to each other, while also shutting down lines of communication with patients and families. As a result, the opportunities for parental support and help were lost, preventing the sharing of valuable information and inhibiting the development of relationships between medical staff and families that promoted responsive care and treatment compliance (Kuo, Bird, & Tilford, 2011; Leff, Chan, & Walizer 1991; Rushton, 1990; Shelton, Jeppson, & Johnson, 1989).

Safran, Miller, and Beckman (2006) provide a comprehensive review and model of relationship-centered organizational cultures and describe their impact on both staff and patient outcomes. They identify the multiple levels at which relationships influence staff and client outcomes, including clinician-patient relationships, clinician-colleague relationships, and clinician-community relationships. Consistent with our efforts to build effective relationships characterized by availability, responsiveness, and continuity using ARC (Dozier, Cue, & Barnett, 1994; Wahler, 1994), the quality of relationships between providers and patients within health care are associated with a variety of positive improvements, including patients' adherence to clinical advice, symptom relief, and both clinical and functional status, as well as indicators of client satisfaction such as enhanced patient retention and loyalty (Dimatteo et al., 1993; Greenfield, Kaplan, & Ware, 1985; Stewart, et al., 2000; Safran, Miller, & Beckman, 2006; Safran, Murray, Chang, Montgomery, & Rogers, 2000; Safran, Taira, Rogers, Kosinski, Ware, & Tarlov,

1998). These studies illustrate that a consistent pattern of high-quality, collaborative relationships among staff and with clients results in improved service outcomes.

The important point is that relationship-centered organizations have social contexts that promote functional relationships among individual service providers that influence the type of relationships that develop between service providers and clients. Pfeffer and Sutton's (2006) conclusions are supported by the Institute of Medicine's (2000) report on health care, "To Err is Human." The report finds that medical errors are less likely the result of individual clinicians' behaviors and incompetence than a result of failures within the organizational systems that provide the care. As explained by Safran et al. (2006), the IM report was interpreted as attributing errors to failures in technologies such as information systems, but the real culprit became evident over time. Failures in health care were increasingly understood to be a function of interaction patterns, communication patterns, and shared goals promoted by team cultures (Donchin et al., 1995; Risser et al., 1999). In related work, Edmondson and colleagues explored health-care team psychological safety and interactions supporting learning, examination of errors, and non-hierarchal relationships that allowed input from all team members in identifying and addressing problems in care (Edmondson, Kramer, & Cook, 2004; Pisano, Bohmer, & Edmondson, 2001). Her research shows that social norms guiding team interactions supporting psychologically safe contexts for sharing information, discussing problems, and openly addressing errors are critical to client care and outcomes.

To summarize, findings from a variety of health-care studies support the effectiveness of relationship-centered organizations (Dimatteo et al., 1993; Donchin et al., 1995; Edmondson, Kramer, & Cook, 2004; Greenfield, Kaplan, & Ware, 1985; Pisano et al., 2001; Stewart, et al., 2000; Risser et al., 1999; Safran et al., 1998, 2000, 2006). Lower mortality rates across health-care environments are associated with collaborative environments that foster increased levels of open interaction, input, and information sharing. Team interventions that improve team collaboration and sharing of information lower mortality rates. Effective team communication, team problem solving, knowledge sharing, and provision of mutual respect among team members predict improved functional outcomes for patients and shorter lengths of stay. Collaborative cultures within surgical teams predict improved outcomes for patients even after surgical care. And positive outcomes extend beyond the patients. Higher morale and lower turnover among health-care providers are consistently linked to collaborative cultures: that is, cultures and settings where interactions emphasize input and integration of knowledge from medical staff and health-care team members.

External social networks in human services. The impact of altering the pattern and nature of relationships within service organizations extends to the creation of networks of relationships outside the boundaries of the formal organization, such as relationships developed in family-centered medical care (Arango, 2011), relying on external peers to assist families in navigating the child mental health-care system (Hoagwood et al., 2008; Olin, Hemmelgarn, Madenwald, & Hoagwood, 2016), or even enabling agricultural extension agents to identify mental health-care needs in rural populations (Molgaard, 1997). Efforts to alter social systems and patterns of relationships including external stakeholders are essential in efforts to establish community-based schools (Capella, Frazier, Atkins, Schoenwald, & Glisson, 2008). Our application of the ARC model has included boundary spanning activities in the community to link key stakeholders (e.g., schools, juvenile courts, and mental health care) in collaborative efforts with the participating service organization (Glisson & Schoenwald, 2005; Glisson et al., 2010; see also Gray, 1985, 1990). Researchers have identified relational networks including mental health and health and other human service systems that lead to success (Provan, Huang, & Milward, 2009; Provan & Milward, 1995). Central to these efforts are attempts to understand how these networks of relationships improve services to clients.

Our experience suggests there are both technical and social benefits from building and sustaining collaborative, relationship-centered contexts that support strong social networks of relationships characterized by availability, responsiveness, and continuity (Glisson, 2012; Glisson, Dukes, & Green, 2006; Glisson & Williams, 2015; Glisson et al., 2010). Expanding networks and enhancing the quality of relationships among providers and between providers and clients is a primary determinant of successful service outcomes (Hoagwood, et al., 2008; Olin, Hemmelgarn, Maddenwald, & Hoagwood, 2016). A review of the effects of collaborative organizational cultures and interventions to promote relationship-centered care in health services emphasize the roles of mindfulness, valuing multiple perspectives, mutual respect, and responsiveness in communication (Safron, Miller, & Beckman, 2006). Creating and expanding relationships characterized by trust and collaboration require participants to take more risks in nurturing relationships with each other, share more information, and grant increased latitude and deference to each other regarding decisions and actions (compare Bachmann & Inkpen, 2011; Butler & Cantrell, 1994; Mayer, Davis, Schoorman, 1995; McAllister, 1995; Schoorman, Mayer, & Davis, 2007; Schneider, Brief, & Guzzo, 1996). These factors lead to technical improvements as decision making, process improvements, and the redesign of roles and responsibilities occur. And these occurrences are based on information sharing, improved communication of ideas and knowledge, and group problem solving. These activities within healthy relationships increase the positive effects of improvement plans and the selection of strategies and tools that collaborative groups use to complete their work.

There are additional benefits when organizational interventions alter the network of social relationships that compose an organization's social contexts (Lawrence, 1969). Creating norms that encourage supportive relationships, interactions characterized by respect and fairness, and increased service provider discretion and control in providing services improve the motivation of service providers and their commitment to engaging clients. Likewise, improving the quality of relationships, patterns of support, and discretion of network members enhances the levels of innovation and tenacity required of service providers, particularly in addressing complex, uncertain, and unpredictable problems (Glisson, 2009).

The impact of the nature of personal relationships within organizations differentiate organizations that are marked by innovation, risk taking, and staff satisfaction from those that are resistant, rigid, and marked by authoritarian patterns of bureaucratic control that restrict innovation, commitment, and satisfaction (Schneider, Brief, & Guzzo, 1996). Social contexts that support collaborative relationships are linked to perceptions of improved status, autonomy, and control, as well as to job satisfaction, lower staff turnover, and improved client outcomes (Aiken, Smith, Lake, 1994; Safran, Miller, Beckman, 2006). Highly stressful work settings and jobs, such as pediatric trauma in emergency rooms or managing crises within mental health services benefit from supportive and responsive relationship networks that buffer individuals from stress and emotional overload (Cohen &Wills, 1985; Hemmelgarn, Glisson, & Dukes, 2001).

EXAMPLES OF RELATIONSHIP-CENTERED ORGANIZATIONS

The members in our previous example, Agency Participation, understood participatory practices and the importance of establishing, both internally and externally, networks of high-quality relationships. These networks contributed to the quality of care provided by the organization and supported beliefs and reasoning regarding collaboration that contributed to success. As shown in the following description of our experience with this agency, organizational leaders viewed their organization as an integrated and comprehensive system based on the central role of relationships that drive effective organizational performance.

At an early meeting with the ARC specialist, one leader explained that, "Our people are our organization. We don't have machinery or assembly lines. We have high quality folks who have to collaborate to do good work." Another leader stated that the work was tough and that they depended on each other for help in serving clients. When asked if their success was dependent on individual efforts, the leader replied with an enthusiastic, "God, no!" She explained that they certainly did all they could to hire great staff, to train them well, and to develop their skills but that it was the spirit of the place and the collaborative efforts between everyone that was the key. Another leader described the organization's employees as a very large family. After joking about its dysfunction at times, he said they were a family that supported each other to get things done. "Our job as leaders is to make sure staff members have the resources, skills, and tools to get their work done. But more importantly, we make sure all of us (meaning all organizational members) support each other to deal with what is difficult and often heartbreaking work."

One of the higher-level executives in the meeting said they believed the only way to succeed with the difficult and complex problems they faced was to work together as a team. He described his own and his colleagues' experiences of watching clients fail and the impact of broken families and poor communities. Because those circumstances made it difficult for their clients to be successful, he asserted, "We can't be one of those families." Others nodded and added, "We can't afford to isolate ourselves like those families." They described how they proactively built relationships with key stakeholders such as courts, funders, community support groups, and others. Their comments underscored a deep commitment to relationships as being central to success, but the meeting provided additional insights. Although the leaders were extremely busy, they had initiated this meeting early in the ARC process. They were investing their time to build a strong relationship with the ARC specialist and to determine whether ARC would support their focus on relationships. The specialist left the meeting with the support of a group of leaders who were committed to the ARC process and to a working relationship with the specialist that was essential to helping them identify and address service barriers.

Behavior in a relationship-centered organization. In a different example, we shared information about ARC with a rural judge's assistant we have named "Richard." We were implementing ARC in a program for juveniles with mental health problems who were referred to juvenile courts in a number of counties. After discussing some of our work and some details on the phone, Richard requested additional information including a description of ARC, evidence for its effectiveness, and details on linking community members to the mental health service provider that served the juvenile court. Richard contacted us after reviewing the materials to set up a meeting with him several days later. He requested that we return to talk to his staff and several other individuals he knew in the community. We were surprised at the second meeting several weeks later when over 20 individuals arrived, including the school superintendent, principals from three county schools, the mayor, several community pastors, two business leaders who supported projects by the court, the judge, and Richard's staff. He had copied and distributed our materials to all of these stakeholders several days before the meeting and had prepared an agenda that included an overview of ARC, questions and answers, as well as discussion on how participants could help support the work we were planning to do in their community to solve problems of delinquency and neglect. In that one meeting, we felt we had completed the equivalent of many months of work to establish linkages with community stakeholders and it was clear that Richard was going to ensure that we practiced what we preached.

We discovered in the meeting that several stakeholders had reservations about the organization that would be providing mental health services. We assured them that we would work with the organization to address their concerns. Fortunately, there was one representative from the mental health organization that the county stakeholders perceived as effective. We established her as a central liaison from the mental health organization to monitor, coordinate, and address issues that occurred while providing direct services to the children and families referred from the courts. With the agreement of the mental health liaison, the court personnel requested that our ARC specialist be routinely involved until an effective collaboration between the courts and other stakeholders was established with the mental health service provider. As evidence of their focus on relationships, the court conducted biweekly meetings for stakeholders. These meetings were used to discuss current cases regarding delinquent youth and jointly establish plans, objectives, and ideas on how best to address each pending case. The court requested that the information and recommendations be included in a joint plan that was agreed upon before the case was heard by the judge. The judge relied heavily on these plans, reviewing them before entering court to hear each case.

As Richard promised, court staff supported the efforts of the mental health organization but required the mental health representative to be at the meetings consistently, to be prepared, and to work with them on an ongoing basis. Although the court's approach was directive, the court personnel were extremely supportive and open to ideas and suggestions; they were also clearly collaborative in making decisions. They integrated input from all stakeholders into each case plan and ensured that they shared ongoing updates on events or additional information that could affect each other. They often backed plans, including those from the mental health provider that placed the court at risk with broader community members if client problems occurred within their community. At the same time, they expected support from others in altering plans if outcomes were poor. Well-constructed plans blended the force of the court with the efforts of the mental health providers in engaging the youth and families in therapeutic change efforts. Relationships improved between the mental health service provider and key stakeholders in the community. The mental health service providers were invited to community events and holiday work parties held by school and court staff, and a mutual commitment to sustaining services for juvenile offenders with mental health problems developed in the community.

Isolation and insularity. Our work in a large urban child welfare office provided the ARC specialist a much different experience. Provided with a cubicle among the caseworkers, the ARC specialist had the opportunity to observe caseworkers who remained in their cubicles for most of the day. They left their cubicles to deliver paperwork to other staff members or to obtain information about mandates that were provided to their immediate supervisors via e-mail from the systems' leaders. The social interaction occurring in the office was limited but included groups of staff who gathered in a secure corner of a cubicle to object to the latest requests from leaders, disparage difficult clients, and discuss their organization's dysfunction. In contrast, those who were more positively engaged in their work with clients sought out their own small groups of colleagues to discuss those efforts. Members of the two camps of engaged and unengaged caseworkers exchanged pleasantries but avoided each other when discussing work or clients. The lack of a communal effort to address problems was reflected in meetings as well. Supervisors held regularly scheduled meetings to present a weekly list of things individuals needed to accomplish and to provide directions to those they believed needed guidance. Little or no facilitation of discussion, collaborative problem solving, or group planning occurred.

The impact of this work environment is best illustrated by a caseworker that spent hours each day playing a computer game as her clients left messages throughout the day requesting information or a return call. Her supervisor walked passed her daily without any comment. He later told the ARC specialist that the caseworker did not perform well and the he had no expectation she would change. But he said he did not have the time to go through the bureaucratic hurdles to address the problem. In discussions with those caseworkers who were more positively engaged in their work, the specialist learned that they just ignored the bureaucracy and worked on their own to do what they could. The engaged caseworkers created informal relationships with each other to provide support but were frustrated that supervisors assigned the most difficult and greatest number of cases to them. They indicated this occurred because supervisors knew they would do the best job with the hard cases. These staff also expressed fatigue, feelings of being treated unfairly, and of wanting to give up and go home early everyday like the disengaged staff. They were frustrated about not being part of a group of individuals who worked collaboratively to address client needs. For those who were not engaged, their work with clients was guided by mandatory minimum contact requirements. The disengaged caseworkers also purposefully contacted clients at times clients were unavailable, leaving a message to return a call, and documenting their contact efforts in their files. For these caseworkers, contacting additional stakeholders or family members was not considered because they believed providing quality care was impossible.

This and previous examples illustrate how social networks and social contexts influence the staff effort and service. The caseworkers cited in the last example had wanted to improve lives when they were hired. Instead of joining supportive and collaborative networks of engaged staff focused on client well-being, they experienced isolation and negative attitudes that insulated staff from clients and their organization. Instead of experiencing encouragement, information sharing, and learning, new caseworkers were influenced by burned out staff members who expected to be unsuccessful. The major barrier to service was social rather than technical, reflecting a broken system of relationships characterized by shared norms, beliefs, and attitudes that ensured poor performance.

USING ARC TO BECOME RELATIONSHIP CENTERED

The authors worked with a regional mental health provider in the Southeast that supported community-based programs for youth, including a school-based program for adolescents in alternative schools. The services included case management to coordinate resources and counseling aimed at reducing behavioral health problems for youth and their families. The school-based program addressed educational, familial, and mental health issues that were interfering with students' educational achievement and mental health. This program served students who were referred by teachers and school counselors for disruptive and noncompliant behavior. The program's service providers complained that a barrier existed in accessing and working with the teachers who made the referrals, creating a roadblock to successful outcomes.

During our initial ARC training and preparatory sessions for supervisors who would be guiding ARC activities in various programs, the school-based program supervisor was clearly disengaged in the process. He was late to the initial training session with no apologies or rationale, engaged in multiple side conversations with another staff member throughout the session, and used phone messages to excuse himself several times. In a second training session in which he was again tardy, he interjected a terse, self-protective reaction when ARC activities explored the application of availability, responsiveness, and continuity for developing effective network relationships to support effective care. He asked, "What if the people you have to work with to be successful aren't available or responsive?" When asked to explain, he said it was impossible for his team to do their job because teachers would not cooperate. He explained that teachers, "when we are able to get them to meet with us," refused to accept or follow through with his staff's recommendations. He concluded: "The teachers just want us to fix the kids magically so they don't disrupt their classes."

In further discussion, it became clear that the supervisor and his staff were not appreciative of the demands faced by the teachers. The supervisor had the unrealistic expectation that teachers would do whatever was asked of them by his staff. The ARC specialist used this event as an opportunity to explain the roles of availability, responsiveness, and continuity in developing a network of relationships to support the mental health services provided by the organization. The ARC specialist asked the school-based supervisor and the broader group of supervisors in training to discuss the challenge of building networks and implementing the ARC process with external stakeholders whose support they needed. Several supervisors were interested because they were having their own difficulties with key external stakeholders. The ARC specialist asked if program supervisors would agree to practice availability, responsiveness, and continuity with each other, specifically, in trying to assist the school-based supervisor and others in addressing stakeholder barriers to their program's success. Supervisors, including the school-based supervisor, agreed.

The ARC specialist led a time-limited discussion of the school-based program supervisor's experiences with teachers along with the other supervisors' experiences and challenges in establishing relationships with stakeholders that included court personnel, police, family members, and others involved in the families' lives. Before the discussion began, the ARC specialist explained that the ARC training sessions would allot time to apply ARC concepts, tools, and processes to address the service barriers they experienced. The ARC specialist described his intention to use the barrier experienced by the school-based program to help organizational members create change by employing ARC tools and concepts to build stronger relationships. The ARC specialist outlined work that would take place over several months as additional ARC tools and processes were introduced and practiced.

In the discussion of the school-based program supervisor's issue, the role of the ARC specialist was limited to listening to the problems and encouraging others to share similar problems they had experienced in establishing relationships with key stakeholders. Two supervisors suggested that their successes in establishing relationships with key stakeholders occurred only after they put themselves in the shoes of the stakeholders and began to share their stakeholders' goals. Prompted by the ARC specialist, these supervisors explained in more detail and discussed their experience in relation to the concepts of availability, responsiveness, and continuity. They explained in their own words that they had become more available and responsive to stakeholders after they focused on their stakeholders' experiences with their shared clients and the demands the stakeholders faced. They acknowledged they took this approach only after they realized there was no other way to gain the stakeholders' support.

Following the discussion, action steps were established with the supervisors. The ARC specialist discussed the importance of being responsive to supervisors in the group who were struggling with building effective relationships with challenging stakeholders. The ARC specialist asked program supervisors who had overcome similar challenges, as well as the ARC liaison, to follow up with the school-based program supervisor who had complained about the teachers' inaction. The supervisors needing support, including the school-based program supervisor, were asked to present at least one idea from their discussions in the next training session to the broader group. They were asked to think about the experience they were having and to provide any specific steps or actions from their colleagues that had helped. These action steps were recorded in meeting notes. It was made explicit that everyone put forth their best effort in being responsive and available to their school-based program colleague and others struggling with these issues. Second, the ARC specialist asked the school-based program supervisor to take notes regarding specific examples that he and his staff experienced that could provide details about the challenges they faced and the impact on their clients' care.

After the meeting, the ARC specialist worked with the ARC liaison to review additional steps for using the school-based program experience to further illustrate the concepts of availability, responsiveness, and continuity in training for the program leaders in upcoming sessions. First, the ARC specialist and internal ARC liaison established a plan to model availability and responsiveness from upper leadership in their relationships with the ARC team supervisors. The liaison agreed that she would work with program directors and organizational leaders to use their existing relationships to help the school-based supervisor. This effort was intended to develop access to teachers and relationships between school personnel and school-based program staff. Second, the ARC liaison and specialist planned to use the training on ARC tools, concepts, and processes to identify and improve other relationships affecting the services provided by the school-based program. Third, the ARC specialist and liaison created a plan to use stakeholder relationships as an example when training on the use ARC tools and processes to address service barriers, in this case building better stakeholder relationships.

In the subsequent ARC training on psychological safety and effective team behavior, participants applied their new skills and behaviors to the school-based program's barrier with teachers. The school-based program supervisor was asked to share examples of how the barrier affected both the program's services and clients' outcomes. The larger group also shared their own practical experiences and strategies, and provided additional ideas that helped their programs overcome similar problems in strengthening their relationships with key stakeholders. The ARC specialist guided the group in exploring changes in their mental models and reasoning that helped them alter and improve their relationships with stakeholders. Examples provided by supervisors included recognizing that they had to put themselves in the place of stakeholders to better understand the stakeholder demands and needs; knowing or believing that success would not occur unless stakeholders and program staff helped each other to reach each other's goals, and understanding that relationships do not work unless each of the parties sees a clear benefit to the relationship.

As planned, the ARC liaison worked with the organization's leaders to identify potential links to school personnel who could support the school-based program's efforts. Leaders committed to developing the links when the program supervisor was ready. Second, the ARC specialist suggested that the group of program supervisors use ARC tools and processes to address the identified service barrier over the next two months. The supervisors and leaders agreed to use the ARC tools in their efforts to improve the school-based program. Third, the ARC specialist led the supervisors in a discussion to explore how availability and responsiveness could be supported by the supervisors, the ARC liaison, the ARC specialist, and leaders. This included listing the examples of availability, responsiveness, and continuity from each level and discussing the experiences of the school-based program supervisor up to that point. The supervisor explained how difficult it was to be the person with the problem that was being discussed but also described conversations with other program staff that were supportive and informed his thinking about different approaches to address the problem. He admitted it remained difficult for him to see that he and his staff were sustaining the problem but agreed they had to change their thinking. Finally, he announced that he no longer felt like he, in his words, was "on the island of misfits."

These early steps engaged the entire group of supervisors who practiced the ARC concepts. This included practicing positive teamwork behaviors (dialogue and inquiry) and maintaining a psychologically safe work environment for sharing ideas, beliefs, and solutions. Through this process, the school-based program supervisor increased his level of engagement in his work and with his colleagues while examining his own beliefs and assumptions. Leaders affirmed their availability and responsiveness in offering their assistance as they had promised. And, the supervisor group placed a priority on building relationships with colleagues, leaders, stakeholders, and clients.

As ARC progressed, the school-based program identified strategies for addressing the service barrier caused by poor relationships with teachers. Working with leaders and the ARC liaison, they prepared a well-thought out proposal for strengthening relationships with teachers in several key schools. The proposal was overwhelmingly supported by the OAT (see Chapters 4–6). Leaders, the ARC liaison, and the program supervisor and staff were provided opportunities for improving relationships with the schools through leaders' efforts to connect with key school personnel. The efforts included developing a relationship with a university educator who was well recognized and highly supported by school personnel and teachers. Jointly, this educator (who had instructed the school-based program supervisor in college), the school-based staff, and several teachers in alternative schools created a series of ongoing training and support meetings for school staff struggling with difficult students. These events were supported by school leaders and led to a joint educational and mental health effort with teachers and school-based counselors that continues annually. Successes occurring with students began to be informally discussed by parents and teachers, leading to increasing interest in the school-based program, increased referrals, and improved availability of teachers throughout the school system for the school-based program staff.

We were pleased to note a change in the description of the school-based program provided on the agency's website several years after we introduced ARC. Unlike its original description when ARC began, the program description now included an emphasis on a highly collaborative teacher-and-clinician led program that partnered with parents and students to provide support for addressing mental health issues influencing academic success. The original ARC liaison who helped facilitate ARC indicated that the program had become successful in achieving desired outcomes and that the term "ARCish" was used to describe staff behaviors associated with psychological safety and with availability, responsiveness, and continuity in working closely with key stakeholders.

14

CONCLUSION AND FUTURE CHALLENGES FOR IMPROVING HUMAN SERVICE ORGANIZATIONS

The previous chapters summarized four decades of our research and practice with hundreds of human service organizations nationwide. Our intention has been to share what we have learned from these experiences about creating effective service organizations. We know from our practice experience, nationwide surveys, and randomized controlled trials that social context explains why some human service organizations are more likely to implement best practices, have lower staff turnover, provide higher-quality service, and achieve better outcomes than other organizations with similar resources and staff. We also know that organizational culture and climate are dimensions of social context that can be improved with organizational strategies and that explain why some organizations are more effective than others. We found that successful organizational strategies include tools for addressing service barriers that are guided by principles of effective service organizations and supported by mental models that promote innovation, psychological safety, and staff participation. However, we also know that not all organizations are equally successful in using these strategies.

The variation in organizational outcomes suggests we need more information about which organizational strategies are most successful in changing different types of organizational social contexts. Also, among those organizations that do adopt these strategies successfully, there is much more to be learned about the mechanisms that explain the strategies' effects and how the strategies can be implemented most efficiently. Given these questions and based on what we know from our work to date, we suggest that future research and development efforts focus on four areas. These four areas are interrelated and together describe how more specific information about the effects of these organizational strategies can increase capacity for improving human services.

First, we view organizations as sociotechnical systems and emphasize the different but complementary roles played by their core technologies (i.e., the knowledge, skills and tools used by the providers who directly serve clients) and their social contexts (i.e., culture, climate, and work attitudes that characterize the organization) in which the technologies are embedded. We have shown that each of these two factors, core technology and social context, affect service quality and outcomes, and in addition, that the characteristics of one can moderate the effects of the other. We therefore argue that the successful implementation of new technologies such as EBTs, outcome monitoring, or continuous improvement processes within an organization is a function of the social context in which the new technologies are introduced.

We conclude from this work that efforts to improve services by introducing new technologies must include strategies for creating social contexts that support the implementation of the new technologies. Furthermore, the adoption of new technologies is an ongoing endeavor in successful organizations. This endeavor is important because best practices such as EBTs continue to be developed and disseminated in all service areas, and effective organizations must consider using the new technologies as they become available. The ongoing dissemination of new technologies means that training staff in the use of a specific new practice is sufficient for a limited amount of time, until a better alternative is available, so organizations can never stop exploring new technologies that address emerging service issues or concerns. The best organizations never become complacent or satisfied with the status quo. The beliefs among its members that there are always more improvements possible in the services they provide are reinforced and supported by their OSCs.

The role of social context in providing effective service that we have documented in our studies, suggests that having staff trained in organizational strategies for improving services is as important to an organization's effectiveness as having staff trained in the latest treatments or practice technologies. In most human services, however, relatively few resources are devoted to training and supporting organizational specialists in strategies for assessing and changing social contexts to improve services. Neither graduate education programs nor human service agencies invest sufficiently in preparing organizational specialists who understand how to improve services with strategies for changing social context. We argue that the current emphasis in health care, behavioral health, social services, and other human services on increasing the use of evidence-based practices should be expanded beyond the focus on core technologies to include strategies that focus on the organization's social context.

Second, the organizational strategies that we have found to be effective in improving services include organizational tools for identifying and addressing service barriers, principles to guide the application of those tools for effective services, and shared mental models that support the organizational improvement effort. The use of multiple tools, principles, and mental models allows for flexibility to emphasize some strategies more than others in working with an organization, depending on the needs of that specific organization. Our experience suggests that not all strategies and their elements are equally useful in all service improvement efforts in all organizations. We have also learned that the respective importance of each strategy and the elements that comprise these strategies is a function of the organization and service barriers that are identified. For example, one organization may already have a well-developed feedback system for monitoring client outcomes while another may not, suggesting that one of ARC's component tools, feedback, varies in its need for development across the two organizations. Or, as described in the case examples introduced in Chapter 2, the leadership of one organization may be open to a constructive critique of the services it provides and the possibility of change, while the leadership of another may be closed to such critique and change. As we explained using the two case examples presented in Chapter 2, both organizations could benefit from improvement, but the array of strategies and their elements that would be most useful would not be the same in each organization.

This is to say that we need more information about which tools, principles, and mental models are most effective for various organizational profiles. Although we maintain that the array of tools, principles, and mental models incorporated in the ARC strategies contribute to organizations functioning at their best, we recognize that the optimal use of those strategies depends on the characteristics of the organization and the issues it faces. Just as effective services require individualized care to clients, they also require tailoring organizational strategies to the needs of specific social contexts. As a result, we have learned that an important first step in an organizational improvement effort is assessing the organization. This includes measuring OSC (as explained in Chapter 3), interviews with key personnel, and observations gathered from initial meetings at all levels. The optimal use of the tools, principles, and mental models composing the ARC strategies depends on the assessment. Similarly, the application of these strategies will vary during the improvement effort. We believe that additional research and development efforts should be committed to identifying the strategies (and key elements of strategies) that are most useful for different organizational profiles and needs at each stage of the improvement process. Although adjustments in the use of the various strategies are made as described in the examples throughout the book, more empirically based information about how and when those adjustments can be made with the greatest impact will contribute to the success of the improvement efforts.

Third, a better understanding of the mechanisms that link the organizational strategies we have described to the desired outcomes is needed to improve the strategies' power and utility in the field. We have identified mechanisms, such as creating a more proficient culture, that mediate ARC strategies' effects on service quality and outcomes. But more work can be done to unwrap the larger array of mechanisms that explain their impact. For example, we need a better understanding of the key mental models and underlying beliefs and assumptions that must be shared among organizational members to promote organizational priorities that align with the ARC principles and effective services. Similarly, we need a better understanding of the social transmission of norms, expectations, and beliefs among organizational members and the relative contribution of these mechanisms to effective change.

A better understanding of the linking mechanisms will contribute to refinements in both the sequence and content of the tools, principles, and mental models applied in the improvement effort. At this point in our practice and research efforts, we know that we can improve service quality and outcomes with the three ARC strategies but cannot identify the full array of linking mechanisms that explain those effects on various outcomes. By tracing the specific linkages from each strategy to each outcome, we will be able to identify which strategies are most needed as a function of the outcomes that are targeted in an organization. For example, we know that proficient culture mediates the effect of the ARC strategies on the adoption of EBTs, but we do not know which of the strategies and their respective elements are most helpful in creating a proficient culture. This type of information would be useful in organizational planning to support specific improvement goals, whether the objective is to increase the use of EBTs, reduce staff turnover, or individualize care.

The important point is that the sequence and content of the tools, principles, and mental models employed during an organizational improvement effort are specified by the ARC model, but variation from organization to organization depends on the targeted outcomes. We view this variation as a function of the unique needs of each organization. At the same time, we believe the ideal sequence and content of the strategies that are employed for a specific organization should be informed by empirical evidence about the mechanisms that link the individual strategies to specific outcomes. This empirical information would contribute to decisions of the ARC specialist and inform the ARC teams' efforts in a way that improves strategy deployment and the achievement of targeted outcomes.

Fourth, we need additional information to understand how to use the ARC strategies in the most efficient manner. As we described in the previous points, knowing which strategies are most effective for specific organizational profiles and knowing the sequence of strategies that are most effective for the targeted outcomes, will allow organizations to tailor improvement efforts with the greatest efficiency. Although there are benefits to building OSCs by incorporating the full set of tools, principles and mental models offered by ARC, organizations face resource and time constraints in their improvement efforts and would welcome the advantage of incorporating those most likely to achieve the precise desired effect. We need more information about how the array of strategies can be used most efficiently by an organization to target outcomes over an extended period and how to determine a priori, the optimal application of the various strategies necessary to achieve success with the least amount of resources.

Efficiency depends on effectiveness, and we argue that the most effective and efficient organizations would employ organizational specialists as staff or consultants who are trained in the full array of strategies that we have described. These specialists provide the organizations with the capacity to use any combination of tools that are needed to address the service barriers identified by an organization at any one time. Depending on the characteristics of the organization's service system at the time and the ability to determine the specific tools, principles, and mental models that would be most efficient, specialists could address service barriers as they arise. As we described in our case examples throughout the book, work on improving services in any organization begins with an analysis of the organization that informs subsequent change efforts and those efforts then evolve over time with the successes and failures that follow. The capacity for change in response to new challenges is increased when specialists work with an organization as staff or consultants over an extended period. The specialists' work is more efficient when there is a history with the organization and the improvement effort is understood to be an ongoing process rather than a segmented event that involves a new specialist starting at square one each time the organizational leaders perceive the need for help. This argues against the well-known pattern of organizational consultants, "blowing in, blowing off and blowing out," as an inefficient approach to organizational improvement.

In summary, although we begin an organizational improvement effort with the idea that the organization can benefit from the full array of strategies included in the ARC model, our experience has illustrated the importance of following the direction of the organizational members who identify the issues that most concern them. Over an extended period, the entire list of tools, principles, and mental models can be used by an organization as it continues to identify and address new service barriers that arise. The process is never complete, however, because there will always be new core technologies, new staff, new client populations, new service opportunities, and new legislative and regulatory mandates that present never-ending challenges for an organization's capacity to align its priorities and activities with the principles of effective service. Our belief is that an organization can respond to these challenges by creating social contexts that expect proficiency, flexibility, and openness to change with an engaged staff who are provided the support and direction they need to do their jobs and improve the services they provide. The ARC strategies are designed to create these types of social contexts and provide an organization with the capacity to mount improvement efforts that identify and address service barriers as they arise.

CONCLUSION

We have more to learn about using organizational strategies to improve human service quality and outcomes. Previously, the efforts and resources of both practitioners and researchers to improve services, whether in health care, behavioral health, social services, or other human service areas have been devoted more to developing and disseminating new core technologies such as EBTs than to strategies for changing organizations. The idea that effective services depend on organizational characteristics is not new, but there are few evidence-based organizational strategies for improving services and proportionately less work has focused on developing such strategies. We have described in the preceding chapters the results of our efforts to develop evidence-based organizational strategies in response to that knowledge gap. We have described strategies for assessing and changing OSCs that were developed through research and practice with a range of different organizations nationwide. We have shown these strategies are helpful in supporting an organization's adoption and implementation of new core technologies, as well as in identifying and addressing a variety of service barriers.

We have explained that creating the OSCs necessary for providing effective services requires three types of strategies. These strategies include organizational tools for identifying and addressing service barriers, principles for aligning priorities to guide improvement, and the development of shared mental models among organizational members to support the principles and tools. The future challenge for both practitioners and researchers is to determine which elements of the ARC component tools, organizational principles, and mental models are most effective for various organizational profiles and characteristics. Likewise, the mechanisms that link each element of each organizational strategy to each desired outcome, and the sequence of strategies that is most effective needs further study. This information will allow an organization to select the combination of strategies that is most likely to meet its needs given the characteristics of the organization and the improvements it seeks. This capacity, in turn, will contribute to the most efficient use of the strategies to meet each organization's goal of improving service quality and outcomes.

REFERENCES

Aarons, G. A., Glisson, C., Green, P., Hoagwood, K., Kelleher, K. J., & Landsverk, J. A. (2012). The organizational social context of mental health services and clinician attitudes toward evidence-based practice: A United States national study. *Implementation Science*, 7(1), 56. doi:10.1186/1748-5908-7-56.

Aarons, G. A., Hurlburt, M., & Horwitz, S. M. (2011). Advancing a conceptual model of evidence-based practice implementation in public sectors. *Administration and Policy in Mental Health*, 38(1), 4–23.

Aarons, G. A., & Sawitzky, A. C. (2006). Organizational climate partially mediates the effect of culture on work attitudes and staff turnover in mental health services. *Administration and Policy in Mental Health*, 33(3), 289–301.

Aarons, G. A., Sommerfeld, D. H., & Walrath-Greene, C. M. (2009). Evidence-based practice implementation: The impact of public versus private sector organization type on organizational support, provider attitudes, and adoption of evidence-based practice. *Implementation Science*, 4(83), 1–13. doi:10.1186/1748-5908-4-83.

Aiken, L. H., Smith, H. L., & Lake, E. T. (1994). Lower Medicare mortality among a set of hospitals known for good nursing care. *Medical Care*, 32(8), 771–787.

Ajzen, I. (1991). The theory of planned behavior. *Organizational Behavior and Human Decision Processes*, 50, 179–211.

Ajzen, I., & Fishbein, M. (1980). *Understanding attitudes and predicting social behavior.* Englewood Cliffs, NJ: Prentice-Hall.

Alper, S., Tjosvold, D., & Law, K. S. (2000), Conflict management, efficacy, and performance in organizational teams. *Personnel Psychology*, 53, 625–642.

Angermeier, I., Dunford, B. B., Boss, A. D., & Boss, R. W. (2009). The impact of participative management perceptions on customer service, medical errors, burnout, and turnover intentions. *Journal of Healthcare Management*, 54(2), 127.

Annie E. Casey Foundation. (2003). The unsolved challenge at system reform—the condition of the Frontline Human Service workforce. Retrieved January 2018 from Annie E. Casey Foundation site, http://www.aecf.org/m//resourcedoc/aecf-theUunsolvedChallengeSystemReform-2003.pdf

Annie E. Casey Foundation. (2004). *HR Turnover Calculator*. Retrieved January 2018 from http://www.cpshr.us/workforceplanning/documents/ToolKitTurnover.pdf

Arango, P. (2011). Family-centered care. *Academic Pediatrics, 11*(2), 97–99.

Argyris, C. (2004). "Double loop learning and organizational change. Facilitating transformational change", in Boonstra, J.J. (Ed.), *Dynamics of Organizational Change and Learning*. Wiley, Chichester.

Argyris, C., & Schon, D. A. (1996). *Organizational learning: Theory, method and practice* (2d ed.). Reading, MA: Addison-Wesley.

Armitage, C. J., & Conner, M. (2001). Efficacy of the theory of planned behavior: A meta-analytic review. *British Journal of Social Psychology, 40*(4), 471–499.

Ashkanasy, N.M., Broadfoot, L. E., & Falkus, S. A. (2000). Questionnaire measures of organizational culture. In N. Ashkanasy, C. Wilderom, & M. Peterson (Eds.), *Handbook of organizational culture and climate* (pp. 131–145). Thousand Oaks, CA: SAGE.

Ashkanasy, N. M., Wilderom, C. P. M., & Peterson, M. F. (Eds.). (2000). *Handbook of organizational culture and climate*. Thousand Oaks, CA: SAGE.

Bachmann, R., & Inkpen, A. C. (2011). Understanding institutional-based trust building processes in inter-organizational relationships. *Organization Studies, 32*(2), 281–301.

Backer, T. E., & Rogers, E. M. (1998). Diffusion of innovations theory and work-site AIDS programs. *Journal of Health Communication, 3*(1), 17–29.

Baer, M., & Frese, M. (2003). Innovation is not enough: Climates for initiatives and psychological safety, process innovations and firm performance. *Journal of Organizational Behavior, 24*(1), 45–68.

Baer, J. S., Wells, E. A., Rosengren, D. B., Hartzler, B., Beadnell, B., & Dunn, C. (2009). Agency context and tailored training in technology transfer: A pilot evaluation of motivational interviewing training for community counselors. *Journal of Substance Abuse Treatment, 37*(2), 191–202.

Bandura, A. (1997). *Self-efficacy: The exercise of control*. New York: Freeman.

Bandura, A. (1977). *Social learning theory*. Englewood Cliffs, NJ: Prentice-Hall.

Bandura, A. (1986). *Social foundations of thought and action: A social cognitive theory*. Englewood Cliffs, NJ: Prentice-Hall.

Bank, W. (2014). Thinking with mental models. In *World Development Report 2015: Mind, Society, and Behavior* (pp. 62–75). Washington, DC: World Bank.

Barends, E., Janssen, B., ten Have, W., & ten Have, S. (2013). Effects of change interventions: What kind of evidence do we really have? *Journal of Applied Behavioral Science, 50*(1), 5–27.

Bargh, J. A., Chen, M., & Burrows, L. (1996). Automaticity of social behavior: Direct effects of trait-construct and stereotype activation on action. *Journal of Personality and Social Psychology, 71*(2), 230–244.

Barnsley, J., Lemieux-Charles, L., & McKinney, M. M. (1998). Integrating learning into integrated delivery systems. *Health Care Management Review, 23*(1), 18–28.

Barraud-Didier, V., & Guerrero, S. (2002). Impact of social innovations on French companies' performance. *Measuring Business Excellence, 6*(2), 42–48.

Bartholomew, N. G., Joe, G. W., Rowan-Szal, G. A., & Simpson, D. D. (2007). Counselor assessments of training and adoption barriers. *Journal of Substance Abuse Treatment, 33*(2), 193–199.

Beer, M (1980). *Organizational change and development: A systems view*. Santa Monica, CA: Goodyear.

Bess, K. D., Prilleltensky, I., Perkins, D. D., & Collins, L. V. (2009). Participatory organizational change in community-based health and human services: From tokenism to political engagement. *American Journal of Community Psychology, 43*(1–2), 134–148.

Beidas, R. S., & Kendall, P. C. (2010). Training therapists in evidence-based practice: A critical review of studies from a systems-contextual perspective. *Clinical Psychology: Science & Practice, 17*, 1–30.

Bennis, W. G. (1966). *Changing organizations.* New York: McGraw-Hill.

Berlowitz, D. R., Young, G. J., Hickey, E. C., Saliba, D., Mittman, B. S., Czarnowski, E., et al. (2003). Quality improvement implementation in the nursing home. *Health Services Research, 38*(1), 65–83.

Bersin, J. (January 18, 2012). 5 keys to building a learning organization. Retrieved from http://www.forbes.com/sites/joshbersin/2012/01/18/5-keys-to-building-a-learning-organization/#4db3fbd04218

Bickman, L., & Noser, K. (1999). Meeting the challenges in the delivery of child and adolescent mental health services in the next millennium: The continuous quality improvement approach. *Applied and Preventive Psychology, 8*(4), 247–255.

Birleson, P. (1998). Building a learning organisation in a child and adolescent mental health service. *Australian Health Review, 21*(3), 223–240.

Blake, R. R., Shepard, H. A., & Mouton, J. S. (1964). *Managing intergroup conflict in industry.* Houston, TX: Gulf.

Blanz, B., & Schmidt, M. H. (2000). Practitioner review: Preconditions and outcome of inpatient treatment in child and adolescent psychiatry. *Journal of Child Psychology and Psychiatry, 41*(6), 703–712.

Blumenthal, D., & Kilo, C. M. (1998). A report card on continuous quality improvement. *Milbank Quarterly, 76*(4), 625–648.

Branch, K. M. (2002). Participative management and employee and stakeholder involvement. *Management Benchmarking Study*, 1–27. Retrieved on January 2018 from http://www.sc.doe.gov/sc5/benchmark/Ch%2010%20Participative-%20Management%2006.08.02.pdf

Britt, E., Blampied, N. M., & Hudson, S. M. (2003). Motivational interviewing: A review. *Australian Psychologist, 38*(3), 193–201.

Broome, K. M., Flynn, P. M., Knight, D. K., & Simpson, D. D. (2007). Program structure, staff perceptions, and client engagement in treatment. *Journal of Substance Abuse Treatment, 33*(2), 149–158.

Brown, S. P., & Leigh, T. W. (1996). A new look at psychological climate and its relationship to job involvement, effort, and performance. *Journal of Applied Psychology, 81*(4), 358–368.

Burke, W. W. (1993). *Organization Development* (2d ed.). Reading, MA: Addison-Wesley.

Burnette, J. L., O'Boyle, E. H., VanEpps, E. M., Pollack, J. M., & Finkel, E. J. (2013). Mind-sets matter: A meta-analytic review of implicit theories and self-regulation. *Psychological Bulletin, 139*(3), 655–701.

Burns, T., & Stalker, G. M. (1961). *The management of innovation.* New York: Oxford University Press.

Butler, J. K., & Cantrell, R. S. (1994). Communication factors and trust: An exploratory study. *Psychological Reports, 74*(1), 33–34.

Caldwell, D. F., & O'Reilly, C. A. (1982). Boundary spanning and individual performance: The impact of self-monitoring. *Journal of Applied Psychology, 67*(1), 124–127.

Callister, R. R., & Wall, J. A. (2001). Conflict across organizational boundaries: Managed care organizations versus health care providers. *Journal of Applied Psychology, 86*(4), 754–763.

Cappella, E., Frazier, S. L., Atkins, M. S., Schoenwald, S. K., & Glisson, C. (2008). Enhancing schools' capacity to support children in poverty: An ecological model of school-based mental health services. *Administration and Policy in Mental Health and Mental Health Services Research, 35*(5), 395–409.

Carlfjord, S., Andersson, A., Nilsen, P., Bendtsen, P., & Lindberg, M. (2010). The importance of organizational climate and implementation strategy at the introduction of a new working tool in primary health care. *Journal of Evaluation in Clinical Practice, 16*(6), 1326–1332.

Carr, J. Z., Schmidt, A. M., Ford, J. K., & DeShon, R. P. (2003). Climate perceptions matter: A meta-analytic path analysis relating molar climate, cognitive and affective states, and individual level work outcomes. *Journal of Applied Psychology, 88*(4), 605–619.

Carver, C. S., & Scheier, M, F. (1981). *Attention and self regulation: A control theory to human behavior.* New York: Springer-Verlag.

Christiansen, S. (1992). Emotional stress and eyewitness memory: A critical review. *Psychological Bulletin, 112*(2), 284–309.

Cohen, S., & Wills, T. A. (1985). Stress, social support, and the buffering hypothesis. *Psychological Bulletin, 98*(2), 310.

Cooke, R. A., & Rousseau, D. M. (1988). Behavioral norms and expectations: A quantitative approach to the assessment of organizational culture. *Group & Organization Studies, 13*(3), 245–273.

Cotton, J. L. (1995). Participation's effect on performance and satisfaction: A reconsideration of Wagner. *The Academy of Management Review, 20*(2), 276–278.

Cotton, J. L., Vollrath, D. A., Froggatt, K. L., Lengnick-Hall, M. L., & Jennings, K. R. (1988). Employee participation: Diverse forms and different outcomes. *Academy of Management Review, 13*(1), 8–22.

Craik, K. (1943). *The nature of explanation.* Cambridge, U.K.: Cambridge University Press.

Cummings, G. G., Estabrooks, C. A., Midodzi, W. K., Wallin, L., & Hayduk, L. (2007). Influence of organizational characteristics and context on research utilization. *Nursing Research, 56*(4), S24-S39. doi: 10.1097/01.NNR.0000280629.63654.95.

Cummings, T. G., & Worley, C. G. (2014). *Organization Development & Change.* Stamford, Ct: Cengage Learning.

Damschroder, L. J., Aron, D. C., Keith, R. E., Kirsh, S. R., Alexander, J. A., & Lowery, J. C. (2009). Fostering implementation of health services research findings into practice: A consolidated framework for advancing implementation science. *Implementation Science, 4*, 50.

Davidoff, J. (2013, December 2). Mission-focused results. Retrieved from http://www.thenonprofittimes.com/news-articles/mission-focused-results/

Dearing, J. W., & And, O. (1994). Portraying the new: Communication between university innovators and potential users. *Science Communication, 16*(1), 11–42.

Deloitte (2013). *Culture of purpose: A business imperative. 2013 core beliefs & culture survey.* Retrieved from http://www2.deloitte.com/content/dam/Deloitte/us/Documents/about-deloitte/us-leadership-2013-core-beliefs-culture-survey-051613.pdf

Deming, W. E. (1986). Out of crisis, Centre for Advanced Engineering study. Cambridge, MA: MIT Press.

Denison, D. R. (1996). What is the difference between organizational culture and organizational climate? A native's point of view on a decade of paradigm wars. *Academy of management review, 21*(3), 619–654.

Denison, D. R., & Mishra, A. K. (1995). Toward a theory of organizational culture and effectiveness. *Organization Science, 6*(2), 204–223.

DiMaggio, P. (1997). Culture and cognition. *Annual Review of Sociology, 23*, 263–287.

DiMatteo, M. R., Sherbourne, C. D., Hays, R. D., Ordway, L., Kravitz, R. L., McGlynn, E. A., et al. (1993). Physicians' characteristics influence patients' adherence to medical treatment: Results from the Medical Outcomes study. *Health Psychology, 12*(2), 93.

Dirkson, C. D., Ament, A. J., & Go, P. M. (1996). Diffusion of six surgical endoscopic procedures in The Netherlands: Stimulating and restraining factors. *Health Policy, 37*(2), 91–104.

Donchin, Y., Gopher, D., Olin, M., Badihi, Y., Biesky, M., Sprung, C. L., et al. (1995). A look into the nature and causes of human errors in the intensive care unit. *Critical Care Medicine, 23*(2), 294–300.

Doran, D., Haynes, B. R., Estabrooks, C. A., Kushniruk, A., Dubrowski, A., Bajnok, I., et al. (2012). The role of organizational context and individual nurse characteristics in explaining variation in use of information technologies in evidence based practice. *Implementation Science, 7*, 122.

Doss, B. D. (2006). Changing the way we study change in psychotherapy. *Clinical Psychology: Science and Practice, 11*(4), 368–386.

Doucouliagos, C. (1995). Worker participation and productivity in labor-managed and participatory capitalist firms: A meta-analysis. *Industrial and Labor Relations Review, 49*(1), 58–77.

Dozier, M., Cue, K. L., & Barnett, L. (1994). Clinicians as caregivers: Role of attachment organization in treatment. *Journal of Consulting and Clinical Psychology, 62*(4), 793.

Druskat, V. U., & Pescosolido, A.T. (2002). The content of effective teamwork mental models in self-managing teams: Ownership, learning and heedful interrelating. *Human Relations. 55*(3), 283–314.

Durham, C. C., Knight, D., & Locke, E. A. (1997). Effects of leader role, team-set goal difficulty, efficacy, and tactics on team effectiveness. *Organizational Behavior and Human Decision Processes, 72*(2), 203–229.

Dweck, C. S., & Leggett, E. L. (1988). A social-cognitive approach to motivation and personality. *Psychological Review, 95*(2), 256–273.

Dyer, W. G. (1977). *Team building: Issues and alternatives.* Reading, MA: Addison-Wesley.

Edmondson, A. C. (2001). *Manage the risk of learning: Psychological safety in work teams.* Cambridge, MA: Division of Research, Harvard Business School.

Edmondson, A. C., Bohmer, R., & Pisano, G. P. (2001). Disrupted routines: Team learning and new technology implementation in hospitals. *Administrative Science Quarterly, 46*(4), 685–716.

Edmondson, A. C., Kramer, R. M., & Cook, K. S. (2004). Psychological safety, trust, and learning in organizations: A group-level lens. *Trust and Distrust in Organizations: Dilemmas and Approaches, 12*, 239–272.

Eisenberger, N. I., Lieberman, M. D., & Williams, K. D. (2003). Does rejection hurt? An fMRI study of socEial exclusion. *Science, 302*(5643), 290–292.

Ensley, M. D., & Pearce, C. L. (2001). Shared cognition in top management teams: Implications for new venture performance. *Journal of Organizational Behavior, 22*(2), 145–160.

Eysenck, M. W. (1992). *Attention and arousal: Cognition and performance.* Berlin: Springer-Verlag.

Fishbein, M., Triandis, H. C., Kanfer, F. H., Becker, M., Middlestadt, S. E., & Eichler, A. (2001). Factors influencing behavior and behavior change. In A. Baum, T. Revenson, & J. Singer (Eds.), *Handbook of health psychology* (pp. 3–17). Mahwah, NJ: Lawrence Erlbaum Associates.

Fiske, S.T., & Taylor, S.E. (2013). *From brains to culture: Social cognition.* Los Angeles: SAGE.

Ferlie, E., Gabbay, J., Fitzgerald, L., Locock, L., & Dopson, S. (2001). Evidence-based medicine and organisational change: An overview of some recent qualitative research In L. Ashburner (Eds.), *Organisational behaviour and organisational studies in health care: Reflections on the future* (pp. 18–42). Basingstoke, U.K.: Palgrave Macmillan.

Florsheim, P., Shotorbani, S., Guest-Warnick, G., Barratt, T., & Hwang, W. C. (2000). Role of the working alliance in the treatment of delinquent boys in community-based programs. *Journal of Clinical Child Psychology, 29*(1), 94–107.

Flower, C., McDonald, J., & Sumski, M. (2005). *Review of turnover in Milwaukee County private agency child welfare ongoing case management staff.* Milwaukee, WI: Bureau of Milwaukee Child Welfare.

Foster-Fishman, P. G., & Keys, C. B. (1997). The person/environment dynamics of employee empowerment: An organizational culture analysis. *American Journal of Community Psychology, 25*(3), 345–369.

French, W. L., & Bell, C. H. (1984). *Organization development: Behavioral science interventions for organization improvement* (3d ed.). Englewood Cliffs, NJ: Prentice- Hall.

Frese, M., & Zapf, D. (1994). Action as the core of work psychology: A German approach. In H. C. Triandis, M. D. Dunnette, & L. M. Hough (Eds.), *Handbook of industrial and organizational psychology* (2d ed., Vol.4, pp. 271–340). Palo Alto, CA: Consulting Psychologists.

Friedmann, P. D., Taxman, F. S., & Henderson, C. E. (2007). Evidence-based treatment practices for drug-involved adults in the criminal justice system. *Journal of Substance Abuse Treatment, 32*(3), 267–277.

Fu, P.O., Kennedy, J., Tata, J., Yukl, G., Bond, M. H., et al. (2004). The impact of societal cultural values and individual social beliefs on the perceived effectiveness of managerial influence strategies: A meso approach. *Journal of International Business Studies, 35*(4), 284–305.

Gao, L., Janssen, O., & Shi, K. (2011). Leader trust and employee voice: The moderating role of empowering leader behaviors. *The Leadership Quarterly, 22*(4), 787–798.

Garvin, D. A. (1993). Building a learning organization. *Harvard Business Review,* July–August, 78–91.

Garvin, D. A., Edmondson, A. C., & Gino, F. (2008). Is yours a learning organization? *Harvard Business Review, 86*(3), 109.

Garvin, D. A. (1993). Borkovec, T. D., Echemendia, R. J., Ragusea, S. A., & Ruiz, M. (2001). The Pennsylvania Practice Research Network and future possibilities for clinically meaningful and scientifically rigorous psychotherapy effectiveness research. *Clinical Psychology: Science and Practice, 8*(2), 155–167.

Gibson, C. B. (2001). Me and us: Differential relationships among goal-setting training, efficacy and effectiveness at the individual and team level. *Journal of Organizational Behavior, 22*(7), 789–808.

Gioia, D., & Dziadosz, G. (2008). Adoption of evidence-based practices in community mental health: A mixed methods study of practitioner experience. *Community Mental Health Journal, 44*(5), 347–357.

Glisson, C.A. (1978). Dependence of technological routinization on structural variables in human service organizations. *Administrative Science Quarterly, 23*(3), 383–395.

Glisson, C. (1992). Structure and technology in human service organizations. In Y. Hasenfeld (Ed.), *Human services as complex organizations* (pp. 184–202). Beverly Hills, CA: SAGE.

Glisson, C. (2007). Assessing and changing organizational culture and climate for effective services. *Research on Social Work Practice, 17*(6), 736–747.

Glisson, C. (2009). Organizational climate and culture and performance in the human services. In R.J. Patti (Ed.), *Handbook of human services management* (2d ed., pp.119–142). Thousand Oaks, CA: SAGE.

Glisson, C. (2010). Organizational climate and service outcomes in child welfare agencies. In M. B. Webb, K. Dowd, B. J. Harden, J. Landsverk, & M. F. Testa (Eds.), *Child welfare and child well-being: New perspectives from the national survey of child and adolescent well-being* (pp. 378–406). New York: Oxford University Press.

Glisson, C., Dukes, D., & Green, P.D. (2006). The effects of the ARC organizational intervention on caseworker turnover, climate, and culture in children's service systems. *Child Abuse & Neglect, 30*(8), 855–880.

Glisson, C., & Durick, M. (1988). Predictors of job satisfaction and organizational commitment in human service organizations. *Administrative Science Quarterly, 33*(1), 61–81.

Glisson, C., & Green, P. (2006). The effects of organizational culture and climate on the access to mental health care in child welfare and juvenile justice systems. *Administration and Policy in Mental Health and Mental Health Services Research, 33*(4), 433–448.

Glisson, C., & Green, P. D. (2011). Organizational climate, services and outcomes in child welfare systems. *Child Abuse & Neglect*, 35(8), 582–591 doi:10.1016/j.chiabu.2011.04.009.

Glisson, C.A. (2012). Interventions with organizations. In C.A. Glisson, C.N. Dulmus, & K.M. Sowers (Eds.). *Social work practice with groups, communities and organizations* (pp.159–190). Hoboken, NJ: John Wiley & Sons, Inc.

Glisson, C., Green, P., & Williams, N. (2012). Assessing the organizational social context (OSC) of child welfare systems: Implications for research and practice. *Child Abuse & Neglect*, 36(9), 621–632. doi: 10.1016/j.chiabu.2012.06.002.

Glisson, C., & Hemmelgarn, A. L. (1998). The effects of organizational climate and interorganizational co-ordination on the quality and outcomes of children's service systems. *Child Abuse and Neglect*, 22(5), 401–421.

Glisson, C., Hemmelgarn, A., Green, P., Dukes, D., Atkinson, S., & Williams, N. (2012). Randomized trial of the ARC organizational intervention with community-based mental health programs and clinicians serving youth. *Journal of the American Academy of Child and Adolescent Psychiatry*, 51(8), 780–787. doi: 10.1016/j.jaac.2012.05.010.

Glisson, C., Hemmelgarn, A., Green, P., & Williams, N. (2013). Randomized trial of the availability, responsiveness and continuity (ARC) Organizational Intervention for Improving Youth Outcomes in Community Mental Health Programs. *Journal of the American Academy of Child and Adolescent Psychiatry*, 52(5), 493–500. doi: 10.1016/j.jaac.2013.02.005.

Glisson, C., Hemmelgarn, A. L., & Post, J. A. (2002). The Shortform Assessment for Children (SAC): An assessment and outcome measure for child welfare and juvenile justice. *Research on Social Work Practice*, 12(1), 82–106.

Glisson, C., & James, L.R. (2002). The cross-level effects of culture and climate in human service teams. *Journal of Organizational Behavior*, 23(6), 767–794.

Glisson, C., Landsverk, J., Schoenwald, S. K., Kelleher, K., Hoagwood, K. E., Mayberg, S., et al. (2008). Assessing the organizational social context (OSC) of mental health services: Implications for implementation research and practice. *Administration and Policy in Mental Health and Mental Health Services Research*, 35(1), 98–113.

Glisson, C., & Schoenwald, S.K. (2005). The ARC organizational and community intervention strategy for implementing evidence-based children's mental health treatments. *Mental Health Services Research*, 7(4), 243–259.

Glisson, C., Schoenwald, S.K., Hemmelgarn, A.L., Green, P.D., Dukes, D., Armstrong, K.S., & Chapman, J.E. (2010). Randomized trial of MST and ARC in a two-level evidence-based treatment implementation strategy. *Journal of Consulting and Clinical Psychology*, 78(4), 537–550. doi: 10.1037/a0019160.

Glisson, C., Schoenwald, S.K., Kelleher, K., Landsverk, J., Hoagwood, K.E., Mayberg, S., et al. (2008). Therapist turnover and new program sustainability in mental health clinics as a function of organizational culture, climate, and service structure. *Administration and Policy in Mental Health and Mental Health Services Research*, 35(1), 124–133.

Glisson, C., & Williams, N. J. (2014). Testing a theory of organizational culture, climate and youth outcomes in child welfare systems: A United States national study. *Child Abuse and Neglect*, 38(4), 757–767.

Glisson, C., & Williams, N. J. (2015). Assessing and changing organizational social contexts for effective mental health services. *Annual Review of Public Health*, 36, 507–523. doi: 10.1146/annurev-publhealth-031914-122435.

Glisson, C., Williams, N.J., Hemmelgarn, A., Proctor, E., & Green, P. (2016a). 'Aligning organizational priorities with ARC to improve youth mental health service outcomes.' *Journal of Consulting and Clinical Psychology*. *84*(8), 713–725. doi: 10.1037/ccp0000107.

Glisson, C., Williams, N.J., Hemmelgarn, A., Proctor, E., & Green, P. (2016b). 'Increasing clinicians' EBT exploration and preparation behavior in youth mental health services by changing organizational culture with ARC. *Behaviour Research and Therapy*, *76*(1), 40–46. doi.org/10.1016/j.brat.2015.11.008.

Godin, G., Belanger-Gravel, A., Eccles, M., & Grimshaw, J. (2008). Healthcare professionals' intentions and behaviors: A systematic review of studies based on social cognitive theories. *Implementation Science*, *3*, 36.

Goes, J. B., & Park, S. H. (1997). Intraorganizational links and innovation: The case of hospital services. *Academy of Management Journal*, *40*(3), 673–696.

Graef, M. I., & Hill, E. L. (2000). Costing child protective services staff turnover. *Child Welfare*, *79*(5), 517–533.

Grant, A. M. (2007). Relational job design and the motivation to make a prosocial difference. *Academy of Management Review*, *32*(2), 393–417.

Gray, B. (1985). Conditions facilitating interorganizational collaboration. *Human Relations*, *38*(10), 911–936.

Gray, B. (1990). Building interorganizational alliances: Planned change in a global environment, *Research in Organizational Change and Development*, *4*, 101–140.

Green, P. S. (1998). Improving clinical effectiveness in an integrated care delivery system. *Journal for Healthcare Quality*, *20*(6), 4–9.

Greener, J. M., Joe, G. W., Simpson, D. D., Rowan-Szal, G. A., & Lehman, W. E. K. (2007). Influence of organizational functioning on client engagement in treatment. *Journal of Substance Abuse Treatment*, *33*(2), 139–147.

Greenfield, S., Kaplan, S., & Ware, J. E. (1985). Expanding patient involvement in care: Effects on patient outcomes. *Annals of Internal Medicine*, *102*(4), 520–528.

Greenhalgh, T., Robert, G., MacFarlane, F., Bate, P., & Kyriakidou, O. (2004). Diffusion of innovations in service organizations: A systematic review and recommendations. *Milbank Quarterly*, *82*(4), 581–629.

Grimshaw, J. M., Thomas, R. E., MacLennan, G., Fraser, C., Ramsay, C. R., Vale, L., et al. (2004). Effectiveness and efficiency of guideline dissemination and implementation strategies. *Health Technology Assessment Report*, *8*(6), 1–84.

Grol, R. P., Bosch, M. C., Hulscher, M. E., Eccles, M. P., & Wensing, M. (2007). Planning and studying improvement in patient care: The use of theoretical perspectives. *Milbank Quarterly*, *85*(1), 93–138.

Groscurth, C. (2014, March 6). Why your company must be mission-driven. Retrieved March 2015 online from The Gallup Business Journal, http://www.gallup.com/businessjournal/167633/why-company-mission-driven.aspx

Gustafson, D. H., Sainfort, F., Eichler, M., Adams, L., Bisognano, M., & Steudel, H. (2003). Developing and testing a model to predict outcomes of organizational change. *Health Services Research*, *38*(2), 751–776.

Guzzo, R. A., Jette, R. D., & Katzell, R. A. (1985). The effects of psychologically based intervention programs on worker productivity: A meta-analysis. *Personnel Psychology*, *38*(2), 275–291.

Hackman, J. R., & Oldham, G. R. (1980). *Work redesign*. Reading, MA: Addison-Wesley.

Harter, J. K., Schmidt, F. L., Agrawal, M. S. & Plowman, S. K. (2013). The relationship between engagement at work and organizational outcomes] Gallup New Directions Consulting.

Hartnell, C. A., Ou, A. Y., & Kinicki, A. (2011). Organizational culture and organizational effectiveness: A meta-analytic investigation of the competing values framework's theoretical suppositions. *Journal of Applied Psychology, 96*(4), 677–694.

Harvey, G., Loftus-Hills, A., Rycroft-Malone, J., Titchen, A., Kitson, A., McCormack, B., et al. (2002). Getting evidence into practice: The role and function of facilitation. *Journal of Advanced Nursing, 37*(6), 577–588.

Herman, J. B., & Hulin, C. L. (1972). Studying organizational attitudes from individual and organizational frames of reference. *Organizational Behavior and Human Performance, 8*(1), 84–108.

Higgins, S. E., & Routhieaux, R. L. (1999). A multiple level analysis of hospital team effectiveness. *Health Care Supervisor, 17*(4), 1–13.

Hemmelgarn, A.L., Glisson, C., & Dukes, D. (2001). Emergency room culture and the emotional support component of family-centered care. *Children's Health Care, 30*(2), 93–110.

Hemmelgarn, A. L., Glisson, C., & James, L. R. (2006). Organizational culture and climate: Implications for services and intervention research. *Clinical Psychology: Science and Practice, 13*(1), 73–89.

Hemmelgarn, A.L., Glisson, C., & Sharp, S. (2003). The validity of the Shortform Assessment for Children. *Research on Social Work Practice, 13*(4), 510–530.

Henderson, C. E., Young, D. W., Jainchill, N., Hawke, J., Farkas, S., & Davis, R. M. (2007). Program use of effective drug abuse treatment practices for juvenile offenders. *Journal of Substance Abuse Treatment, 32*(3), 279–290.

Henggeler, S. W., Chapman, J. E., Rowland, M. D., Halliday-Boykins, C. A., Randall, J., Shackelford, J., et al. (2008). Statewide adoption and initial implementation of contingency management for substance-abusing adolescents. *Journal of Consulting and Clinical Psychology, 76*(4), 556–567.

Hoagwood, K. E., Green, E., Kelleher, K., Schoenwald, S., Rolls-Reutz, J., Landsverk, J., et al. (2008). Family advocacy, support and education in children's mental health: Results of a national survey. *Administration and Policy in Mental Health and Mental Health Services Research, 35*(1–2), 73–83.

Hodges, S. P., & Hernandez, M. (1999). How organizational culture influences outcome information utilization. *Evaluation and Program Planning, 22*, 183–1997.

Hofstede, G. (1998). Attitudes, values, and organizational culture: Disentangling the concepts. *Organization Studies, 19*(3), 477–492.

Hofstede, G., Neuijen, B., Ohayv, D. D., & Sanders, G. (1990). Measuring organizational cultures: A qualitative and quantitative study across twenty cases. *Administrative Science Quarterly, 35*, 286–316.

Hoy, W. K. (1990). Organizational climate and culture: A conceptual analysis of the school workplace. *Journal of Educational and Psychological Consultation, 1*(2), 149–168.

Hulpia, H., Devos, G., & Rosseel, Y. (2009). The relationship between the perception of distributed leadership in secondary schools and teachers' and teacher leaders' job satisfaction and organizational commitment. *School Effectiveness and School Improvement, 20*(3), 291–317.

Hysong, S. J., Best, R. G., Pugh, J. A., & Moore, F. I. (2005). Not of one mind: Mental models of clinical practice guidelines in the Veterans Health Administration. *Health Services Research, 40*(3), 829–847.

Iacoboni, M., Lieberman, M. D., Knowlton, B. J., Molnar-Szakacs, I., Moritz, M., Throop, C. J., et al. (2004). Watching social interactions produces dorsomedial prefrontal and medial parietal BOLD fMRI signal increases compared to a resting baseline. *NeuroImage, 21*(3), 1167–1173.

Institute of Medicine (2000). *To err is human: Building a safer health system.* Washington, DC: National Academy.

Ismail, A., Zainuddin, N. F. A., & Ibrahim, Z. (2010). Linking participative and consultative leadership styles to organizational commitment as an antecedent of job satisfaction. *UNITAR e-Journal, 6*(1), 11–26.

Jaccard, J., Litardo, H. A., & Wan, C. K. (1999). Subjective culture and social behavior. In J. Adamopoulos & Y. Kashima (Eds.), *Social psychology and cultural context* (pp. 95–106). Thousand Oaks, CA: SAGE.

James, L. A., & James, L. R. (1989). Integrating work environment perceptions: Explorations into the measurement of meaning. *Journal of Applied Psychology, 74*(5), 739–751.

James, L. R., Demaree, R. G., & Wolf, G. (1984). Estimating within-group interrater reliability with and without response bias. *Journal of Applied Psychology, 69*(1), 85–98.

Jensen-Doss, A., Hawley, K. M., Lopez, M., & Osterberg, L. D. (2009). Using evidence-based treatments: The experiences of youth providers working under a mandate. *Professional Psychology: Research and Practice, 40*(4), 417–424.

Johnson, F. (2015, November 21). This is what real work flexibility looks like. Retrieved from http://www.theatlantic.com/business/archive/2014/11/this-is-what-real-work-flexibility-looks-like/425823/

Johnson-Laird, P. N. (1983). *Mental models: Towards a cognitive science of language, inference, and consciousness* (No. 6). Cambridge, MA: Harvard University Press.

Johnson-Laird, P. N. (1994). Mental models, deductive reasoning, and the brain. In M. S. Gazzaniga (Ed.), *The cognitive neurosciences* (pp. 999–1008). Cambridge, MA: MIT Press.

Jones, A. P., & James, L. R. (1979). Psychological climate: Dimensions and relationships of individual and aggregated work environment perceptions. *Organizational Behavior and Human Performance, 23*(2), 201–250.

Jones, R. A., Jimmieson, N. L., & Griffiths, A. (2005). The impact of organizational culture and reshaping capabilities on change implementation success: The mediating role of readiness for change. *Journal of Management Studies, 42*(2), 361–386.

Jonassen, D. H., & Henning, P. (1996). Mental models: Knowledge in the head and knowledge in the world. In *Proceedings of the 1996 international conference on learning sciences,* (pp. 433–438). International Society of the Learning Sciences. Evanston, IL.

Joyce, W. F., & Slocum, J. W. (1984). Collective climate: Agreement as a basis for defining aggregate climates in organizations. *Academy of Management Journal, 24*(4), 721–742.

Katz, E. (1961). The social itinerary of technical change: Two studies on the diffusion of innovation. *Human Organization, 20*(2), 70–82.

Kazdin, A. E. (2007). Mediators and mechanisms of change in psychotherapy research. *Annual Review of Clinical Psychology, 3,* 1–27.

Kazdin, A. E. (2009). Understanding how and why psychotherapy leads to change. *Psychotherapy Research, 19*(4–5), 418–428.

Kazdin, A. E. (2015). Treatment as usual and routine care in research and clinical practice. *Clinical Psychology Review, 42,* 168–178.

Kelly, H. H. (1972). Attribution in social interaction In E. E. Jones, D. E. Kanouse, H. H. Kelly, R. E. Nisbett, S. Valins, & B. Weiner. (Eds.), *Attribution: perceiving the causes of behavior.* (pp. 1–26). Morristown, NJ: General Learning.

Khemlani, S. S., Barbey, A. K., & Johnson-Laird, P. N. (2014). Causal reasoning with mental models. *Frontiers in Human Neuroscience, 8,* 849.

Klein, K. J. & Sorra, J. S. (1996). The challenge of innovation implementation. *Academy of Management Review, 24*(4), 1055–1080.

Kluger, A.N. & DeNisi, A. (1996). The effects of feedback interventions on performance: A historical review, a meta-analysis, and a preliminary feedback intervention theory. *Psychological Bulletin, 119*(2), 254–284.

Knight, D., Durham, C. C., & Locke, E. A. (2001). The relationship of team goals, incentives, and efficacy to strategic risk, tactical implementation, and performance. *Academy of Management Journal, 44*(2), 326–338.

Kuo, D. Z., Bird, M. T., & Tilford, J. M. (2011). Associations of family-centered care with health care outcomes for children with special health care needs. *Maternal and Child Health Journal, 15*(6), 794–805.

Larren, H. (2014, September 24). 6 reasons why everyone should work for a Mission-driven Company. Retrieved from http://www.huffingtonpost.com/herve-larren/6-reasons-why-everyone-sh_b_5611747.html

Latham, G. P., Winters, D. C., & Locke, E. A. (1994). Cognitive and motivational effects of participation: A mediator study. *Journal of Organizational Behavior, 15*(1), 49–63.

Lawrence, P. (1969). How to with resistance to change. *Harvard Business Review,* Jan–Feb, 1–10.

Leff, P. T., Chan, J. M., & Walizer, E. M. (1991). Self-understanding and reaching out to sick children and their families: An ongoing professional challenge. *Children's Health Care, 20*(4), 230–239.

Lemieux-Charles, L., Murray, M., Baker, G. R., Barnsley, J., Tasa, K., & Ibrahim, S. A. (2002). The effects of quality improvement practices on team effectiveness: A meditational model. *Journal of Organizational Behavior, 23*(5), 533–553.

Lewinsohn, S., & Mano, H. (1993). Multi-attribute choice and affect: The influence of naturally occurring and manipulated moods on choice processes. *Journal of Behavioral Decision Making, 6*(1), 33–51.

Levesque L. L., Wilson, J. M., & Wholey, D.R. (2001). Cognitive divergence and shared mental models in software development project teams. *Journal of Organizational Behavior, 22*(2), 135–144.

Li, X., & Qian, J. (2016). Stimulating employees' feedback-seeking behavior: The role of participative decision making. *Social Behavior and Personality: An International Journal, 44*(1), 1–8.

Liker, J. K., & Morgan, J. M. (2006). The Toyota way in services: The case of lean product development. *Academy of Management Perspectives, 20*(2), 5–20.

Lindberg, A., & Meredith, L. (2012). Building a culture of learning through organizational development: The experiences of the Marin County health and human services department. *Journal of Evidence-based Social Work, 9*(1–2), 27–42.

Locke, E. A., Latham, G. P., & Erez, M. (1988). The determinants of goal commitment. *Academy of Management Review, 13*(1), 23–39.

Locke, E. A., & Latham, G. P. (Eds.). (2013). *New developments in goal setting and task performance.* London: Routledge.

Locke, E. A., & Latham, G. P. (2002). Building a practically useful theory of goal setting and task motivation: A 35-year odyssey. *American Psychologist, 57*(9), 705–717.

Leung, K., & Bond, M. H. (2004). Social axioms: A model for social beliefs in multicultural perspective. *Advances in Experimental Social Psychology, 36*, 119–197.

Lundberg, C. C. (1990). Surfacing organisational culture. *Journal of Managerial Psychology, 5*(4), 19–26.

Lundgren, L., Chassler, D., Amodeo, M., D'Ippolito, M., & Sullivan, L. (2012). Barriers to implementation of evidence-based addiction treatment: A national study. *Journal of Substance Abuse Treatment, 42*(3), 231–238.

Lynggaard, M., Pedersen, M. J., & Andersen, L. B. (first published online September 28, 2016). Exploring the context dependency of the PSM–performance relationship. *Review of Public Personnel Administration*. Retrieved from https://doi.org/10.1177/0734371X16671371

Mancini, M. A., & Miner, C. S. (2013). Learning and change in a community mental health setting. *Journal of Evidence-based Social Work, 10*(5), 494–504.

March, J. G., & Simon, H. A. (1958). *Organizations*. New York: John Wiley.

Marks, M.A., Sabella, M. J., Burke, C. S., & Zaccaro, S. J. (2002). The impact of cross-training on team effectiveness, *Journal of Applied Psychology, 87*(1), 3–13.

Martin, P., & Glisson, C. (1989). Perceived structure: Welfare organizations in three societal cultures. *Organization Studies, 10*(3), 353–380.

Martin, L. M., Peters, C. L., & Glisson, C. (1998). Factors affecting case management recommendations for children entering state custody. *Social Service Review, 72*(4), 521–544.

Mathieu, J. E., Heffner, T. S., Goodwin, G. F., Salas, E., & Cannon-Bowers, J. A. (2000). The influence of shared mental models on team process and performance. *Journal of Applied Psychology, 85*(2), 273–283.

Mayer, R. C., Davis, J. H., & Schoorman, F. D. (1995). An integrative model of organizational trust. *Academy of Management Review, 20*(3), 709–734.

McAllister, D. J. (1995). Affect-and cognition-based trust as foundations for interpersonal cooperation in organizations. *Academy of Management Journal, 38*(1), 24–59.

McDonald, R. E. (2007). An investigation of innovation in nonprofit organizations: The role of organizational mission. *Nonprofit and Voluntary Sector Quarterly, 36* (2), 256–281.

McGregor, D. M. (1960). *The human side of enterprise*. New York: McGraw-Hill.

McHugh, R. K., & Barlow, D. H. (2010). The dissemination and implementation of evidence-based psychological treatments: A review of current efforts. *American Psychologist, 65*(2), 73–84.

Merlani, P., Garnerin, P., Diby, M., Ferring, M., & Ricou, B. (2001). Quality improvement report: Linking guideline to regular feedback to increase appropriate requests for clinical tests: Blood gas analysis in intensive care. *British Medical Journal, 323*(7313), 620–624.

Meyer, A. D., & Goes, J. B. (1988). Organizational assimilation of innovations: A multilevel contextual analysis. *Academy of Management Journal, 31*(4), 897–923.

Meyers, P. W., Sivakumar, K., & Nakata, C. (1999). Implementation of industrial process innovations: Factors, effects, and marketing implications. *Journal of Product Innovation Management, 16*(3), 295–311.

Michie, S., van Stralen, M. & West, R. (2011). The behaviour change wheel: A new method for characterising and designing behaviour change interventions. *Implementation Science, 6*(1), 112. https://doi.org/10.1186/1748-5908-6-42

Mikulincer, M. (1994). *Human learned helplessness: A coping perspective*. New York: Plenum.

Miller, E. K., & Cohen, J. D. (2001). An integrative theory of prefrontal cortex function. *Annual Reviews of Neuroscience, 24*, 167–202.

Mills-Scoefield, D. (2012, November 26). It's not just semantics: Managing output versus outputs. *Harvard Business Review*, Retrieved from https://hbr.org/2012/11/its-not-just-semantics-managing-outcomes

Mohammed, S., Ferzandi, L., & Hamilton, K. (2010). Metaphor no more: A 15-year review of the team mental model construct. *Journal of Management, 36*, 876–910.

Molden, D. C., & Dweck, C. S. (2006). Finding 'meaning' in psychology: A lay theories approach to self-regulation, social perception, and social development. *American Psychologist, 61*(3), 192–203.

Molgaard, V. K. (1997). The extension service as key mechanism for research and services delivery for prevention of mental health disorders in rural areas. *American Journal of Community Psychology, 25*(4), 515–544.

Morling, B., & Masuda, T. (2012). Social cognition in real worlds: Cultural psychology and social cognition. In S.T. Fiske, & C.N. Macrae (Eds.), *Sage handbook of social cognition* (pp. 429–450). Thousand Oaks, CA: SAGE.

Morris, A., Bloom, J. R., & Kang, S. (2007). Organizational and individual factors affecting consumer outcomes of care in mental health services. *Administration and Policy in Mental Health, 34*(3), 243–253.

Morris, J. H., & Sherman, J. D. (1981). Generalizability of an organizational commitment model. *Academy of Management Journal, 24*(3), 512–526.

Mowday, R., Porter, L., & Steers, R. (1982). Organizational linkages: The psychology of commitment, absenteeism, and turnover. New York: Academic Press.

Murphy, G. D., & Southey, G. (2003). High performance work practices: Perceived determinants of adoption and the role of the HR practitioner. *Personnel Review, 32*(1), 73–92.

National Institute of Mental Health. (2015). *Strategic Plan for Research*. Washington, DC: National Institutes of Health.

Neuman, G. A., Edwards, J. E., & Raju, N. S. (1989). Organizational development interventions: A meta-analysis of their effects on satisfaction and other attitudes. *Personnel Psychology, 42*(3), 461–489.

Norquist, G. S. (2001). Practice research networks: Promises and pitfalls. *Clinical Psychology: Science and Practice, 8*(2), 173–175.

Nugent, W., & Glisson, C. (1999). Reactivity and responsiveness in children's service systems. In E. K. Proctor, N. Morrow-Howell, & A. Stiffman (Eds.), *Mental health services and sectors of care* (pp. 41–60). New York: Haworth.

Oakhill, J., & Garnham, A. (1996). *Mental models in cognitive science*. East Sussex, U.K.: Psychology P.

O'Brien, J. L., Shortell, S. M., Hughes, E. F., Foster, R. W., Carman, J. M., Boerstler, H., et al. (1995). An integrative model for organization-wide quality improvement: Lessons from the field. *Quality Management in Healthcare, 3*(4), 19–30.

Ogbonna, E., & Harris, L. C. (2000). Leadership style, organizational culture and performance: Empirical evidence from UK companies. *International Journal of Human Resource Management, 11*(4), 766–788.

Olin, S. S., Williams, N. J., Pollock, M., Armusewicz, K., Kutash, K., Glisson, C., et al. (2014). Quality indicators for family support services and their relationship to organizational social context. *Administration and Policy in Mental Health and Mental Health Services Research, 41*(1), 43–54. doi: 10.1007/s10488-013-0499-z.

Olin, S. C. S., Hemmelgarn, A. L., Madenwald, K., & Hoagwood, K. E. (2016). An ARC-informed family centered care intervention for children's community based mental health programs. *Journal of Child and Family Studies, 25*(1), 275–289.

Onken, L. S., Blaine, J. D., & Battjies, R. J. (1997). Behavioral therapy research: A conceptualization of a process. In S.W. Henggeler & A.B. Santos. (Eds.), *Innovative approaches for difficult-to-treat populations*, (pp. 477–485). Arlington, VA: American Psychiatric Association.

Osborne, D., & Gaebler, T. (1992). Reinventing government. Reading, MA: Addison-Wesley.

Parker, C. P., Baltes, B. B., Young, S. A., Huff, J. W., Altmann, R. A., Lacost, H. A., et al. (2003). Relationships between psychological climate perceptions and work outcomes: A meta-analytic review. *Journal of Organizational Behavior, 24*(4), 389–416.

Parmelli, E., Flodgren, G., Beyer, F., Baillie, N., Schaafsma, M. E., & Eccles, M. P. (2011). The effectiveness of strategies to change organizational culture to improve healthcare performance: A systematic review. *Implementation Science, 6*(33).

Parnell, J. A., & Bell, E. D. (1994). The propensity for participative decision making scale: A measure of managerial propensity for participative decision making. *Administration & Society, 25*(4), 518–530.

Parnell, J. A., & "Rick" Crandall, W. (2003). Propensity for participative decision-making, job satisfaction, organizational commitment, organizational citizenship behavior, and intentions to leave among Egyptian managers. *Multinational Business Review, 11*(1), 45–65.

Pasmore, W., Francis, C., Haldeman, J., & Shani, A. (1982). Sociotechnical systems: A North American reflection on empirical studies of the seventies. *Human Relations, 35*(12), 1179–1204.

Pate-Cornell, M.E. (1990). Organizational aspects of engineering system safety: The case of offshore platforms. *Science, 250*, 1210–1217.

Patten, T. (1981). *Organizational development through team building.* New York: Wiley.

Patterson, M. G., West, M. A., Shackleton, V. J., Dawson, J. F., Lawthom, R., Maitlis, S., et al. (2005). Validating the organizational climate measure: Links to managerial practices, productivity and innovation. *Journal of Organizational Behavior, 26*(4), 379–408.

Paul, R., & Elder, L. (2007). *Thinker's guide to the art of Socratic questioning.* Tomales, CA: Foundation for Critical Thinking.

Perkins, M. B., Jensen, P. S., Jaccard, J., Gollwitzer, P., Oettingen, G., Pappadopulos, E., et al. (2007). Applying theory-driven approaches to understanding and modifying clinicians' behavior: What do we know? *Psychiatric Services, 58*, 342–348.

Pfeffer, J., & Sutton, R. I. (2006). *Hard facts, dangerous half-truths, and total nonsense: Profiting from evidence-based management.* Cambridge, MA: Harvard Business Press.

Petty, M. M., Beadles, N. A., Chapman, D. F., Lowery, C. M., & Connell, D. W. (1995). Relationships between organizational culture and organizational performance. *Psychological Reports, 76*(2), 483–492.

Pieterse, A. N., Van Knippenberg, D., Schippers, M., & Stam, D. (2010). Transformational and transactional leadership and innovative behavior: The moderating role of psychological empowerment. *Journal of Organizational Behavior, 31*(4), 609–623.

Pink, D. H. (2011). *Drive: The surprising truth about what motivates us.* New York: Penguin.

Pisano, G. P., Bohmer, R. M., & Edmondson, A. C. (2001). Organizational differences in rates of learning: Evidence from the adoption of minimally invasive cardiac surgery. *Management Science, 47*(6), 752–768.

Pollock, M., & Colwill, N. L. (1987). Participatory decision making in review. *Leadership & Organization Development Journal, 8*(2), 7–10.

Porras, J. I. (1986). Organization development. In G. E. Germane (Ed.), *The executive course: What every manager needs to know about the essentials of business* (pp. 261–293). Reading, MA: Addison-Wesley.

Porras, J. I., & Robertson, P. J. (1992). Organizational development: Theory, practice, and research. In M. D. Dunnette & L. M. Hough (Eds.), *Handbook of industrial and organizational psychology* (2d ed., Vol. 3, pp. 719–822). Palo Alto, CA: Consulting Psychologists.

Proctor, E. K., Landsverk, J., Aarons, G., Chambers, D., Glisson, C., Mittman, B. (2009). Implementation research in mental health services: An emerging science with conceptual, methodological, and training challenges. *Administration and Policy in Mental Health and Mental Health Services Research. 36*(1), 24–34. doi: 10.1007/s10488-008-0197-4.

Provan, K. G., & Milward, H. B. (1995). A preliminary theory of interorganizational network effectiveness: A comparative study of four community mental health systems. *Administrative Science Quarterly*, *40*(1), 1–33.

Provan, K. G., Huang, K., & Milward, H. B. (2009). The evolution of structural embeddedness and organizational social outcomes in a centrally governed health and human services network. *Journal of Public Administration Research and Theory*, *19*(4), 873–893.

Quinn, R.E., & Rohrbaugh, J. (1983). A spatial model of effectiveness criteria: Towards a competing values approach to organizational analysis. *Management Science*, *29*(3), 363–377.

Raghavan, R., Inkelas, M., Franke, T., & Halfon, N. (2007). Administrative barriers to the adoption of high-quality mental health services for children in foster care: A national study. *Administration and Policy in Mental Health and Mental Health Services Research*, *34*(3), 191–201.

Rasmussen, J. (1979). *On the structure of knowledge—A morphology of mental models in a man-machine system context.* (Tech. Rep. No. Riso-M-2192). Roskilde, Denmark: Riso National Laboratory.

Reichers, A. E., & Schneider, B. (1990). Climate and culture: An evolution of constructs. In B. Schneider (Ed.), *Organizational climate and culture* (pp. 5–39). San Francisco: Jossey-Bass.

Rentsch, J. R. (1990). Climate and culture: Interaction and qualitative differences in organizational meanings. *Journal of Applied Psychology*, *75*(6), 661–668.

Rentsch, J. R., & Klimoski, R. J. (2001). Why do 'great minds' think alike? Antecedents of team member schema agreement. *Journal of Organizational Behavior*, *22*(2), 107–120.

Rentsch, J. R., & Mot, I. R. (2012). Elaborating cognition in teams: Cognitive similarity configurations. In E. Salas, S. M. Fiore, & M. P. Letsky (Eds.), *Applied psychological series: Theories of team cognition: Cross-disciplinary perspectives* (pp. 145–155). London: Routledge.

Risser, D. T., Rice, M. M., Salisbury, M. L., Simon, R., Jay, G. D., Berns, S. D., et al. (1999). The potential for improved teamwork to reduce medical errors in the emergency department. *Annals of Emergency Medicine*, *34*(3), 373–383.

Robert, G., Greenhalgh, T., MacFarlane, F., & Peacock, R. (2009). *Organizational factors influencing technology adoption and assimilation in the NHS: A systematic literature review. Report for the National Institute for Health Research Service Delivery and Organization Program.* London: HMSO.

Robertson, P. J., Roberts, D. R., & Porras, J. I. (1993). Dynamics of planned organizational change: Assessing empirical support for a theoretical model. *Academy of Management Journal*, *36*(3), 619–634.

Robey, D., & Altman, S. (1982). *Organization development: Progress and perspectives.* New York: Macmillan.

Rock, D. (2008). SCARF: A brain-based model for collaborating with and influencing others. *NeuroLeadership Journal*, *1*(1), 44–52.

Rogers, E. M. (1995). *Diffusion of innovations.* New York: Free Press.

Rogers, E. M. (2003). *Diffusion of innovations* (5th ed.). New York: Free Press.

Ross, M. (2015, December 14). 5 Reasons why mission driven leaders are the most successful. Retrieved from http://www.corporateculturecreator.com/2015/12/14/5-reasons-why-mission-driven-leaders-are-the-most-successful/

Rouse, W. B., & Morris, N. M. (1986). On looking into the black box: Prospects and limits in the search for mental models. *Psychological Bulletin*, *100*(3), 349.

Rousseau, D. M. (1977). Technological differences in job characteristics, employee satisfaction, and motivation: A synthesis of job design research and sociotechnical systems theory. *Organizational Behavior and Human Performance*, *19*(1), 18–42.

Rushton, C. H. (1990). Family-centered care in the critical care setting: Myth or reality? *Children's Health Care, 19*(2), 68–78.

Sackmann, S. A. (2011). Culture and performance. In N. M. Ashkanasy, C. P. M. Wilderom, & M. F. Peterson (Eds.), *The handbook of organizational culture and climate* (2d ed., pp. 188–224). Thousand Oaks, CA: SAGE.

Safran, D. G., Miller, W., & Beckman, H. (2006). Organizational dimensions of relationship-centered care. *Journal of General Internal Medicine, 21*(S1), S9–S15.

Safran, D. G., Murray A., Chang, H., Montgomery, J., Rogers, W. H. (2000). Linking doctor-patient relationship quality to outcomes. *Journal of General Internal Medicine, 15*, 116.

Safran, D. G., Taira, D. A., Rogers, W. H., Kosinski, M., Ware, J. E., & Tarlov, A. R. (1998). Linking primary care performance to outcomes of care. *Journal of Family Practice, 47*(3), 213–221.

Sage, M. D. (2010). Child welfare workforce turnover: Frontline workers' experiences with organizational culture and climate, and implications for organizational practice. *Dissertations and Theses.* Portland State University, ProQuest Dissertations Publishing.

Scanlon, D. P., Darby, C., Rolph, E., & Doty, H. E. (2001). The role of performance measures for improving quality in managed care organizations. *Health Services Research, 36*(3), 619–641.

Schein, E. H. (1985). *Organizational culture and leadership.* San Francisco: Jossey-Bass.

Schein, E. H. (2004). *Organizational culture and leadership.* San Francisco: Jossey-Bass.

Schneider, B., & Bowen, D. (1995). *Winning the service game.* Boston: Harvard Business School Press.

Schneider, B., Brief, A. P., & Guzzo, R. A. (1996). Creating a climate and culture for sustainable organizational change. *Organizational Dynamics, 24*(4), 7–19.

Schneider, B., White, S. S., & Paul, M. C. (1998). Linking service climate and customer perceptions of service quality: Tests of a causal model. *Journal of Applied Psychology, 83*(2), 150–163.

Schneider, G., & Gunnarson, S. K., & Niles-Jolly, K. (1994). Creating the climate and culture of success. *Organizational Dynamics, 23*(1), 17–29.

Schoenwald, S. K., Carter, R. E., Chapman, J. E., & Sheidow, A. J. (2008). Therapist adherence and organizational effects on change in youth behavior problems one year after multisystemic therapy. *Administration and Policy in Mental Health, 35*(5), 379–394.

Schoenwald, S. K., Chapman, J. E., Sheidow, A. J., & Carter, R. E. (2009). Long-term youth criminal outcomes in MST transport: The impact of therapist adherence and organizational climate and structure. *Journal of Clinical Child and Adolescent Psychology, 38*(1), 91–105.

Schoorman, F. D., Mayer, R. C., & Davis, J. H. (2007). An integrative model of organizational trust: Past, present, and future. *Academy of Management Review, 32*(2), 344–354.

Schorr, L. B. (1997). *Common purpose.* New York: Doubleday.

Scott, W. R. (2008). *Institutions and organizations* (2d ed.). Thousand Oaks, CA: SAGE.

Senge, P. M., Kleiner, A., Roberts, C., Ross, R. B., & Smith, B. J. (1994). *The fifth discipline fieldbook: Strategies and tools for building a learning organization.* New York: Doubleday.

Senge, P. M. (2006). *The fifth discipline: The art and practice of the learning organization.* New York, Doubleday.

Sheeran, P. (2002). Intention-behavior relations: A conceptual and empirical review. In W. Stroebe & M. Hewstone (Eds.), *European review of social psychology* (Vol. 12, pp. 1–36). London: Wiley.

Shelton, T., Jeppson, E., & Johnson, B. (1989). *Family-centered care for children with special health care needs* (2d ed.). Washington, DC: Association for the Care of Children's Health.

Shortell, S. M., Bennett, C. L., & Byck, G. R. (1998). Assessing the impact of continuous quality improvement on clinical practice: What it will take to accelerate progress. *Milbank Quarterly, 76*(4), 593–624.

Shortell, S. M., O'Brien, J. L., Carman, J. M., Foster, R. W., Hughes, E. F. X., Boerstler, H., et al. (1995). Assessing the impact of continuous quality improvement/total quality management: Concept versus implementation. *Health Services Research, 30*(2), 377–401.

Simons, T. (2002). Behavioral integrity: The perceived alignment between managers' words and deeds as a research focus. *Organization Science, 13*(1), 18–35.

Smith, E. R., & Branscombe, N. R. (1987). Procedurally mediated social inferences: The case of category accessibility effects. *Journal of Experimental Social Psychology, 23*(5), 361–382.

Smith, M. K. (2001). Peter Senge and the learning organization. In *The encyclopedia of informal education*. http://www.infed.org/ thinkers/senge.htm. Accessed 5 February 2008.

Stewart, M., Brown, J. D., Donner, A., McWhinney, I. R., Oates, J., Weston, W. W., & Jordon, J. J. (2000). The impact of patient-centered care on outcomes. *The Journal of Family Practice, 49*(9), 796–804.

Solomons, N. M. & Spross, J. A. (2011). Evidence-based practice barriers and facilitators from a continuous quality improvement perspective: an integrative review. *Journal of Nursing Management, 19*(1), 109–120.

Spreitzer, G. M. (2008). Taking Stock: A review of more than twenty years of research on empowerment at work. In C. Cooper & J. Barling (Eds.), *Handbook of organizational behavior* (pp. 54–73). Thousand Oaks, CA: SAGE.

Spreitzer, G. M., & Doneson, D. (2005). Musings on the past and future of employee empowerment. In *Handbook of organizational development*. Thousand Oaks, CA: SAGE.

Steel, R. P., & Shane, G. S. (1986). Evaluation research on quality circles: Technical and analytical implications. *Human Relations, 39*(5), 449–468.

Stevenson, S. (2014, May 11). Don't go to work. Slate Magazine. Retrieved from http://www.slate.com/articles/business/psychology_of_management/2014/05/best_buy_s_rowe_experiment_can_results_only_work_environments_actually_be.html

Stiverson, L. (2014, June 17). Mission Driven? Neil Blumental, Warby Parker. Excerpts from Stew Friedman interview on Work and Life radio program, Wharton School. Retrieved from http://worklife.wharton.upenn.edu/2014/06/mission-driven-neil-blumenthal-warby-parker/

Strang, D., & Soule, S. A. (1998). Diffusion in organizations and social movements: From hybrid corn to poison pills. *Annual Review of Sociology, 24*, 265–290.

Strolin-Goltzman, J., Kollar, S., & Trinkle, J. (2010). Listening to the voices of children in foster care: Youths speak out about child welfare workforce turnover and selection. *Social Work, 55*(1), 47–53.

Sue-Chan, C., & Ong, M. (2002). Goal assignment and performance: Assessing the medicating roles of goal commitment and self-efficacy and the moderating role of power distance. *Organizational Behavior and Human Decision Processes, 89*(2), 1140–1161.

Tasi, W. (2001). Knowledge transfer in intraorganizational networks: Effects of network position and absorptive capacity on business unit innovation and performance. *Academy of Management Journal, 44*(5), 996–1004.

Taylor, F. W. (1911). *The principles of scientific management*. New York: Harper Brothers.

Taylor. S. E. (1991). Asymmetrical effects of positive and negative events: The mobilization—minimization hypothesis. *Psychological Bulletin, 110*(1), 67–85.

Terziovski, M. (2002). Achieving performance excellence through an integrated strategy of radical innovation and continuous improvement. *Measuring Business Excellence, 6*(2), 5–14.

Thompson, J. D. (1967). *Organizations in action*. New York: McGraw-Hill.

Travis, D. J., & Mor Barak, M. E. (2010). Fight or flight? Factors influencing child welfare workers' propensity to seek positive change or disengage from their jobs. *Journal of Social Service Research, 36*(3), 188–205.

Trice, H. M., & Beyer, J. M. (1993). *The cultures of work organizations.* Englewood Cliffs, NJ: Prentice-Hall.

Trist, E. (1985). Intervention strategies for interorganizational domains. In R. Tannenbaum, N. Margulies, & F. Massarik (Eds.), *Human systems development* (pp. 167–197). San Francisco: Jossey-Bass.

Trist, E. L., Higgin, G. W., Murray, H., & Pollock, A. B. (1963). *Organization choice: Capabilities of groups at the coal face under changing technologies: The loss, re-discovery, and transformation of a work tradition.* London: Tavistock

Tucker, R. W., McCoy, W. J., & Evans, L. C. (1990). Can questionnaires objectively assess organisational culture? *Journal of Managerial Psychology, 5*(4), 4–11.

Tushman, M. (1977). Special boundary roles in the innovation process. *Administrative Science Quarterly, 22,* 587–605.

Tyson, E. H., & Glisson, C. (2005). A cross-ethnic validity study of the Shortform Assessment for Children (SAC). *Research on Social Work Practice, 15*(2), 97–109.

Vallacher, R. R., & Wegner, D. M. (1987). What do people think they're doing? Action identification and human behavior. *Psychological Review, 94*(1), 3–15.

Van de Ven, A. H., & Poole, M. S. (1995). Explaining development and change in organizations. *Academy of Management Review, 20*(3), 510–540.

Verbeke, W., Volgering, M., & Hessels, M. (1998). Exploring the conceptual expansion within the field of organizational behavior: Organizational climate and organizational culture. *Journal of Management Studies, 35*(3), 303–329.

Wagner, J. A. (1994). Participation's effects on performance and satisfaction: A reconsideration of research evidence. *Academy of management Review, 19*(2), 312–330.

Wahler, R. G. (1994). Child conduct problems: Disorders in conduct or social continuity?. *Journal of Child and Family Studies, 3*(2), 143–156.

Walton, R. E. (1987). *Managing conflict: Interpersonal dialogue and third-party roles.* Reading, MA: Addison-Wesley.

Weick, K. E. (1979). *The social psychology of organizing.* Reading, MA: Addison-Wesley.

Weisz, J. R., Doss, A. J., & Hawley, K. M. (2005). Youth psychotherapy outcome research: A review and critique of the evidence base. *Annual Review of Psychology, 56,* 337–363. http://dx.doi.org/10.1146/annurev.psych.55.090902.141449

Weisz, J. R., & Jensen, P. S. (1999). Efficacy and effectiveness of child and adolescent psychotherapy and pharmacotherapy. *Mental Health Services Research, 1*(3), 125–157.

Weisz, J. R., Krumholz, L. S., Santucci, L., Thomassin, K., & Ng, M. Y. (2015). Shrinking the gap between research and practice: Tailoring and testing youth psychotherapies in clinical care contexts. *Annual Review of Clinical Psychology, 11,* 139–163.

Weisz, J. R., Ugueto, A. M., Cheron, D. M., & Herren, J. (2013). Evidence based youth psychotherapy in the mental health ecosystem. *Journal of Clinical Child and Adolescent Psychology, 42*(2), 274–286.

Weldon, E., & Yun, S. (2000). The effects of proximal and distal goals on goal level, strategy development, and group performance. *Journal of Applied Behavioral Science, 36*(3), 336–344.

White, S. S., & Locke, E. A. (2000). Problems with the Pygmalion effect and some proposed solutions. *The Leadership Quarterly, 11*(3), 389–415.

Wilkins, A. L., & Ouchi, W. G. (1983). Efficient cultures: Exploring the relationship between culture and organizational performance. *Administrative Science Quarterly, 28*, 468–481.

Williams, N. J., & Glisson, C. (2013). Reducing turnover is not enough: The need for proficient organizational cultures to support positive youth outcomes in child welfare. *Children and Youth Services Review, 35*(11), 1871–1877. doi: 10.1016/j.childyouth.2013.09.002.

Williams, N. J., & Glisson, C. (2014a). The role of organizational culture and climate in the dissemination and implementation of empirically-supported treatments for youth. In R. Beidas, & P. Kendall (Eds.), *Child and adolescent therapy: Dissemination and implementation of empirically-supported treatments.* New York: Guilford.

Williams, N. J., & Glisson, C. (2014b). Testing a theory of organizational culture, climate and youth outcomes in child welfare systems: A United States national study. *Child Abuse and Neglect, 38*(4), 757–767. doi: 10.1016/j.chiabu.2013.09.003.

Williams, N.J., Glisson, C., Hemmelgarn, A., & Green, P. (2016). Mechanisms of change in the ARC organizational strategy: Increasing mental health clinicians' EBP adoption through improved organizational culture and capacity. *Administration and Policy in Mental Health and Mental Health Services Research 43*(3), 1–15. doi:10.1007/s10488-016-0742-5.

Wood, R., & Bandura, A. (1989). Impact of conceptions of ability on self-regulatory mechanisms and complex decision making. *Journal of Personality and Social Psychology, 56*(3), 407.

Worren, N. A. M., Ruddle, K., & Moore, K. (1999). From organizational development to change management. *Journal of Applied Behavioral Science, 35*(3), 273–286.

Wright, B. E. (2007). Public service and motivation: Does mission matter? *Public Administration Review, 67*(1), 54–64.

Young, G. J. (2000). Managing organizational transformations: Lessons from the Veterans Health Administration. *California Management Review, 43*(1), 66–83.

Yousef, D. A. (2000). Organizational commitment: A mediator of the relationships of leadership behavior with job satisfaction and performance in a non-Western country. *Journal of Managerial Psychology, 15*(1), 6–28.

Zohar, D., & Hofmann, D. A. (2012). Organizational culture and climate. In S. W. J. Kozlowski (Ed.), *The Oxford handbook of organizational psychology.* New York: Oxford University Press. http://dx.doi.org/10.1093/oxfordhb/9780199928309.013.0020

INDEX